Linguistic Complexity
and
Text Comprehension:
Readability Issues Reconsidered

LINGUISTIC COMPLEXITY AND TEXT COMPREHENSION:
Readability Issues Reconsidered

Edited by

ALICE DAVISON
University of Wisconsin

GEORGIA M. GREEN
University of Illinois

 LAWRENCE ERLBAUM ASSOCIATES, PUBLISHERS
1988   Hillsdale, New Jersey   London

Lawrence Erlbaum Associates, Inc., Publishers
365 Broadway
Hillsdale, New Jersey 07642

Library of Congress Cataloging in Publication Data
Linguistic complexity and text comprehension.

Includes bibliographies and indexes.
1. Psycholinguistics.   2. Reading comprehension.
I. Davison, Alice.   II. Green, Georgia M.
P37.L46   1988   401'.9   87-24545
ISBN 0-89859-541-X

Printed in the United States of America
10 9 8 7 6 5 4 3 2 1

Contents

Acknowledgments

We would like to thank Rand J. Spiro, Center for the Study of Reading, for encouraging us to put together this volume and for helpful advice at several stages in the evolution of the contents. We received valuable editorial and critical comments from Mark Aronoff, Harry Blanchard, Gabriella Hermon, Susan Kemper, Sue Ann Kendall, William Nagy, Jean Osborn, Rona Smith and Andrea Tyler, at the Center for the Study of Reading, and we are grateful to Margaret Olsen for her perceptive suggestions and diligence in preparing the subject index. Many of the chapters were typed—and retyped in successive drafts—by the tireless and expert processors of words at CSR, Rita Gaskill and Delores Plowman, whom we thank for their care and their patience.

   Support for the editing of this book and for the writing of the chapters by Anderson and Davison, Bruce and Rubin and Green and Olsen was received from the National Institute of Education under contract NIE-400-81-0030, awarded to the Center for the Study of Reading, University of Illinois at Urbana-Champaign and Bolt Beranek and Newman, Inc. We would like to express our appreciation for participating in the interdisciplinary discussion of language and comprehension made possible by the existence of the Center, which in large measure contributed to this book. Of course, the views expressed in the chapters in this book are those of the authors, and do not necessarily reflect the views of this agency.

Linguistic Complexity
and
Text Comprehension:
Readability Issues Reconsidered

Introduction

One of the reasons for putting together the chapters in this volume is to bring together work defining an interesting class of research problems. Some of the chapters point out the inadequacy of readability formulas for the prediction or definition of text difficulty; others discuss in detail the linguistic features of words and sentences in a text which must enter into comprehension, defining how these features do or do not contribute to difficulty in understanding. There are important practical ramifications to the question of what features of language influence the understanding of a text. But the relation between language and understanding is an important theoretical issue in its own right. In the last 20 years, research in the psychology of language and of learning, and in linguistics, has progressed to a point where theories and empirical results may be built upon in trying to find a satisfactory model of language understanding. This kind of research has intrinsic interest and value in illuminating theories of language and cognition far greater than refining the statistical correlations between word properties and the results of cloze tests, for example.

Research began in the 1920s on the problem of how language is processed and effectively comprehended. Rather than build psychological models of language comprehension, researchers instead looked for statistical correlations between objectively observable features of texts and the reading levels of readers, as measured by standardized tests. This research led to the development of a number of readability formulas (see Chall (1958) and Klare (1963) for overviews of the early history of readability formulas). Formulas represented a technical and conceptual advance at the time they were originated, making use of new techniques for measuring word frequency and reading ability and for computing statistical correlations. Yet from their inception, researchers have also been aware of the limitations of using formulas, which are equations involving certain constants and two or more measures derived from the text in question. The text properties usually are average sentence length, normally based on samples of 100 words, and an estimate of word difficulty, typically based on syllable length or occurrence on a list of high-frequency words. Many factors pertaining to both the text and the reader are not measured although they could be of great importance in determining the comprehensibility of a text. Further, the measurements which enter into formulas are often inaccurate reflections of the difficulty of some texts. Finally, the emphasis on word difficulty and sentence length which is implicit in formulas—although this was probably not intended by their originators—has misled some users into thinking that these factors somehow directly cause difficulty in comprehension. For discussion of these problems, see the works by Chall and Klare cited above, and Gray and Leary (1935).

What might be a more reliable and accurate approach to the problem of text difficulty? In particular, what model of language understanding and what characterization of texts and the language in them might explain why some readers have difficulty in comprehending a text? Not much research has been done which addresses these questions. Users of formulas, if they were aware of limitations and problems, either have hoped that these problems did not seriously affect the texts they were working with, or were deterred from further investigation by the magnitude of the task of answering the real questions behind readability formulas. Certainly no single individual dissatisfied with readability formulas should be expected to replace them with something conceptually better and also equally simple to use. Yet even though the question of text difficulty is one with both practical consequences and intrinsic theoretical interest for those in disciplines studying cognition, research in the whole field of readability has remained more or less isolated from work done in cognitive psychology, linguistics and other disciplines.

It is not clear why things have turned out this way. Researchers on readability such as Klare and Bormuth make reference in their work to research on information theory by Zipf, Carnap, and Bar-Hillel, as well as Shannon and Weaver and Yngve's work on natural language parsing (Klare 1963, Bormuth (1966)). Yet the research on readability which made reference to work in cognitive psychology, information theory and linguistics was not pursued after these initial approaches in the 1960s and early 1970s.

In the introductory chapters of this book, Bruce and Rubin define the tasks which people actually call upon formulas to perform, and show how the formula approach is not the best one to use for these purposes. Anderson and Davison describe the assumptions about language and the conception of statistical correlation behind formulas, showing that these assumptions are inappropriate given what is now known about the interactive nature of a reader's comprehension of a text.

Several chapters look at the predictions of formulas for specific types of text. Baker, Atwood, and Duffy show that simplification of technical texts according to the criteria which formulas measure does not in itself promote increased comprehension. Both total novices and experts are unaffected, while text simplifications aid readers with only general background knowledge. Charrow compares two kinds of revisions in technical texts, one which simplifies sentences and words, and another which makes changes which are motivated by specific goals, increasing the clarity of the text structure or its internal coherence, for example. The second kind of change resulted in improved comprehension among readers who were of the sort the document was intended for. Kemper's study defines a feature of texts which contributes directly to difficulty in reading, the presence or absence of explicit information which connects events described in the text. Green and Olsen show that readability-inspired changes in stories intended for elementary school readers do not always result in improved comprehension even for the poorer readers, and may result in a text which is less attractive to the intended readers than the original.

Lyn Frazier gives a comprehensive and critical overview of recent psycholinguistic studies which she relates to discussion of the theoretical models of human language processing. She defines the various kinds of information which must be processed and related to each other in understanding natural language. As there are many sources of complexity in language which may result in difficulty of comprehension, a single metric of complexity would be difficult to achieve, and perhaps impossible if different sources of information interact or are of such different natures that they are not combinable into a single measure. This point is also made in Carlota Smith's chapter, which approaches the issue in a somewhat different way.

Crain and Shankweiler study the comprehension of a single complex sentence structure, restrictive relative clauses, considering the interaction of text decoding with higher-level linguistic processes. They show that, given the appropriate contextual support, the presence of a restrictive relative clause is not a barrier to comprehension, and in any case, poorer readers have access to the same linguistic information as better readers. Poorer readers have less attentional capacity for word recognition, and as a consequence their comprehension of relative clauses is not as accurate as it is for better readers. Hence it is unlikely that sentence complexity in itself is actually a cause of poor comprehension.

Janet Randall shows that word complexity is not a simple notion, and its relation to difficulty of comprehension is not simple either. While long or infrequent words add to the difficulty of a text according to readability formulas, and such words are often morphologically complex, it is not the case that morphologically complex words cause difficulty in comprehension. Randall shows that when children are learning to analyze complex words, they learn a great deal of syntactic information when they learn an affix like the agentive -er. Furthermore, since morphologically complex words contain subparts like -er which the child knows, there is often more familiar and helpful information in a complex word than in a similar unknown word which cannot be broken down into parts. Hence it is not possible to generalize from the correlation of long or infrequent words with text difficulty to some model of what causes difficulty. Such a generalization may be spurious, given the linguistic features of words.

Carlota Smith shows that there is no simple, one to one correlation between sentence length and difficulty of comprehension, in a study of sentence comprehension which used two different measures of comprehension, each of which was sensitive to a different level of complexity and depth of processing. Sentences which are hard for young children to process accurately by one measure of comprehension, are easy to process by another, and vice versa. It is not possible to characterize sentence complexity by a single measure, as sentence structure involves complexity at different levels of description and may arise from the interrelation of different components of sentence structure.

The impetus behind this collection of chapters on language processing and readability is the conviction that two mostly independent groups of researchers have a common concern, in spite of the external differences in the questions they ask. On the one hand, some researchers want to know how language is understood by hearers (or readers). How do people identify and interpret linguistic forms, how do they derive information from a linguistically encoded message, and how do they integrate new information with previously known information? These are questions which have occupied researchers in cognitive psychology, linguistics and artificial intelligence, and though much progress has been made, at least in defining the questions and the techniques for exploring them, the answers are far from complete.

On the other hand, other researchers have asked whether it is possible to assess the difficulty of a text by looking at some features of the text, especially those which can be measured objectively. Do features of the text reflect its difficulty, and do linguistic features—such as word difficulty and sentence complexity in themselves present barriers to comprehension? Why do some readers, and not others, find a text difficult—is it because of a deficit of knowledge, or of language or of attentional capacity for efficient processing of language? These are questions which should be investigated both by educational and cognitive psychologists as well as educators, writers and publishers concerned with very practical problems of matching texts and readers.

REFERENCES

Bormuth, J. R. (1966). Readability: A new approach. *Reading Research Quarterly, 1,* 79–132.

Chall, J. S. (1958). *Readability: An appraisal of research and application.* Columbus, OH: Bureau of Educational Research, Ohio State University.

Gray, W. S., & Leary, B. E. (1935). *What makes a book readable?* Chicago: University of Chicago Press.

Klare, G. R. (1963). *The measure of readability.* Ames: Iowa State University Press.

Alice Davison
Georgia Green

1 Readability Formulas: Matching Tool and Task

Bertram Bruce
Andee Rubin
BBN Laboratories, Cambridge, MA

In the past few years, American education has again become the subject of intense public scrutiny. Numerous individuals and commissions (Davidson & Montgomery, 1983) have offered their analyses and recommendations for American schools. Although these documents vary in their recommendations, one common theme is "back to basics." Another theme is accountability, especially that based on numerical scales, such as achievement tests and teacher competency exams. The centrality of *texts* in these reports and the emphasis on *quantifiable* standards suggest a renewed role for readability formulas, a method by which numbers reflecting text characteristics can be generated. Thus it is important to examine the uses of readability formulas and their impact on classrooms and students.

This chapter illustrates why an increased role for readability formulas in education is misguided. We first describe readability formulas and their most common uses, then analyze five tasks in which readability formulas are employed. In each case, we find that important assumptions underlying the correct use of the formulas are violated. We conclude that readability formulas should always be used in ways consistent with their underlying assumptions.

MOTIVATION FOR READABILITY FORMULAS

A readability formula is a method of assigning to a text a numerical estimate of "readability," variously defined as "ease of reading," "interest" or "ease of understanding" (Gilliland, 1972). Because it is intended as a quick and convenient measurement, the typical readability formula takes into account only easily

5

measurable aspects of a text such as word difficulty and average sentence length. A weighted combination of these measurements yields a number for each text. Some readability formulas produce estimates that represent grade levels; others range over a 100 point scale where higher numbers indicate greater readability.

Readability formulas were first developed in the 1920s for use by textbook writers; in the past 60 years hundreds have been proposed (Klare, 1976). One of the most popular readability formulas in current use is the Dale–Chall (Dale & Chall, 1948). Using it requires choosing three 100 word selections from a book, measuring the percentage of uncommon words (based on a 3000-word list of familiar words compiled in 1948) and the average number of words per sentence in the passages, then combining the two numbers according to the equation:

$$\text{Reading grade} = .16 \ (\% \text{ uncommon words}) + .05 \ (\text{average number of words per sentence})$$

A similar formula—the FOG index (Gunning, 1964)—uses a syllable count as an estimate of vocabulary difficulty:

$$\text{Reading grade} = .4 \ (\text{average sentence length} + \% \text{ words of more than two syllables})$$

To see how these formulas are applied, consider the first few sentences of *The Phantom Tollbooth,* a children's book by Norton Juster (Juster, 1961).

There was once a boy named Milo who didn't know what to do with himself—not just sometimes, but always.

When he was in school he longed to be out, and when he was out he longed to be in. On the way he thought about coming home, and coming home he thought about going. Wherever he was he wished he were somewhere else, and when he got there he wondered why he'd bothered. Nothing really interested him—least of all the things that should have.

In this 86-word passage, there are 5 sentences, for an average sentence length of 17.2. According to the Dale–Chall list, there is 1/86 or 1.1% unfamiliar words, so by the Dale-Chall formula:

$$\text{Reading grade} = .16(1.1) + .05(17.2) = 176 + .86 = 1.03 + 3.63 = 4.7$$

There are only 2 words (2.3%) of more than two syllables in the passage, so by the FOG formula:

$$\text{Reading grade} = .4(17.2 + 2.3) = 7.8$$

(Note that the grade levels assigned to this passage differ by three grades. This may be due in part to the fact that a single sample from a text is inadequate for assessing readability.)

Readability formulas are widely used in a variety of situations where estimates of text complexity are thought to be necessary. One obvious use is by educational publishers designing basal and remedial reading texts; some states, in fact, will consider using a basal series only if it fits within certain readability formula criteria. Basal publishers are asked to provide such information as the average readability for each book, the highest and lowest readability scores in each book, the number of samples on which each score is based and the actual readability worksheets. Makers of standardized reading comprehension tests use criteria similar to those included in readability formulas to rate the grade level of test passages.

Increasingly, public documents such as insurance policies, tax forms, contracts and jury instructions must also meet criteria stated in terms of readability formulas. In Massachusetts, for example, the State Insurance Commission requires that insurance policies score at least 50 on the Flesch Reading Ease Scale (one of the most commonly used readability formulas, Flesch, 1948); a similar law in Minnesota specifies a Flesch score of 40 (Redish, 1979). Agencies which design documents use the idea of an ''objective'' standard to argue that testing their products by having prospective users read them would be superfluous. The Internal Revenue Service, for example, refused to field test their revised 1040 forms (rated by formula as readable at an 8th-grade level), claiming that the process would be too expensive and the results would be redundant.

PROBLEMS WITH READABILITY FORMULAS

To be able to measure the readability of a text with a simple formula is an enticing prospect. Unfortunately, readability formulas fail in many of their applications. This is due to an interaction between two fundamental problems. First, from a theoretical point of view, readability formulas contradict much of current knowledge about reading and the reading process. They thus have a central invalidity that, at best, limits their usefulness. Second, they have been used in many ways that make the situation worse, violating assumptions that are necessary for any proper use of the formulas. Taken together, these considerations suggest that readability formulas are inappropriate as practical tools either for matching individual children to texts or for providing guidelines for writers, two of their most common uses. These kinds of criticisms have been leveled at readability formulas from many quarters (Bruce, 1984; Gilliland, 1972; Kintsch & Vipond, 1979; Redish, 1979; Rubin, 1984; Taylor, 1953).

One problem is that readability formulas do not measure all the factors that influence the comprehensibility of a text. Because most of the formulas include only sentence length and word difficulty as factors, they can account only indirectly for factors which may make a particular text difficult, such as syntactic complexity, discourse cohesion characteristics, the number of inferences required, the number of items to remember, the complexity of ideas, rhetorical structure, and dialect. Further, because the formulas are measurements based on a text isolated from the context of its use, they can not reflect such reader-specific factors as motivation, interest, values, or purpose. Nor can they reflect different readers' cultural backgrounds or the effect of the circumstances in which a passage is read.

Each reading event is a transaction (Rosenblatt, 1978). The meaning which emerges depends on far more than simple text factors. To see this, consider the following four scenarios in which someone is reading the beginning of *The Wizard of Oz* (Baum, 1956):

> Dorothy lived in the midst of the great Kansas prairies, with Uncle Henry, who was a farmer, and Aunt Em, who was the farmer's wife. Their house was small, for the lumber to build it had to be carried by wagon many miles.

Scenario 1. A 10-year-old child, living in what remains of the Kansas prairie, is reading the book alone for the first time. Her parents have read parts of it to her before. It is a rainy afternoon—a perfect time to stay inside and read. Her mother is nearby available for help.

Scenario 2. A 10-year-old child, living near downtown Pittsburgh, is reading the book for a school assignment. It is late at night and she must have the first chapter (6 pages) read by 8 AM. Her mother is at work, her father asleep in front of the television. She has trouble keeping her eyes open and is frustrated even in the first sentence by the word "prairie."

Scenario 3. A test-maker is searching for reading comprehension test passages which focus on "main idea." He considers *Wizard of Oz* a good source because it is familiar to students, yet complex enough to be challenging. He has trouble, however, imagining what the main idea of the first paragraph might be, so he goes on to skim the next several chapters.

Scenario 4. A 10-year-old child in New York who has seen the movie *Wizard of Oz* every year on television since he was five, is reading it in class for the first time. The teacher calls on each student to read three sentences, but the student is enthusiastically looking for pictures of the scarecrow, his favorite character, and can't find the place when it's his turn to read.

While these scenarios were constructed to illustrate the greatest contrasts, they are not atypical. The crucial point is that the text in each case is identical; the particular reader and situation define the differences. It is clear that the text has no inherent degree of readability, apart from considerations of the reader and his or her purpose. Nevertheless, readability formulas, which evaluate texts out of the context of the reader-text interaction, continue to be widely used. One reason is that a number of tasks exist for which a simple measure of text difficulty would be enormously useful: designing texts appropriate to the level of a child in school (including the writing, selecting and adapting of texts), choosing among trade books for children, choosing passages for tests, evaluating difficulties in reading, making writing clear for adults, designing materials for special populations, and writing and evaluating materials to be used in research.

We consider here a few such tasks and the problems that arise when either the formulas themselves or similar considerations of vocabulary and sentence length are used for these purposes. For each task we ask: Is the example idiosyncratic, or does it illustrate the violation of an assumption underlying the appropriate use of a readability measure? After looking at several examples, we attempt to define the necessary criteria for a valid and valuable use of readability formulas.

Task No. 1: Choosing Elementary-School Trade Books

Trade books written for elementary-school children are often graded via readability formulas so that they can be matched by teachers, librarians, and parents with the reading abilities of children. Even though it might be argued that young children have very individual tastes, these readability ratings are made on a uniform basis, focusing on vocabulary and sentence length. Some readability formula advocates argue that these word-level considerations are of primary importance for young children whose reading vocabulary is sharply limited. Some pitfalls of this approach can be seen by looking at a popular trade book:

Example: Don't Forget the Bacon. (Hutchins, 1976) is an elementary-school trade book which scores between grades 1 and 2 on the Fry scale. The book concerns a little boy whose mother is sending him on a shopping errand. On the first page we are shown the mother holding a basket and coin purse and saying to the little boy (via a cartoon-type balloon) "Six farm eggs, a cake for tea, a pound of pears, and don't forget the bacon." On the next page the little boy is pictured carrying the basket and coin purse, walking along a street where there are three fat people standing on the corner, and thinking (via a cloud figure) "six fat legs, a cake for tea, a pound of pears, and don't forget the bacon." The next page shows the boy passing another boy, who is wearing a cape, this time thinking "six fat legs, a cape for me, a pound of pears, and don't forget the bacon." The story proceeds in this fashion, with the text consisting only of the little boy's thoughts and a few similarly structured instances of speaking to the storekeeper and to his mother. Predictably, his shopping mission goes awry. He confuses the things he sees with the things he is supposed to remember. By the time he reaches the store he has a totally garbled list of items to buy. Returning home, he one by one remember the items on the list.

Problems.   Many 3rd and 4th-graders find this book (but *not* the individual words) difficult. One reason is that much of the information in the book is communicated in the pictures. Even the fact, for instance, that the little boy is walking down the street is not explicitly stated and the various scenes which change his memory of what to buy are pictured, not described.

Another reason for difficulty is that enjoyment of this story relies heavily on appreciating its symmetrical structure. The little boy forgets the items on his list one by one by going through a series of transformations of the linguistic material he is trying to remember, then remembers the items in the opposite order, until he arrives back at the original list. There is also a potentially confusing, but critical, distinction between thought and speech, indicated by the standard balloons and clouds used in cartoons. Finally, an appreciation of rhyme and how people use it as a memory aid is an important component of comprehending this text. Thus, the potential sources of difficulty for the book are not attributable to its word difficulty or sentence complexity, but to properties of the text as a whole.

This example illustrates a general problem with readability formulas, namely their underlying assumption that lexical and syntactic factors are highly correlated with such characteristics as overall structure, conceptual load, pictures, graphic conventions and rhyme. It is these latter features in general that determine difficulty. Thus a text being measured must fortuitously have such a high correlation.

This example also illustrates a fairly widespread misuse of readability formulas as a method for matching individual books and children. Unfortunately, one cannot predict how difficult a particular child will find a specific book based on formula estimates. In the case of *Don't Forget the Bacon,* we have already noted that for many children the book is too difficult, at least on initial independent reading. However, children already exposed to the rhyming and literary conventions used in this book may understand it quite easily. Thus, no statistically derived quantity will be an adequate predictor in an individual case. This fact suggests caution in the use of readability formulas for one-to-one matching.

Task No. 2.: Constructing Reading Comprehension Tests

Reading comprehension tests are another domain in which written material must be graded or scaled. Either readability formulas per se or related considerations of vocabulary and sentence difficulty routinely come into play in the screening, selection, ordering and norming process. The following example illustrates some mistaken assumptions about the process of reading and comprehending texts which are common to both reading tests and readability formulas.

Example.   The following passage is from a reading comprehension test (Educational Testing Service, 1960):

As to clever people's hating each other, I think a little extra talent does sometimes make people jealous. They become irritated by perpetual attempts and failures, and it hurts their tempers and dispositions. Unpretending mediocrity is good, and genius is glorious; but a weak flavor of genius in an essentially common person is detestable. It spoils the grand neutrality of a commonplace character, as the rinsings of an unwashed wine glass spoil a draught of fair water. No wonder the poor fellow who belongs to this class of slightly favored mediocrities is puzzled and vexed by the strange sight of a dozen men of high capacity working and playing together in harmony.

One of the comprehension questions asked about this passage is the following:

The writer suggests that persons of exceptionally great ability

A. tend to like and appreciate one another.
B. dislike the company of ordinary men.
C. are likely to be jealous of one another.
D. are essentially common except for their genius.

Problems.   Although the writers of the test consider A to be the correct answer, some people choose (and can justify) C as their answer. People who select C interpret the first sentence to mean that clever people are jealous of one another (the same interpretation those who choose A make), but then equate "clever people" with "geniuses." Although there are other indications in the passage that the author does *not* consider clever people to be geniuses, this evidence does not change their opinion, so they assert that "persons of exceptionally great ability are likely to be jealous of one another." In our sample protocol analyses, those who chose C considered themselves to be ordinary people, thus members of the lowest of the three groups of people identified by the author (ordinary people, slightly gifted people, and geniuses). One is tempted to conclude that they were therefore less conscious of the intended differences between geniuses and clever people. Even if this interpretation proves incorrect, it points out how quite personal differences (in this case, in self-image) might affect comprehension.

Users of readability formulas for test construction must assume that the intended reader and the rater of a passage do not differ on measures (vocabulary, life experience, purpose for reading) that are relevant to the evaluation of the text. In the case of a reading comprehension test, the "rater" may be a person, a committee or a norming process; with readability formulas, rater characteristics are derived from the population on which texts are graded and are reflected, for example, in the choice of words for vocabulary lists. Where differences exist, the use of readability formulas (or standardized comprehension tests) is less justified.

This passage also illustrates the importance of applying readability formulas only to "honestly written" material. If readability formulas are to be useful at all, they must be applied to material that was written for a real communicative purpose, not for the purpose of satisfying a readability level. A corollary to this edict is that a passage being evaluated should be taken as much as possible in its entirety, as excerpting can significantly change the complexity of a text. The material in this item was obviously not written to be excerpted, but was intended as part of a larger text, so any measure of its difficulty will be flawed.

Finally, this passage illustrates the potential pitfall into which many test constructors fall: the temptation to make a passage less complex by shortening sentences or simplifying syntax. This particular text is, in fact, quite complex and is not likely to be simplified by such local measures.

Task No. 3: Writing Remedial Reading Texts

Junior-high and high-school age students who have trouble in reading present a difficult problem: Their reading skills may be inadequate for the texts directed at their age level, while texts which they could read easily are typically directed toward much younger children and may be boring or embarrassing for them to read. One proposed solution to this problem is to identify a set of texts that score low on readability formulas but have high interest value for the older student.

There are several criticisms to be made of the high-interest/low readability score solution. First, it is extraordinarily difficult to select high-interest texts for an individual student, especially one who is not much of a reader. Giving the student the power to choose (and reject) texts might be more effective and just as pedagogically sound. Second, it might be more useful to search for a meaningful text and task in which the student would be willing to invest some effort. Third, a low readability score is no guarantee of true ease of reading. This is particularly the case for texts constructed or adapted to fit a readability formula.

Nevertheless, readability formulas or their kin are widely used in designing and choosing remedial reading texts. The following two examples illustrate the results of this approach. Both passages score about grade 5 on the Fog readability formula.

Example 1.   The first example is called "Indian Occupation" (Education Progress Corporation, 1979).

The Indians had not heard from the government. The suit for Alcatraz was still not settled. The Indians were discouraged and angry. They did not know if their goal could be reached. Some people wanted to tear down the buildings. "The White Man is our foe," they said. "He took our land 300 years ago. It's true! The White Man wrote treaties, but they were all a hoax."

Other Indians said, "Wait! We must build a place here that we can boast about. We must have a school. It's dangerous for our children to roam through these old buildings. We need food, too. We must hoe the soil and plant tomatoes, potatoes, and fruit."

Suddenly someone roared, "Fire! Fire!" A fire had started in an old building. Unfortunately, the boards made good fuel. The flames soared high. There was no water to soak the buildings. The only water on Alcatraz was the drinking water brought by the boats. The Indians had no pumps to bring water out of the bay. Finally, the roaring fire was reduced to coals and burned itself out. There were no clues to tell how it started.

Other problems came up. Food and water did not come when they were due. Boats cruised by, but they didn't stop at the island. Some of the Indians began to loaf. They forgot about their oath to work together. Richard Oakes decided to leave the island. Others said, "If he goes, we'll go too." Nobody could coax them to stay.

Problems.   There are several problems with this text that can be traced to an overreliance on surface-level text features. Many of the subjects in the first few sentences (e.g., "the Indians," "the suit") are introduced with no referent and no specification. On the other hand, one of the few specific characters in the text—Richard Oakes—is not mentioned until the end of the selection. Random collections of nouns ("tomatoes, potatoes and fruit") are included that make little semantic sense. Some of the text is even contradictory; not until the last paragraph do we have a sense that the Indians had "an oath" to work together.

Much of the difficulty with this text clearly results from an overriding effort to introduce the written forms of particular sounds, especially long *o* and *u*. This, plus the word and sentence restrictions of readability formulas, results in an incoherent story. This example illustrates again the underlying problem with readability formulas: their discounting of higher-level structural features of text (e.g., in this case, any sense of story).

The misuse of formulas illustrated by this example is quite common. Readability formulas have been used here to guide the writing of a text, rather than to evaluate it after it has been written. Thus the text is not "honestly written"—or very communicative. In fact, it is likely to be more difficult to comprehend than its readability estimate might indicate, owing to the strange constructions and vocabulary made necessary by the need to introduce certain sounds.

Example 2.   A second remedial reading passage intended for older children is "Shine" from the *Bridge* series (Simpkins, Holt, & Simpkins, 1977). The following is an excerpt:

Shine was a stoker on the *Titanic*. The Brother, he shovel coal into the ship furnace to make the engines go. Now dig. Check what went down on the day the *Titanic* sunk. Shine kept on going up to the captain of the ship. He kept on telling the captain that the ship was leaking.

Shine run on up to the captain and say, "Captain, Captain, I was down in the hole looking for something to eat. And you know what? The water rose above my feet."

Problems.   While the text from which this passage is taken does seem to be better as a story than the preceding one, it could pose a problem for some White students because it relies on familiarity with Black English Vernacular (BEV). Some misinterpretations white students made when reading passages from the *Bridge* series were (1) to read "brother" as meaning "male sibling," (2) to read "Russ say," as "Someone made/is making Russ say," and (3) to fail to understand such expressions as "they wheels" (Standard English, "their car"). The use of imperatives directed to the reader, such as "Now dig," is characteristic of Black folk tales or BEV, but may be unfamiliar to the White student.

By presenting a text that draws from a nonmajority culture, this example highlights the cultural variables that readability formulas ignore. A readability formula is a measure which makes no reference to the cultural background and values of the reader. This property causes difficulty with a passage like "Shine," since there is no consideration of students' different degrees of familiarity with BEV or the conventions of Black folk tales. Since a major determinant of true readability is the match between the cultural attitudes, beliefs and values of the author and those of the reader, a readability extimate for this passage would surely be inaccurate for either White or Black students. In fact, many readability formulas subtly include a cultural bias against Blacks by including in their lists of familiar words mostly words that are familiar to the majority culture (Bruce, Rubin, Starr, & Liebling, 1984).

Task No. 4: Preparing Basal Readers

Basal readers are texts whose main purpose is to be used in teaching reading. Most of the basal readers feature a "controlled vocabulary," which permits only a slow, paced introduction of new words. They also exercise controls over sentence length and syntactic complexity. The language standards for basal readers are similar to readability formulas, and many of the series explicitly apply explicit formulas as well, in either the writing or selection of passages.

Example.   The following is an example from a 2nd-grade basal reader (Clymer et al., 1976):

"See the sights!" called the tall man.
Every day the tall man came to 5th Street.
Every day he called, "See the sights! See the sights!"

One day Dan was walking on 5th Street.
The tall man was there.
He was calling. "See the sights! See the sights!"
Dan saw a big sight-seeing bus stop on 5th Street.
There was a sign on the back of the bus.
The sign said, "See the Sights! See the Sights!"

"What sights?
Where *does* that bus go?" Dan thought.
The next day Dan walked up to the tall man.
"I want to see the sights," he said.
"When can I take the bus?"
"You're too late today," said the man.
"Come back next Saturday.
Saturday you can see the sights!"

Problems.   This selection lacks coherence even though readability formulas indicate it is easy to read. In the process of controlling vocabulary, sentence length, syntactic complexity, and so on, the basal reader authors have had to ignore other crucial characteristics of the text. As a result, a child who looks for a familiar narrative structure, for example, conflict and resolution, will find a story which violates that expectation. Laying aside for a moment the question of the aesthetic or pleasure value of such a story, it may simply be harder to read because of its inadequacies in terms of characteristics such as conflict, suspense, surprise, and humor. Children fed a steady diet of stories such as this may develop a conception of stories which discourages them from exploring other texts and which does not match the passages they encounter elsewhere.

Steinberg and Bruce (1980) report on a study of story characteristics that is relevant to this problem. Stories were coded for rhetorical structure, point of view, conflict, and amount of insight into characters' thoughts and feelings. One finding was a dramatic shift from lower-primary-level basal stories to upper-primary-level stories in the amount of inside view (insight into characters' thoughts and feelings). A similar situation obtains with regard to interpersonal or internal conflict; the upper-primary basals were rated much higher on this parameter. Again, there is a major difference between the kinds of educational reading materials children receive in lower primary grades and those they receive in upper primary grades. This difference is likely related to the fact that the lower level stories are constructed to conform to readability formula constraints, whereas the upper level stories are typically selected and adapted from trade books.

These selections from basal readers demonstrate again that higher-level factors such as conflict and inside view cannot be ignored in assessing readability. Stories that exclude these characteristics may actually be *more* difficult to read. In addition, they provide little preparation for students who will later be reading more complex stories. It may well be that children who have not learned in basal texts to understand, for example, patterns of conflict in stories may not be adept at dealing with these factors in upper-level texts. The basic problem is that one cannot know by simple measures whether such higher-level factors are correlated with the formula factors.

Task No. 5: TV Captioning

Hearing-impaired adults in this culture are doubly isolated from mainstream society—not only is it difficult for them to communicate with most other people around them, but they also lack access to the television programs so many people watch. TV captioning, which is also done for foreign language dialogue, is a partial solution to this problem.

The process of captioning TV shows must take into account two characteristics of hearing-impaired adults' language capabilities for which readability formulas could plausibly provide some assistance. First, hearing-impaired adults' reading rates are generally lower than those of hearing adults and significantly lower than the rate of oral presentation, so that a simple transcription of the audio portion of a show may not be readable in the time available. Second, hearing-impaired adults are believed to have more limited syntactic and vocabulary abilities than hearing adults. Since readability formulas focus on these aspects of text, they are obvious candidates for evaluating captions. The following illustrates what happens when captioning is done with prime consideration given to word choice and sentence construction. (More recent efforts at TV captioning for the hearing-impaired are moving towards literal transcription.)

Example. The following texts are two versions of introductory comments to a television documentary on Arab-Israeli relations. The show starts with a picture of Marilyn Berger speaking on location in the Middle East. Throughout the passage, we see the same scene, so virtually no information is communicated in the video portion of the show. The first version below is the captioned text; the second is the original.

(a) [1] I'm Marilyn Berger. [2] I first came to the Middle East 11 years ago after the 6-day war. [3] Many Israelis thought it would be the last war. [4] This program is not about armies or diplomats. [5] It is about 2 families caught in the Middle East conflict. [6] The program was filmed 3 years ago. [7] But the same feelings remain today as they have for the last 30 years. [8] The feelings remain although there was hope from the historic visit to Israel by Egypt's President Anwar Sadat. [9] This program was the idea of an Israeli TV producer, and a Harvard professor. [10] They worked with an Egyptian newsman. [11] There is no attempt to decide who is right or wrong. . . . .

(b) I'm Marilyn Berger. I first came to the Middle East 11 years ago, just after the 6-day war—the war so many Israelis thought was the one to end all wars. What you are about to see is the first in a series about the Middle East. It is not about armies, or governments or diplomats. It's about people and families caught in the conflict. The program was filmed in Egypt, in Syria, in Jordan and Lebanon and here in Israel some 3 years ago. But the same feelings, the same dilemmas persist today, as they did 3 years ago—indeed as they have for the last 30 years. They persist despite Egyptian President Anwar Sadat's historic visit to Israel last fall, and all the hopes

16

that visit aroused here and around the world. Before we begin this series, a word about how it all came to be, and about some of the unusual people who were involved in it. Back in 1973, Zvi Dor Ner, an Israeli television producer, and Professor Roger Fisher, of Harvard, who shared a concern for the Middle East and an interest in television had an idea. By July, 1974, the idea had taken shape in a series of broadcasts. Fisher and Dor-Ner became part of a team that included Professor Nadav Safran of Harvard, a leading Middle East scholar, Mohammed Salmawy, an Egyptian newspaper man, and a group from WGBH in Boston. Each program in their series is devoted to a specific aspect of the Middle East conflict. It does not try to resolve who is right or wrong, if indeed there is a right and a wrong. . . . .

The readability level of the original text is 11.4, that of the adapted text 7.4 on the Fog readability scale.

Problems.   The problems with this adaptation arise mainly because the higher-level discourse structure of the text was neglected in its construction. Thus, although individual sentences are "simplified," the overall text is less coherent. For example, the deletion of the repeated phrase "the war" from the original text causes a shift in focus in the adapted text (between sentences [2] and [3] to the Israelis' beliefs. The result is a garden path reading of sentence [3] which at first suggests "Many israelis thought it would be Marilyn Berger's last visit." In the original, the focus is maintained.

A similar problem is the rough transition between "Anwar Sadat" (sentence [8]) and "This program" (sentence [9]). Organizational material from the original ("Before we begin the series, a word. . .") has been deleted, leaving it to the reader to forge some connection between Anwar Sadat and the program.

Third, in the adapted version it is unclear who is not attempting to decide in "There is no attempt to decide who is right or wrong" (Sentence [11]). Is it the producer, the professor, the newsman, or Anwar Sadat? The original contained sufficient context to make the answer clear.

In general, the problems with this selection appear to follow partly from the rate constraints imposed on captioners. Captions are written in general for a reading rate of 120 words per minute regardless of the content of the caption or the video. Since in this particular case the screen showed only a talking head, one approach might have been to increase the length of captions (and therefore the presentation rate) so that the text would have been more coherent.

This example is just one illustration of the problems introduced by adaptations that use readability formulas as guides. (Many more are detailed in Davison & Kantor, 1982.) As in this example, connectives are often deleted in the adaptation, resulting in interpretation problems. Other common adaptations include deletion of organizing material and unprincipled splitting of sentences. Because the final product to which the readability formula is being applied is no longer "honestly written," there is no guarantee its estimate will be accurate.

ASSUMPTIONS ABOUT READABILITY MEASURES
AND THEIR USE

The preceding examples have illustrated various ways in which readability formulas give faulty predictions or even lead to the writing of passages which are harder to read. In each case, one can point to an assumption about the use of the formulas which has been violated. We are led to the conclusion that the formulas are valid *only if* certain conditions hold. Our list of assumptions has arisen from examination of cases where the formulas fail, but similar lists have been put forth by designers of the formulas themselves. For example, explanatory material included with the Raygor Readability Estimator states some of these limitations:

> Reader interest level, reader experience, or any other personal or ethnic variables are not measured by this or any other estimators of readability. Readability estimators do not measure style or syntax.

> Making materials less difficult by shortening sentences and substituting shorter or more common words for longer and more difficult sentences and words may not, in fact, reduce the difficulty level indicated when the formula is applied to the new material. The new material may appear easier and show a lower grade level with the estimate but the concept level may still be high. Readability estimates use variables that predict but do not necessarily control the difficulty of the material. Estimates work best on discursive or narrative prose. Applying estimates to poetry, test items, or other types of non-prose material may produce inaccurate results.

Examples such as the ones presented in this paper provide evidence that these cautions should be observed. Nevertheless, it appears that many uses of readability formulas violate the basic assumptions on their applicability. Our examples have indicated that readability formulas should be used only where the following criteria are met:

1. *Material may be read freely*—The time spent on reading and the manner of reading are determined by the reader, not external factors (such as with TV captions).

2. *Text is honestly written*—The material is written to satisfy a communicative goal, not formula constraints.

3. *Higher-level text features are highly correlated with sentence and word features*—Features such as higher-level organization, conceptual load, and information about character intentions, must be generally predictable from the word and sentence characteristics of the text. This general point applies to all uses of readability formulas.

4. *Purpose in reading is similar to that of readers in the validation studies*—The reader's purpose and strategies in reading should not be altered from that of the validation studies. (This would occur in cases where a reader is skimming, taking a test or reading for pleasure.)

5. *The formula results are not being applied to individual cases*—Readability scores are statistical averages applicable to large numbers of texts and readers and are not intended to provide useful information regarding the appropriateness of an individual text for an individual person.

6. *Readers of interest are the same as the readers on whom the readability formula was validated*—Any attempt to expand the use of the formula to evaluate materials for readers whose background, dialect, purpose in reading, etc. differs from that of the readers used in validation is likely to lead to difficulties.

Rigorous adherence to these assumptions effectively prevents use of readability formulas for TV captioning, text adaptation, selection of texts for readers of different cultural backgrounds, designing special texts for children, selection of text passages, choosing trade books, or designing remedial readers.

Recent studies support the validity of restrictions on readability formula use. One study (Bruce, Rubin, Starr, & Liebling, 1983) compared the oral vocabularies of children of different ethnic and socioeconomic groups with the word lists used in two popular readability formulas (Spache and Dale-Chall). The results indicated two kinds of bias in the lists: one in favor of middle-class as opposed to working-class children, and another in favor of White as opposed to Black children. That is, more of the words on the readability formula vocabulary lists were familiar to middle-class and/or White children than to working-class and/or Black children (than is predictable on the basis of overall vocabulary size differences). Of course, further research is needed to determine if the biases in the word lists are indicative of mismatches in other text dimensions as well. However, since a vocabulary measure is one of the principal factors in some readability formulas, the biases highlight a major drawback in readability formulas: They do not reflect differences in readers' social and cultural backgrounds.

CONSEQUENCES OF VIOLATING THE ASSUMPTIONS

The readability formula focus on variables such as sentence length contravenes much of what we know about how purpose, background, and inference affect communication. The justification for readability formulas must therefore rest on statistical validation. But the validations have been restricted to a narrow class of readers, texts, and purposes for reading. This becomes a problem when readability formulas are applied carelessly. Despite the warnings of many readability researchers (Gilliland, 1972; Kintsch & Vipond, 1977; Redish, 1979), the formulas are used for individual readers and passages; they are applied to types of texts never intended, and they are used in a prescriptive fashion to alter otherwise honestly written text.

To some extent, the formulas encode cultural bias, since the word lists they use are derived from school materials and other texts that are strongly representative of White middle-class America. The extent to which the readability formula word lists fail to match the vocabularies of other cultural and social groups reflects the failure of school texts to match the background, experience, and culture of many of the children who use them. Thus, for a reader of the appropriate cultural background a readability formula estimate may be more accurate than it is for another. Since cultural difference is correlated with reading difficulty, the formulas give their least accurate estimates for the poorest readers.

The formulas may thus interact strongly with standardized tests and curricula in a circular way which fails to address the needs of many children. Standardized tests identify students of low aptitude for success in school. These tests are of the type once used to validate readability formulas. Now, in a circular fashion, readability formulas are used to adjust passage difficulty on the tests. Books for beginning readers once served as the source for the word lists for readability formulas; now the formulas have been used in the preparation and editing of basal readers. While basal publishers do not in general give authors explicit instructions to tailor their stories to readability formulas, the formulas are used to choose the most appropriate passages, adapt them to particular grade levels, and sequence them in order of increasing complexity. Moreover, the skills taught in the basal readers and emphasized throughout the basic curriculum are those tested on the standardized tests. To the extent that readability formulas are valid, they measure the difficulty of a text with respect to the skills, such as word identification, that are emphasized in the tests, the basal readers, and the standard reading curriculum.

In the public document arena, readability formulas perform a similar function. A contract that has been rewritten to comply with a readability formula benchmark may or may not be more readable, but a defender of it can argue that it is, by scientific criteria, a readable document. A party to that contract has no one to blame if the contract remains obscure. In reality, though, the readability of the contract, or any text, depends on such issues as the desire of the author to communicate, the social context in which the text is read, and the way in which the text meets the needs of the reader. In these cases, readability formulas divert attention from the real problems to the text itself, then transfer responsibility from the text to the reader by arguing that the text is comprehensible, even when it is not.

CONCLUSION

The ultimate judge of readability is the reader, not a formula. Formulas do not guarantee readable texts, even less do they grant people power or access in educational, medical, or legal information systems. Unfortunately, they have often helped to perpetuate cultural bias and protect existing power relationships. Any use of readability formulas should be carefully circumscribed. They are best viewed as statistical approximations, which provide rough categorizations of difficulty for honestly written texts, but which may easily fail to be valid in any specific context.

ACKNOWLEDGMENT

This research was supported by the Office of Educational Research and Improvement under Contract No. 400-81-0030.

REFERENCES

Baum, L. F. (1956). *The Wizard of Oz*. Chicago: Rand McNally.

Bruce, B. C. (1984). A new point of view on children's stories. In R. C. Anderson, J. Osborn, & R. J. Tierney (Eds.), *Learning to read in American schools: Basal readers and content texts*. Hillsdale, NJ: Lawrence Erlbaum Associates.

Bruce, B., Rubin, A., Starr, K., & Liebling, C. (1984). Sociocultural differences in oral vocabulary and reading material. In W. S. Hall, W. Nagy, & R. Linn (Eds.), *Spoken words: Effects of Situation and Social Group on Oral Word Usage and Frequency* (pp. 466–480). Hillsdale, NJ: Lawrence Erlbaum Associates.

Clymer, T. et. al. (1976). *One to grow on* (720 Reading Series, Level 6). Lexington, MA: Ginn.

Dale, E., & Chall, J. S. (1948). A formula for predicting readability. *Educational Research Bulletin, 27*, Jan. 11–20, and Feb. 37-54.

Davidson, J. L., & Montgomery, M. (1983). *An Analysis of reports on the status of education in America: Findings, recommendations, and implications*. Tyler, TX: Tyler Independent School District.

Davison, A., & Kantor, R. N. (1982). On the failure of readability formulas to define readable texts. *Reading Research Quarterly, 17*, No. 2, 187–209.

Education Progress Corporation. (1979). *Clue Magazine*, No. 2.

Educational Testing Service. (1960). *Cooperative English Test of Reading Comprehension*. Menlo Park, CA: Addison-Wesley.

Flesch, R. F. (1948). A new readability yardstick. *Journal of Applied Psychology, 32*, 221–233.

Gilliland, J. (1972). *Readability*. London: University of London Press.

Gunning, R. (1964). *How to take the fog out of writing*. Chicago: Dartnell.

Hutchins, P. (1976). *Don't forget the bacon*. New York: Greenwillow Books.

Juster, N. (1961). *The phantom tollbooth*. New York: Random House.

Kintsch, W., & Vipond, D. (1977). Reading comprehension and readability in educational practice and psychological theory. In Lars-Goran Nilsson (Ed.), *Proceedings of the Conference on Memory*. Hillsdale, NJ: Lawrence Erlbaum Associates.

Klare, G. R. (1976). A second look at the validity of readability formulas. *Journal of Reading Behavior, 8*, 129–152.

Redish, J. (1979). Readability. In D. A. McDonald (Ed.), *Drafting documents in plain language*. New York: Practicing Law Institute.

Rosenblatt, L. M. (1978). *The reader, the text, the poem*. Carbondale: Southern Illinois University Press.

Rubin, A. (1984). What can readability formulas tell us about text? In J. Osborn, P. T. Wilson, & R. C. Anderson (Eds.), *Foundations for a literate America*. Lexington, MA: Lexington Books.

Simpkins, G., Holt, G., & Simpkins, C. (1977). *Bridge - A cross-culture reading program.* Boston: Houghton Mifflin.

Steinberg, C. S., & Bruce, B. C. (1980). Higher level features in children's stories: Rhetorical structure and conflict. In *The National Reading Conference Yearbook.* Clemson, S.C.: The National Reading Conference.

Taylor, W. L. (1953). Cloze procedure: A new tool for measuring readability. *Journalism Quarterly, 30,* 415.

2 Conceptual and Empirical Bases of Readability Formulas

Richard C. Anderson
Alice Davison
Center for the Study of Reading, University of Illinois

The question of what features of a text make the text difficult or easy for a reader is interesting from many different perspectives. In this chapter we examine this question and its implications from the specific perspective of *readability formulas*, pointing out the basic choices and assumptions made in their development and use. These assumptions are discussed in relation to the larger question of text comprehensibility in which the use of formulas is embedded. We question to what degree readability formulas actually do what they were intended to do: to gauge whether particular texts can be read and understood by particular readers or groups of readers, on some particular use or occasion of reading.

We argue that readability formulas are not the most appropriate measures for this purpose. To preview these arguments, the aggregate statistical model which readability formulas are based on is inappropriate. As a consequence, formulas do not make reliable predictions of comprehension for individual readers. Formulas are misleading guides for editing a text to reduce its difficulty. They measure features of a text which are at best correlated with difficulty, without being a more specific causal model. Such a model would define what features of language actually contribute directly to difficulty in comprehension. These formulas cannot be used to diagnose what is difficult about the language in a text. Formulas are applied by calculating the average sentence length and word difficulty in short samples of texts. Features of a text not among the features of sentence and word difficulty almost certainly make a much greater difference to comprehension than the features which are measured in the application of a formula. The criteria of comprehension associated with formulas are comprehension measures which are generally the *least* sensitive to specific features of language, of the experimental measures currently in use. Finally, to the extent that formulas do capture some plausible intuitions about the working memory capacity of a reader, these notions need to be made more explicit in the context of basic research using on-line measures of attention and comprehension. These points are discussed in more detail in the remainder of the chapter.

We begin by describing one of the earliest readability formulas, proposed in Vogel and Washburne (1928), and noting the characteristics which have persisted in the formulas now in use. Vogel and Washburne based their formula on a sample of 700 books which had been mentioned by 37,000 children as ones they had liked. The scores of these children on the paragraph meaning section of the Stanford Achievement test allowed them to be placed in grade-level rankings. The linguistic features of the books were measured and correlated with the reading scores of the children who had read and liked the books. From this information, a formula was designed which is used to predict what reading scores are necessary for a reader to read a certain book.

The *Vogel and Washburne Formula* consists of the following:

1. number of different words in a 1000-word sample;
2. total number of prepositions in the 1000-word sample;
3. total number of words not on the Thorndike list of the 10,000 most frequent words;
4. the number of clauses in 75 sample sentences.

These factors enter into a regression equation:

Reading test score: $= .085x_1 + .101x_2 + .604x_3 - .411x_4 + 17.43$

The reading score levels which the formula predicted for books correlated .85 with the average reading test scores of the children in the sample who had read and liked the books (Chall, 1958, p. 19 and *passim,* Klare, 1963, p. 39).

This early formula illustrates the features which are still typical of readability formulas as a class, and it should be noted that these features represented advances in research and research methods of that period. Thorndike's (1921) list of word frequencies was the first large-scale study of English vocabulary use on an objective empirical basis. Regression analysis was a new statistical procedure that allowed large amounts of data to be integrated. Standard achievement tests, which had been recently developed, provided an objective way of comparing students and ranking them. The measures of language in a text sample focused on fairly easily defined units (words, sentences, prepositions) which occur in large numbers in a text. The sample of students and books which were studied included a wide range of variation, and the correlations of features of text and student scores were very high. Note that, unlike much subsequent readability research, the books sampled were not school texts edited to a certain grade, nor short passages contrived to test reading achievement.

The early formulas like the Vogel and Washburne formula just described represented a considerable advance in research at that time. While formulas have undergone considerable development since 1928, the general conception has remained the same. Some specific features have changed, however, such as methods of sampling texts and measuring comprehension. The independent measure of student performance has typically been the ability to answer correctly 50% or more of multiple choice comprehension questions, or to retrieve 30% or more of the deleted words in a cloze test. Different formulas have used different text variables and ways of counting them, but all formulas use some measure of word difficulty and of sentence complexity. (For more complete discussion of specific formulas, see the overviews in Chall (1958), Klare (1963, 1984), and the discussion of many text variables and cloze as a comprehension measure in Bormuth (1966)). But the formulas have not changed in any fundamental way, in the basic assumptions behind them, or in the way that the problem of text difficulty is conceived.

Anyone who reads surveys of formulas and the problems of measuring text difficulty will be struck by the fact that scholars who do research on readability formulas are aware of the range of features that make a text complex or easy for a reader. These scholars present lucid and perceptive discussions of those aspects of texts and readers which are not measured by formulas such as writing style, text organization, and background knowledge of the reader (Chall, 1958, 1984; Gray & Leary, 1935; Klare, 1963, 1984, for example). These writers are quite clear about what formulas are sensitive to and what results can be expected from them. Both Chall (1958, pp. 97ff) and Klare (1963, pp. 20, 122ff.) note that efforts to increase the readability of texts by simplifying the vocabulary and sentences does not consistently lead to improved comprehension as measured by ability to answer questions, to recall important features of content, and to retain information over time. Nevertheless, both Chall and Klare interpret available evidence as demonstrating that vocabulary and sentence complexity account for a large proportion of the variance in the understanding of texts (cf. Chall, 1984, as well as Chall, 1958; Klare, 1963).

Scholars of readability are also aware of the impossibility of reducing all text properties or reader properties to formula variables. To accommodate formulas to the great variety in texts, they attach external conditions to formulas. These take the form of injunctions not to use the formulas for revising texts or for assessing certain kinds of text (poetry, mathematics, unusual texts of various kinds), and not to take formula values as anything but rough predictions of text ease or difficulty. But these injunctions are not built into formulas, as an intrinsic and unavoidable part of them. It is easy to overlook hedges and restrictions added onto a mathematical formula, which has the immense lure of statistical correlation behind it.

The world at large, including publishers and purchasers of textbooks, have not heeded the responsible and well-founded warnings of writers like Chall and Klare. The formula variables—word difficulty and sentence length/complexity—*look* like factors that could cause a load upon a reader's capacity to process linguistic information. Writers and editors who ignore the difference between correlation and causation persist in seeing a formula as a model of what causes a text to be difficult, so that when under pressure to revise a text which might be difficult for a variety of reasons, they simplify hard words and split up complex sentences in the hope that these factors have enough causal power to make a difference in comprehension (cf. Davison & Kantor, 1982, and Green & Olsen, this volume). The damage done to text cannot be blamed on scholars like Chall and Klare, cited above, or even entirely on people who misunderstand the meaning of correlation. The problem is that there are no clear or widely accepted alternatives to the formula-like approach to the problem of linguistic variables and text comprehensibility, although field-testing on a sample of readers and the judgment of experienced readers are possibilities (Klare, 1984). The research on linguistic and other properties of texts that influence comprehension has not yet provided a comprehensive model of how the language of a text is understood which would be more insightful and effective than formulas. There is, however, a substantial body of research which has made considerable progress in illuminating important aspects of texts and readers; this is surveyed in later sections of this chapter, and in other chapters of the book.

INAPPROPRIATE STATISTICAL MODEL

Arguments against readability formulas are sometimes treated as though crushed by the weight of accumulated evidence. It is true that formulas can account for as much as 60% to 80% or more of the variance in student response measures representing the ease or difficulty of texts, but the weightiness of this evidence is an illusion. The problem with formulas is that readability researchers analyze their data using the wrong statistical model, one in which data are aggregated by grade. This is a problem because almost all users of formulas, such as, for instance, teachers and librarians, are attempting to match books to individuals, small groups within a class, or, maybe, the collection of individual students at a certain grade level in a specific school. For example, a group consisting of students reading at the 2nd grade level and the 6th grade level might have an average level of 4th grade, but a 4th grade level text (also averaged over sample passages) would not necessarily be suitable for each individual student.

In studies such as Vogel and Washburne (1928) and Bormuth (1966) in which readability formulas were validated, texts of a very wide range of difficulty were investigated. Of course, the wider the range of text difficulty the higher the correlations of text features with the student response measure. However, such correlations are unrealistic since a 7th grade teacher, for instance, will not be considering high school physics texts or 1st grade primers. When Rodriguez and Hansen (1977) replicated Bormuth's (1966) study using 7th grade students and texts appropriate for 7th graders, they found that the text features accounted for only 20% to 40% of the variance in the student response measure, instead of the 80% to 85% in the original Bormuth study.

It is well-known that aggregating data leads to a big increase in the percentage of variance that is apparently explained. But when formula authors aggregate while users individuate, the increase in variance explained is misleading. The user is left with an inflated impression of the power of the formula to predict the difficulty of texts for individual readers.

The correct approach would be to analyze the total variance, treating both texts *and* individuals as random variables. This research remains to be done. If it were done, we would not be surprised to find that the best formulas explained, say, 10% of the variance [of individual scores] instead of 80% of the variance [of grade-level averages].

Reading is now understood to be an interactive process (see chapters in Spiro, Bruce, & Brewer, 1980). What this means for readability research is that there should be interactions between characteristics of texts and characteristics of readers. Detecting interactions of this type is impossible when data are aggregated. Moreover, if such interactions do exist, this would mean that a formula that gave a seemingly good prediction of grade-level averages could be grossly inaccurate when used to select material for any individual reader. The sections that follow summarize evidence showing several strong interactions between text characteristics and reader characteristics and suggest other probable interactions that have not yet been documented in empirical studies.

To encapsulate our conclusion, because an inappropriate statistical model has been used, the right unit for assaying the weight of the evidence from readability research is the ounce instead of the ton. Unless a formula were to include terms representing interactions, not only among text features, but also between text features and reader characteristics, it could not do justice to comprehension as we now understand it.

In the next sections, we survey research which has sought to determine the contribution of word and sentence difficulty to comprehension of texts. We conclude that these factors, which enter into all formulas, do not directly influence comprehension very much. If their presence in formulas is taken seriously as a model of text comprehension, incorrect predictions will be made.

WORD DIFFICULTY

The major variable in every readability formula is some operational definition of word difficulty, such as the percentage of words that do not appear on a list of words familiar to children, the length of words in syllables, or the length of words in letters. It may seem intuitively obvious that long, rare words are an important cause of text difficulty, but close analysis shows that this intuition is open to serious question.

Nagy and Anderson (1984) estimated that there are about 240,000 words in printed school English. About 139,000 of these are semantically transparent derivatives or compounds, that is, words that a person could figure out from knowledge of the parts with little or no help from context. Below are several examples, along with the frequency with which each word occurred in the 5,088,721 word corpus that formed the basis for the *American Heritage Word Frequency Book* (Carroll, Davies, & Richman, 1971):

unladylike	2
girlish	0
rustproof	2
distasteful	4
helplessness	4
caveman	1

For comparison's sake, consider that *people* occurred 7989 times in the corpus or that *sentence* occurred 3122 times.

Though not all derivatives and compounds are as easy as the ones above, these examples do illustrate the fact that long, rare words are not necessarily, or even usually, hard words. An estimated additional 43,000 words in printed school English are semantically opaque derivatives and compounds. In most of these cases, the word parts provide guides to pronunciation and partial clues to meaning. Some examples are: *apartment, saucepan, shiftless,* and *foxtrot.*

Nagy and Anderson (1984; see Table 6, p. 320) found that semantically transparent derivatives are disproportionately found in the lower end of the frequency distribution, far more often than morphologically basic words [words that cannot be divided into parts with consistent meanings] and semantically opaque derivatives. Only 10% of the most frequent words in printed school English are transparent derivatives. As one moves downward in frequency, however, the proportion of transparent derivatives increases steadily, until among the least frequent words there are nearly twice as many transparent derivatives as there are basic words and opaque derivatives.

Thus, most long, rare words are derivatives and compounds, and the great majority of these are phonologically and semantically transparent. What inference can be drawn from this fact about the extent to which long, rare words are a *cause* of text difficulty? We present evidence below suggesting that they are not a cause of difficulty for most readers. Our conjecture is that these words are a cause of difficulty only for a special subclass of readers, those who are poor decoders, specifically those who have trouble segmenting words into useful parts such as basic words, prefixes, suffixes, and syllables, and perhaps into parts whose status is more problematical such as bound morphemes and phonograms—words like *raspberry, caterpillar,* and *minister,* which cannot be analyzed into meaningful units, even though they might appear to be made up of separate parts.

Children are able to deal with words productively composed of parts. One of the best established and most interesting findings of developmental psycholinguistics is that preschool children overextend the rules of inflectional morphology (Berko, 1958; Cazden, 1968). At one time or another, most children 3 or 4 years of age can be heard to say, for instance, *foots* instead of *feet* or *eated* instead of *ate*. Far from indicating that they don't yet know English, these overextensions are a sign that the children are making crucial inductive generalizations about word composition.

Recently, we have uncovered preliminary evidence that knowledge of derivational morphology develops later than knowledge of inflectional morphology. Anderson and Freebody (1983) gave 5th graders a checklist vocabulary task in which real words varying widely in familiarity were to be discriminated from close-to-English nonwords. The fascinating finding was that almost all of the false alarms of the good readers were with ''pseudo-derivatives,'' where a pseudo-derivative was defined as a letter string that does not occur in English consisting of a real word and suffix. Among the top quartile of readers, for instance, who checked an average of only 6.4% of the nonwords, 70% checked *loyalment,* 48% checked *conversal,* and 19% checked *forgivity*. Anderson and Freebody (1983, p. 254) characterized these good readers as ''aggressive'' in applying morphological principles to attack the meanings of unfamiliar words. Notice that, whereas the checklist task in a sense tricked the children into making mistakes, aggressiveness in using morphology would be highly functional during normal reading.

Findings from research in progress suggest that overextensions of the type just illustrated [involving neutral suffixes like *-ness* that attach to stems with no shift in pronunciation or spelling] peak at about the 6th grade (see Tyler & Nagy, 1986). Fewer overextensions encompassing pseudo-derivatives are observed with 4th graders, presumably because generalizations about derivational morphology are fragmentary among most children at this level. Further, overextensions are no more frequent among 8th graders than 4th graders, presumably at this level, though, because 8th graders have learned more of the sometimes subtle selection restrictions on the use of derivational suffixes. Just as the young child eventually learns that you say *ate* instead of *eated* so, too, it is reasonable to suppose, does the typical 8th grader tacitly know that *forgivity* is not right because *-ity* attaches only to adjective stems of latinate origin.

The tentative conclusion we draw from the foregoing is that for the child in the 5th or 6th grade making average, or even somewhat below average progress in reading, the lion's share of long, infrequent words do *not* cause increased text difficulty. It is beyond our imagination that the typical child able to read at this level would have any more than the slightest problem with even previously unencountered transparent compounds and derivatives, provided the base words were known. Of course, long, infrequent words may cause problems for, perhaps, the bottom quartile of middle grade readers, because they cannot reliably decode the words and segment them into useful parts, and probably have a shaky command of derivational morphology. For similar reasons, long, infrequent words can be expected to cause problems for a larger proportion of children in the primary grades.

We turn now to words that are really difficult for children, not *unladylike* and *helplessness*, but *rambunctious, tort,* or *buffoon.* Do words such as these *cause* texts to be difficult? Available research bearing on the answer has yielded weak and inconsistent results. First, there is the readability research, discussed later in this paper, showing that splitting long sentences and substituting short, frequent words for longer, less frequent words generally produces little improvement in text comprehension.

Better evidence, in principle at least, comes from studies in which children were taught truly difficult words and then tested to see whether comprehension of texts containing the difficult words improved. Several studies of this kind have produced negative results. For instance, Jenkins, Pany, and Schreck (1978) explored several methods for teaching the meanings of 12 difficult words. All the methods were at least somewhat better than no instruction. The most effective method with both normal and learning disabled children involved intensive drill and practice on the words in isolation. However, even when children had definitely learned the meanings of all the difficult words, they did no better than uninstructed children, who definitely did not know the words, on a cloze test or in retelling a brief story that contained the difficult words.

That instruction in difficult vocabulary *can* produce improvement in text comprehension has been demonstrated by Beck and her associates (Beck, McCaslin, & McKeown, 1980; Beck, Perfetti, & McKeown, 1982; McKeown, Beck, Omanson, & Perfetti, 1983). They hypothesized that instruction on difficult words will improve comprehension only if the words are learned thoroughly, so that the word's meaning can be accessed automatically, and so that the word is embedded in a rich mental network of associations. In two studies, involving 75 half-hour lessons over a 5 month period, during which 4th graders encountered 108 difficult words—such as *glutton, filch, lurch,* and *jovial*—10 to 40 times in a range of cleverly designed instructional activities, Beck and her colleagues did find significant increases in comprehension of texts loaded with the words that had been taught. Thus, the hypothesis was confirmed, though the fact that it took such an heroic effort ought to give pause to advocates of direct vocabulary instruction.

A different tack for assessing the influence of difficult vocabulary is described in Freebody and Anderson (1983a, 1983b). They compared the comprehensibility of nine 6th grade social studies texts containing fairly easy vocabulary with alternate versions of the same texts in which either 1/6 or 1/3 of the content words were replaced with more difficult synonyms—for instance, *descending* for *falling, pulverize* for *grind, flora* for *plants,* and *minute* for *tiny.* In this study, and three other studies (1983a, Experiment 2; 1983b) in which 1/4 of the words in several texts were replaced, vocabulary difficulty accounted for an average of only 4% of the variance in three measures of text comprehension. Freebody and Anderson (1983a, p. 36) concluded "that it takes a surprisingly high proportion of difficult vocabulary items to create reliable decrements in performance."

The properties of words and texts that influence the incidental learning of word meanings during normal reading were investigated by Nagy, Herman, and Anderson (1985). Twelve passages, including both expository and narrative texts, were selected from textbooks at the 3rd, 5th, and 7th grade levels. The passages contained 212 difficult "target" words [words which would be tested later] judged to be unfamiliar to most children, and were read by a total of 352 3rd, 5th, or 7th graders. Word properties examined included length, morphological complexity, part of speech, conceptual difficulty, and the strength of contextual support for each word. Text properties included readability as measured by four standard formulas, and several measures of the density of difficult words.

Among the word properties, only conceptual difficulty was related to learning the target words. A word was defined as conceptually difficult if the concept associated with it was judged as not known by children in a certain grade, and learning the concept required new factual information or learning a system of related concepts. For example, the noun *divide,* in the sense of a boundary between drainage basins, cannot be learned apart from other concepts about river systems.

Among the text properties, learning from context was most strongly influenced by the proportion of target words that were conceptually difficult, and by the average length of target words. These two variables, both of which suppressed learning, were fairly highly intercorrelated, but appeared to contribute independently to predicting word learning.

Interestingly, none of the readability formulas applied by Nagy, Anderson, and Herman significantly predicted the learning of word meanings during reading, *unless* proportion of conceptually difficult words entered the equation in a multiple regression analysis. This variable accounted for 4% of the variance. Before it entered, the four readability formulas accounted for an average of 1% of the variance; after it entered, they accounted for an average of 2%.

In summary, word difficulty does not seem to be as important a direct cause of text difficulty as might be assumed looking at readability formulas. First, most long, infrequent words are transparent derivatives and compounds that would not be expected to be difficult for the typical student by the time he or she reaches the middle grades. Second, whether or not a transparent derivative or compound is actually difficult for a particular child will depend on the child's level of understanding of derivational morphology and on even more basic abilities in decoding and segmenting words. Hence, this is clearly one of the cases where interactions are expected, and where it can be anticipated that formulas fit to grade-level averages will do a poor job of predicting individual understanding. Third, even words that readers definitely do not know do not appear to cause big problems in comprehension, unless the text is dense with such words, and the words meet strict criteria of conceptual difficulty. Fourth, as an inference from the foregoing, the prominent role that measures of word "difficulty" play in readability formulas probably means that the measures are largely *indirect* reflections of the deeper factors that cause comprehension difficulty. To preview the argument that is developed in a later section, a text with a lot of unfamiliar words is usually about an unfamiliar topic, and it is mainly lack of knowledge of this unfamiliar topic that makes comprehension difficult.

Finally, we cannot resist the observation that after 60 years of research and an estimated 1000 or more books and articles (Klare, 1984), an adequate and theoretically defensible analysis of word difficulty, the principal variable in every formula, has not heretofore issued from readability research. We attribute this embarrassing fact to shallow empiricism arising from a preoccupation with what "works."

Sentence length

No recent study has focused specifically on the contribution of sentence length per se to comprehension. Preliminary findings from a study by Davison, Wilson, and Hermon (1985) show that sentence length alone accounts for a very small percentage of the variance in the comprehension of texts. Average sentence length is correlated with complexity of internal clause structure, which in turn is correlated with the presence of markers of subordination and of connectives (*so, or, because, when, if,* and even *and,* etc.) which make explicit the meaning relation between clauses. Hence, long sentences usually consist of syntactically connected clauses with conjunctions or other markers of connection. The results of the study of 7th grade readers by Davison, Wilson, and Hermon suggest that texts with long sentences are comprehended as well as short sentences, except for poor readers, those in the bottom third of students at this grade level.

Connectives in sentences are not necessarily what makes a long sentence difficult. There is a body of evidence which suggests that, far from being a source of difficulty, the presence of conjunctions facilitates comprehension, particularly when two clauses could be connected in more than one way, such as in a "reversible" way. For example, the two sentences in (1) may bear more than one relation to one another. These different interpretations are paraphrased in (2a) and (2b), in which an explicit connective is used.

1.   I moved the switch. The lights went off.

2a. I moved the switch, because the lights went off (to turn them back on).

2b. The lights went off because I moved the switch (turning them off).

If there is no connective, the reader is not always able to make the correct inference, especially if it is not clear from the context which inferences (if any) should be made. In another example, the two sentences in (3) can convey two very different meanings, (4a) and (4b).

3. Let's fill the bird-feeder with seed. The cat hasn't been active lately.
4a. Let's make the cat more active by filling the bird feeder.
4b. It's safe to fill the feeder because the cat isn't active.

The presence of explicit connectives is often helpful to the reader if the context does not make sentence connections obvious to the reader.

Pearson (1974–1975) has shown that children prefer sentences containing an explicit connective such as *because,* and understand them better than implicitly connected sentences. Irwin (1980) showed for somewhat longer texts that both 5th graders and college students comprehended reversible causal relationships among sentences better if an explicit conjunction was used. In a subsequent study, Irwin and Pulver (1984) found that for 5th and 8th grade students, comprehension of reversible causal relationships was improved if the conjunction was explicit, and not simply left to be inferred. The presence of a conjunction thus facilitates comprehension, even though it adds to average sentence length in the text. The presence of a conjunction affected students independently of reading ability. If sentence length is a factor in comprehension, it would be expected that longer sentences would pose a greater problem for students who are poor readers than those with better reading ability. Irwin and Pulver found no interaction between sentence length and reading ability, however.

Increases in sentence length do not necessarily impede understanding. Beck, McKeown, Omanson, and Pople (1984) systematically revised two basal reader stories to improve comprehensibility. The revisions were directed at eliminating difficult surface forms, such as pronouns with unclear antecedents; clarifying references to concepts the readers might not know; and clarifying relationships among parts of the story. In recall of the central elements of the story, both skilled and less skilled 3rd grade students did better after reading the revised versions, even though the readability level was raised by the revisions one grade level on the Fry scale.

A study of adults' comprehension of difficult and unfamiliar material by Charrow and Charrow (1979) compared revisions of the jury instructions done according to the implicit guidelines of readability formulas, or according to a set of guidelines based on psycholinguistic research and a careful analysis of the content of the instructions. One set of revisions was done by simplifying words and shortening sentences, so as to decrease the readability score computed for the passages. The other set of revisions focused on the important pieces of information in the instruction, eliminating distracting less important phrases and drawing attention to the central concepts. The language was revised to make the sentence structures match the content more clearly, and to use passive, embedded and preposed structures only when they were supported by the surrounding context.

For example, compare the original and revised versions of part of the definition of *contributory negligence:*

5a. (original)
An essential factor in contributory negligence is that it contributes as a proximate cause of the injury. (Charrow & Charrow, p. 1354) (17 words)
5b. (revised version)
If the plaintiff was contributorily negligent, he actually helped cause his own injury, through his own negligence. (Charrow & Charrow, P. 1355) (17 words).

Here, clarifications of sentence structure and vocabulary caused increased comprehension. Nevertheless the sentences in (5a) and (5b) are the same length and the vocabulary in both cases is technical and infrequent. The revisions of the type illustrated in (5b) were not much different in readability level from the originals, but they significantly improved the subjects' ability to recall and paraphrase the instructions. On the other hand, revisions which aimed at lower readability scores resulted in no greater recall than the original forms, or in some cases even poorer recall.

In this next section we discuss some cases in which comprehension of a sentence is made more difficult by some features of the sentence itself. We show, however, that difficulty of comprehension is not linked in a simple way to complex features of sentence syntax. That is, complex features of sentence structure do not necessarily present a problem every time they occur. For example, if the context fits the complex structure and justifies its use, the structure may not be difficult to comprehend. But in other cases, there may be a mismatch between the features of a sentence and the context in which it occurs, and in that case, it may well be difficult for a reader. Or if processing a complex structure in some way exceeds the attentional resources of the reader, it will be difficult. As we will see, difficulty of sentence structure is not an absolute value, and depends on interactions with other text features, and with features of the reader.

The sentence length variable may reflect some kind of semantic complexity in the text, but as we have seen in the studies just reviewed, there is no general causal relation between how long a sentence is and how easy it is to understand. This is not to say that sentence structure has no effect on how well a sentence can be understood. It is easy to imagine many ways in which the length and complexity of a sentence could make it hard to understand, and conversely, how sentences may be written so as to make their meaning easy to understand. What is not easy to characterize is some general definition of sentence complexity. The reason for this is that sentence complexity is not an absolute value. Specific sentence features do not always introduce difficulty into the processing of the sentence that contains them. Sentence features interact with other sentence features, and with features of readers, in many cases where difficulty of comprehension has been revealed by experimental measures, as in the Irwin and Pulver study (1984) cited earlier.

A long sentence may be hard to understand simply by virtue of its length, all other things being equal, just because it contains a large number of words to identify and access. But we may compare sentences of exactly the same length, with the same words, and find that they differ in complexity. For example, Irwin and Pulver used sentence pairs like the following:

6. Because Mexico allowed slavery, many Americans and their slaves moved to Mexico during that time.
7. Many Americans and their slaves moved to Mexico during that time, because Mexico allowed slavery.

The subjects, who were asked to answer comprehension questions about these sentences, were 3rd, 5th, and 8th grade students, as well as college students. As noted earlier, the versions of the sentences with connectives, though longer, were understood better than the single clause sequences. What surprised the experimenters, however, was that the version with the preposed adverbial clause, (6), was difficult for the younger subjects, those in the 3rd and 5th grades. They predicted that (6) would always be *easier* than (7) because the order in which the clauses are mentioned coincides with the general cause-before-effect ordering that is generally preferred. This was the case for older and more skilled readers, who had no trouble in matching the order of mention with the meaning of *because*. But apparently the younger and less skilled readers did not use the cause-effect ordering in the same way to overcome the difficulty they had in understanding the sentence structure.

Why should a preposed clause be more complex than a similar clause which follows the main verb and its objects? A very broad explanation comes from work by Yngve (1960), who wanted to define what is involved in producing or understanding a sentence. The parts of a sentence consist of words grouped into smaller and larger phrases, belonging to different categories whose features are defined by the rules of the language. For example, words like *the* occur only in phrases with nouns, and precede the noun. This word is a *left branch* within a Noun Phrase, and its appearance signals the beginning of a phrase of the NP category. Hence it is stored in working memory while the next constituents are searched for, including the noun. Yngve proposed that for this reason, left branches always require more memory capacity to produce or understand than right branches. Preposed adverbial clauses are left branches, large phrases which must be held in working memory until the main clause constituents are found (Bever & Townshend, 1979).

Kemper (in press-a, in press-b; Kynette and Kemper, in press) investigated people at the other end of the age range than in the Irwin and Pulver study, elderly adults who have less working memory capacity than younger adults. She

compared their ability to paraphrase or recall sentences with left branching or right branching structures. The sentences in (8a) – (10a) all have left branching structures, while those in (8b) – (10b) have right branching structures.
Free relative clauses:

8a. [What I did] interested my grandchildren.
8b. My grandchildren watched [what I did].

Finite *that* clauses:

9a. [That the cookies were brown] surprised me.
9b. I believed [that the cookies were brown].

Relative clauses modifying noun phrases:

10a. The cookies [that I baked] were delicious.
10b. My children enjoyed the cookies [that I baked].

In a study of journals written over a span of many years, Kemper found that the writers produced very few left-branching structures of these types as they became elderly, compared with middle age. She also found that elderly adult subjects had more trouble paraphrasing sentences with the left-branching structures than the right-branching ones. In another study, the subjects, when asked to read connected texts, recalled fewer left-branching structures than their right-branching counterparts. Interestingly, the subjects had less difficulty with left-branching sentences when they expressed the most important information in the passage. This is another instance of an interaction within a passage.

Under some conditions, then, left-branching structures appear to be more complex than right-branching structures. Nevertheless, there have been numerous objections to Yngve's general proposal that left branches always introduce complexity in the position in the sentence where they occur (for a general discussion see Frazier, 1984). For example, sentences like (11) are read no differently than sentences like (12), according to the eye-movement data in Frazier, Rayner, and Carlson (ms, cited in Frazier, 1984):

11. [That the traffic in this town is unregulated] bothers me.
12. It bothers me [that the traffic in this town is unregulated.]

If a pronoun occurs in the embedded clause, however, sentences of the type in (13) were read more slowly than those in (14):

13. [That people look at him strangely] bothers Mary.
14. It bothers Mary [that people look at him strangely].

The young adult subjects in Frazier's study had difficulty with a left branch only if there was an additional relation such as anaphora to be processed at the same time.

A single left branch structure is not as difficult to process as multiply embedded ones, as in (15):

15. That that men were appointed didn't bother the liberals wasn't remarked upon by the press. (Frazier (1984, p. 163))

Frazier (1984) speculates that the correct interpretation of such a complex sentence requires a great deal of abstract (and left-branching) structure in proportion to the number of words in surface structure. This amount of structure containing internal sentence phrase nodes overloads temporary processing capacity. Frazier reports that sentences like (16) appear to many readers to be well-formed even though one verb phrase is missing:

16. That that men were appointed didn't bother the liberals. (Frazier (1984, p. 179)).

The first *that* needs to be matched with a predicate (e.g., *wasn't reported*), whose subject is the internal sentence *that men were appointed didn't bother the liberals*. To detect this anomaly requires that a lot of structure be kept in working memory, too much even for most normal adults.

Even complex structures like these are not *absolutely* difficult to process. The presence of conjunctions with specific syntactic properties and semantic content makes it easier to understand sentences like (12) and to detect missing phrases (cf. Frazier, 1984, p. 178–180).

17. Since if you light a match the gas will explode, you should be careful.

This sentence contains two left-branching structures, one nested within the other. It is nevertheless not as difficult to understand as (15), which has the same general features.

Though some sentences like (15) are harder to understand than others like (16), it is not always clear what makes the difference. The hypothesis, however, is that left-branching structures may cause an overload on working memory, with resulting problems of comprehension, *if* the reader has some problems with short-term memory, as with very young or very old readers. People with normal capacity may also have problems with left-branching structures if some other factor makes demands on short-term memory and there are no additional surface cues which add information. The tendency of left-branching structure to make a sentence hard to understand is the result of an interaction between the demands on short-term memory caused by left-branching structures and a number of other factors.

Yngve's proposal that left-branching and deeply embedded structures are complex has been used to construct a predictor of complexity, which automatically assigns weightings to syntactic structures from which a complexity profile could be derived for a whole sentence, or text (Botel & Granowsky, 1972; and Botel, Dawkins, & Granowsky, 1973). While this approach is interesting, it was never pursued in detail at the time it was proposed, nor used to make specific predictions tested with comprehension measures. Perhaps if it had been, there would have been some alternative conceptions to readability formulas. If sentence complexity is the product of interactions rather than an absolute value, however, it is still unlikely that refinements of the measure of sentence complexity in formulas would have led to more accurate predictions.

Another attempt to refine the measure of sentence complexity was in the form of a taxonomy of structures which seemed to be acquired late in childhood or to cause difficulties in comprehension for young children, according to psycholinguistic studies of language acquisition and comprehension in the 1960s and early 1970s (Dawkins, 1975). There are several problems with this approach. First, more refined experimental methods have shown that children can understand complex structures at an earlier age than previously thought. For example, Sheldon (1974) reported that young children interpreted restrictive relative clauses like (18) as though they were conjoined structures describing successive events (19):

18. The dog which bit the cat ran away.
19. The dog bit the cat and ran away.

But Hamburger and Crain (1981), found that if sentences are placed in a natural discourse context, young children correctly understand a sentence like (18) as a way of picking out which of several dogs is being referred to.

Second, the complexity of a particular construction like the passive or relative clauses does not always cause it to be hard to understand. It is hard to imagine why a language has both an active and a passive form for clauses without there being some difference in their functions. It would be strange if the only use for passive clauses was to express information in a more complex or obscure way than in active clauses. In fact, as many experimenters have shown (Glucksberg, Trabasso, & Wald, 1973; Olson & Filby, 1972, for example), passive sentences require less reading time and are more accurately comprehended when the preceding verbal context contains an antecedent for the passive subject, which is the topic of the target (passive) sentence. The relation between syntactic features of a sentence and the topic is discussed in relation to context in Davison and Lutz (1984) and Davison (1984). The two sentences in (20) differ in that the subordinate clause subject in (20a) has normal subject properties, while the corresponding word *him* in (20b) is semantically a subject, but has properties of an object.

20a. We believe that *he* is intelligent.
20b. We believe *him* to be intelligent.

The constituent *him* in (20b) is like the subject of a passive sentence, since *him* has the syntactic markers of one grammatical role and the semantic properties of another role. So if we assume that sentence structures are more complex if the outward markers of grammatical roles do not directly correspond to the semantic relations, the structure in (20b) is more complex than the synonymous structure in (20a).

The difference can be seen by placing the more and less complex versions of a sentence in a discourse context. For example, consider the sentence (21) to be the context preceding either (22a) or (22b):

21. People are afraid to go out at night.
22a. We believe that a flying saucer is exploring Chicago.
22b. We believe a flying saucer to be exploring Chicago.

The subordinate clause subject *a flying saucer* in the second version (22b) is more like an object. The sentence fits this context less well than the less complex version (22a). There is some lack of continuity between (21) and (22b), as though the existence of a specific flying saucer has to be assumed, although it had not been mentioned. For (22a), there is no such assumption conveyed. In the case of (21) – (22b), however, the reader must make an inference linking the two sentences, in somewhat the same way as when the definite article *the* is used (Clark & Haviland, 1977). The difference in discourse continuity originates in the difference of sentence structure. It appears, then, that there is an interaction between sentence structures and the context in which the sentence occurs. If the context contains discourse antecedents for certain phrases which the syntax marks as special, then the more complex structures are not necessarily harder to understand. In fact, the more complex structures may facilitate comprehension by showing how the new sentence is to be linked to the context. Complexity may arise only when a linguistic form like *do so* requires a matching structure in a previous sentence, and none is found (Tanenhaus & Carlson, 1985).

There is also an interaction between complex words and difficult syntactic structures. Complex words like *indecisive* and *indecision* have a transparent structure, so that their meanings are composed from their parts. Part of their structure includes a suffix which marks the syntactic category of the word, *-ive* for an adjective and *-ion* for a noun. Tyler (1986) found that some subjects may ignore this information in the understanding of certain types of sentences, even when they correctly use the words in another task. In sentences like (23) and (24), the suffixes in *indecisive* and *indecision* are associated with quite different sentence structures:

23. People were afraid of a general *indecision* about nuclear war.
24. People were afraid of a general *indecisive* about nuclear war.

The subjects in Tyler's study chose the paraphrase appropriate for (23) as the preferred interpretation for both (23) and (24), ignoring the adjective suffix *-ive* which makes this interpretation inappropriate for (24). The reason seems to be that the sentences are ambiguous between two syntactic phrase structures up to the point where the target word appears. Parsing strategies which tend to maximize the choice of the simpler interpretation lead to a preference for the interpretation [$_{NP}$ a general N . . .] rather than the more complex interpretation [$_{NP}$ [$_{NP}$ a general] [Adj...]]] (cf. Frazier & Fodor, 1978). These parsing strategies lead to a syntactic decision about the phrase structure of the sentence *before* the target word is encountered. If we assume that abandoning a decision which is already made and reprocessing the sentence adds to complexity of processing, then it is not surprising that the initial choice for N is retained, even when the word has adjective features. So even someone who can normally make use of the information in affixes may ignore it in the face of other factors which add to the complexity of the sentence being understood.

In this section we have discussed a number of cases in which syntactic features of a sentence may make the sentence difficult to understand. But the complexity which is introduced is the result of the interaction of several factors all being processed at once in some limited space in working memory [as we note in the section which follows]. The features of sentence structure cannot be used as absolute indicators that the sentence will be complex, so that it is not possible to replace the length measure with some other direct measure of complexity, however detailed and sensitive it might be. Whatever is measured in this way *might* pose a problem for some readers if other factors are present. While there are explanations for why some sentence features may overload processing capacity in some cases, we are a long way from a general characterization of sentence complexity and how it arises.

Sentence length and word complexity are measured in a sample of text in computing its readability. These variables do not, however, directly reflect the properties of a text which make it difficult for a reader to read and comprehend. As is well-known, the application of a formula in reverse, revising a text to make the sentences shorter and the words simpler, does not increase comprehension. The complexity of a text *may* be directly indicated by the linguistic factors which are measured by formulas. The studies just cited show that the same factors, complex morphology and sentence connectives, actually convey information about meaning in an explicit way, and so are not barriers to comprehension for most readers. They may appear to be powerful indicators of complexity because of the inappropriate use of an aggregate statistical model, not taking into account the interaction of properties of the individual with other properties of the text. In the next section we discuss how some of these other factors, not measured by formulas, have a direct influence on comprehension.

LIMITATIONS ON PROCESSING CAPACITY

Thus far we have presented evidence and arguments that point to the inescapable conclusion that readability formulas permit an exaggerated impression of the role of word difficulty and sentence complexity in text comprehension. However, it would be foolish to suppose that these elements of language have no influence on comprehensibility.

Connected written text has many features, including content, style, and organization. But at the most basic level it is composed of words organized into sentences, which conform to the grammatical rules of the language in question. Ultimately it must be interpreted on that level, so that the text as a whole must pass word by word and sentence by sentence through the "bottleneck" of the linguistic processor, in the metaphor used by Perfetti and Lesgold (1977). The comprehension of words and sentences requires linguistic knowledge. This knowledge is not wholly or even largely predictable from contextual factors. The meaning of complex expressions is composed from the meaning of the parts, and the ways they are put together according to the rules of the language. The ability to understand a text at this fundamental level requires linguistic knowledge.

Words and sentences in a text are the raw material entering into a *full* interpretation, which is only partially determined by the words and sentence meanings. These meanings enter into higher level cognitive processes such as making inferences, combining propositions about the same referent, and integrating propositions with knowledge which the reader already possesses. If, as we have shown, linguistic factors do exert some influence on how difficult a text may be for a reader, we need to relate word difficulty and sentence complexity to a sound model of how language is processed.

If some features of words or sentence structure delay comprehension, or simply make it more difficult, the influence of these factors will not necessarily be reflected in failure to answer comprehension questions correctly. The ability to answer such questions will be based on an interpreted representation of meaning, perhaps combining the meaning of a specific sentence with other information. Even cloze questions, which consist of gaps in texts, are answered after the surrounding sentences have been interpreted. Answering comprehension or cloze questions, therefore, is based more on a memory of representation of a sentence than on a sentence piece by piece while it is being processed.

The linguistic form of a sentence is not always available after it has been stored in memory. In a study which has strongly influenced conceptions of language interpretation, Bransford, Barclay, and Franks (1972) showed that subjects do not always recognize a sentence in exactly the same form in which it was presented; instead, they reliably remember the meaning of a sentence but not its exact surface form. It appears that once a sentence has been interpreted, it is usually no longer necessary to retain a representation of its form. To do so would require extra memory resources. It appears from Jarvella's classic study (1971) that working memory resources are used very economically. If subjects are interrupted while reading and asked to decide if they have seen a certain word before, they can make this decision much more rapidly if the word occurred in the clause currently being read, than if it occurred in a previous clause or preceding sentence. Assuming that retrieval from current working memory is faster than from longer-term memory, it appears that sentences are processed in chunks the size of a clause or possibly smaller (Marslen-Wilson, Tyler, & Seidenberg, 1980).

Marslen-Wilson's (1975) finding that syntactic or semantic errors are very rapidly detected and corrected also shows that processing of oral language is extremely rapid, and the same must be true of written language, at least for fluent readers. While many important details are unclear, a model of language process-ing which is consistent with these findings assumes a temporary working memo-ry with a limited capacity which has the function of breaking a linguistic input into chunks and applying lexical and other linguistic knowledge to the chunks to derive an interpretation. This interpretation, whose form is not directly observ-able, lacks some if not all features of surface structure. As a meaning representa-tion of the sentence is constructed, it is stored in long-term memory and can be combined with other semantic material.

The best time to look for the influence of linguistic factors on language understanding is at the moment of processing, rather than after the interpreted meaning of the sentence has been stored, and therefore subject to reinterpretation or revision from other information from the text or background knowledge. For this reason, the measures used in experiments where linguistic factors are a variable tend to be either those very sensitive to details of comprehension, such as immediate recall, or on-line measures which are sensitive to direct loads on attention and processing capacity. These measures include reading time for spe-cific words or sentences, decision time and accuracy for tasks which immediately follow reading or recordings of the fixations and movements of the eye (cf. Frazier & Rayner, 1982).

To the extent that readability formulas measure factors of sentence and word complexity which have some direct influence on comprehension, they are crude approximations of a model of processing capacity. Studies reviewed in earlier sections showed that some complex linguistic factors interfere with comprehen-sion when they place heavy demands on immediate processing capacity, causing difficulty in comprehension. Certain kinds of readers such as young children or elderly people, are likely to have less immediate processing capacity than others. Others have difficulty if they must deal with a great deal of material at one time, though what causes difficulty is not well understood at present since many linguistic factors may interact to cause or to mitigate and remove processing difficulty. Perfetti and Lesgold (1977), among others, argue that word decoding places a very heavy burden on processing capacity in poor readers, such a heavy burden that either resources are exhausted for higher level processing, or the scheduling of the processing operations is disrupted. This is a promising hypothesis which needs to be understood in more detail, as do other cases where interactions of different factors influence comprehension.

Such is also the case for factors which improve comprehension, such as interest and rich background knowledge [see the sections which follow]. Do these features of the reader in conjunction with the text somehow increase processing capacity for the initial interpretation of the linguistic material? Or do they increase the efficiency of higher-level processes, leading to fewer wrong inferences, more direct interpretation of anaphoric relations, better integration with material in the context? Or does interest simply increase the reader's motivation to go through the processes of interpretation, making best use of whatever capacity to understand language which he or she may possess. Not very much is known about these issues, or about how good and poor readers differ, if they do, in general knowledge of language, as opposed to decoding and other processes specific to written language (cf. Perfetti & Lesgold, 1977).

While much remains to be investigated, it appears to us that the issues discussed above are far more promising questions to pursue than those asked in traditional studies associated with readability and readability formulas, which are concerned with ease of application and what "works." These studies have sought to show greater or lesser correlations of comprehension measures with linguistic variables as measured in various ways. The strongest predictors of comprehension, measured retrospectively with comprehension or cloze questions, have always turned out to be sentence length and word complexity, which are not truly independent of one another, in any case. While these studies may satisfy short-term goals, they are utterly unrevealing of anything of interest about the functioning of cognitive processes applied to understanding language. They don't illuminate why a text is difficult to understand, or how comprehension is affected by interactions of features in the text, the language and the reader. We turn now to some other aspects of texts which affect comprehension.

PRIOR KNOWLEDGE

The knowledge a reader already possesses about a topic exerts a powerful influence on comprehension of texts about that topic. That this is so has been demonstrated with readers of every age and all manner of topics. A sampling: Pearson, Hansen, and Gordon (1979) found that 2nd graders who knew a lot about spiders comprehended more from a text about spiders than 2nd graders who were comparable in IQ and reading level but knew little about spiders. Spilich, Vesonder, Chiesi, and Voss (1979) asked college students high and low in knowledge of baseball, but equivalent in verbal ability, to read and recall a story about a half inning from a fictitious baseball game. Those with high baseball knowledge recalled more information than those with low knowledge, particularly information of tactical significance to the game. Sticht, Armijo, Weitzman, Koffman, Roberson, Chang, and Moracco (1986) showed that Navy personnel with high scores on a test of Navy technical knowledge could comprehend Navy texts five grade levels higher, as determined by the Flesch-Kincaid formula, the formula officially prescribed by the Navy, than personnel with low scores on the test of knowledge.

Comprehension will vary depending upon the match between readers' actual knowledge and the knowledge presupposed by texts. That this is so has also been demonstrated a number of times. For instance: Steffensen, Joag-dev, and Anderson (1979) had natives of India and the United States read and recall letters about an Indian wedding and an American wedding. Each group read what for them was the native passage text more quickly than they read the foreign text; they recalled more propositions from the native text, especially propositions rated as important by fellow natives; and they introduced more culturally appropriate elaborations of the native text but more culturally inappropriate distortions of the foreign text. In a similar study, Lipson (1983) gave American middle-grade Catholic and Jewish students texts about a first communion and a bar mitzvah. Prior religious knowledge strongly influenced measures of comprehension. Each group read the culturally familiar text in less time, recalled more propositions from the culturally familiar text, and made more appropriate inferences and introduced fewer errors when recalling the culturally familiar text. Comparable findings have appeared in research with college students, depending on their major field of study (Anderson, Reynolds, Schallert, & Goetz, 1977), and junior high school students, depending upon whether they were black or white (Reynolds, Taylor, Steffensen, Shirey, & Anderson, 1982).

The knowledge a person possesses depends on age, sex, amount and kind of education, race, religion, occupation or occupation of parents, hobbies, country of origin and residence, and region within country, among factors that come readily to mind. Thus, interactions between the knowledge readers possess and the knowledge demands of texts are bound to be the rule rather than the exception, and the complaint made earlier against statistical models in which data are aggregated has more than hypothetical force.

We believe that the reason vocabulary difficulty is the principal component of every readability formula is primarily that it serves as a proxy for background knowledge (see Anderson & Freebody, 1981, and Anderson, Mason, & Shirey, 1984, for earlier statements of this hypothesis). This position can be illustrated using words from the Indian wedding text employed by Steffensen et al. (1979). Only two words in the text, *sari* and *dhoti,* would have been unfamiliar to any of the American readers. Neither word figured importantly in the text, so not knowing them could not have had much effect on comprehension. Nonetheless, a test examining knowledge of the two words would have been an excellent predictor of performance. All the Indians would have known both words; some of the Americans would have known *sari* but few would have known *dhoti*. It is apparent that the test would have divided subjects in terms of their knowledge of Indian culture, which of course was the real reason for the large advantage Indians had on the various measures of comprehension, learning, and remembering.

What we wish to argue is that there is a correlation between the knowledge demands of texts and the use of long, infrequent words and long, complex sentences. We argue, further, that in made-for-school texts the correlation is higher than any necessity requires. Since the dawn of the readability movement 60 years ago, the heavy controls placed on school texts for the early grades have made the language in them progressively more simple, unnaturally simple, we believe. In turn, as new readability research has been done, it has fed back in ever stronger form the conclusion that the younger the reader the simpler the language ought to be. The result of generations of inbreeding is, in the words of Anderson et al. (1984, p. 35), "that the confounding of knowledge demands and language complexity has been exacerbated . . . [T]he formulas now in use egregiously overestimate the importance of surface features of language. Probably most third-grade students could get the gist of a story about a girl and her puppy even if it were dressed up in fancy language, whereas no amount of simplification of [the language of] an economics treatise would permit very many third-grade students to grasp the concept of the multiplier effect."

INTERESTINGNESS

As important, or perhaps even more important than the influence of prior knowledge is the influence of interest on comprehension. In four experiments involving over 400 3rd and 4th graders, Anderson, Shirey, Wilson, and Fielding (1986) compared the learning and recall of sentences that children find interesting, such as *The huge gorilla smashed the school bus with his fist* and *The hungry children were in the kitchen helping mother make donuts,* with ones they find uninteresting, such as *The old shoes lay in the back of the closet* and *The fat waitress poured coffee into the cup.* The newsworthy finding was that interest, as rated by other children, accounted for over *thirty times* as much variance in sentence recall as readability. It should be emphasized that the sentences were selected so that interestingness and readability were independent and so that there was a wide range of readability. According to the Fry scale, sentence readability ranged from the 1st to the 7th grade.

Studies using texts have revealed similar, if less dramatic, results. Notably, in a series of well-designed studies, Asher and his associates (Asher, 1979, 1980; Asher & Geraci, 1980; Asher, Hymel, & Wigfield, 1978; Asher & Markell, 1974) determined children's interests by having them rate photographs representing a wide array of topics (e.g., ballet, basketball, cats, airplanes, circus). Later, the children read *Britannica Junior Encyclopaedia* selections on topics that they had individually rated as high or low in interest. Briefly, the findings were, first, that the children indicated far greater desire to read selections on highly rated topics. Second, children's comprehension was superior on high-interest material; in each study, children attained higher cloze scores on their high-interest selections. Third, in two of the studies (Asher & Geraci, 1980; Asher & Markell, 1974), boys' performance was facilitated more than girls' performance by high-interest material, a finding since replicated by Anderson et al. (1986) and Baldwin, Peleg-Bruckner, and McClintock (1985).

A worry is that prior knowledge and interest are not clearly separable. One would suppose that people would be knowledgeable about topics they are interested in, and maybe vice versa. However, Baldwin et al. (1985) found only a slight correlation between tests of knowledge of ten topics and interest in the topics among a sample of 7th and 8th graders of above-average ability. They explained this seemingly counterintuitive finding in the following way (p. 502): "[S]chool children . . . are forced to study a variety of topics whether they like them or not. It should not be surprising then to find that a group of above average students could be fairly knowledgeable about space exploration and American Indians, for example, without having any real enthusiasm for those subjects." Baldwin et al. also found that both knowledge and interest independently predicted comprehension of encyclopedia passages on the ten topics.

Systematic empirical study of the features of language, style, plot, characterization, content, and theme that make texts more or less interesting to various readers is in its infancy (for a sampling of work, see Anderson et al., 1984; Bettleheim,1976; Blom, Waite, & Zimet, 1970; Bruce, 1984; Green & Olsen, 1980; Jose & Brewer, 1983). While this field matures, one should not neglect the insights of rhetoricians nor undervalue the craft of skillful writers, as Graves and Slater (1986) have demonstrated in striking fashion. They persuaded three teams of writers to revise a passage from a high school history textbook on the war in Vietnam, described by one of the teams as "some of the driest prose we had ever had the displeasure of reading."

Graves and Slater's first team was made up of a pair of "text linguists" whose revisions were directed at such matters as clarity, coherence, and emphasis. Below is the material on the Communist guerrillas in the text linguists' revision, which is unchanged from the original except for the addition of the phrase, "in particular:"

> In South Vietnam in particular, Communist forces (the Viet Cong) were aided by forces from Communist North Vietnam in a struggle to overthrow the American-supported government.

The next team consisted of two college composition instructors. In their words, "The six main purposes we had in mind . . . were simplifying information, adding background information, clarifying information, supplying transitions, emphasizing key material, and keeping the passage smooth and readable." Here is what they produced on the guerrillas:

> In South Vietnam, Communist guerillas called the Viet Cong were aided by forces from Communist North Vietnam in a struggle to overthrow the American-supported government.

The last team, a pair of veteran *Time/Life* editors, revised the passage in a radically different way. In the words of one of them, "To intensify the action, I replaced weak verbs such as 'tried to get,' 'moved,' 'fight,' and 'increased' with words such as 'tried to gain,' 'hustled,' 'grappled with,' and 'skyrocketed.' I added metaphors [and] colloquialisms . . . However, tinkering with the language did not give the passages a *Time/Life* quality: They were still too panoramic, too impersonal. . . . To enrich the content, I inserted 'nuggets' gleaned from library sources. Nuggets are vivid anecdotes and details that remind us that PEOPLE, not events, make history. A *Time/Life* story is not so much a sequence of events as a string of nuggets. . . . I also quoted from Presidents Eisenhower and Kennedy. After all, why should the textbook quote Kennedy's statement that South Vietnam was of 'vital interest' to the U.S. when Kennedy so graphically called the country 'the cornerstone of the Free World in Southeast Asia, the keystone to the arch, the finger in the dike'?" Below is what this team said about the guerrillas:

> Aided by Communist North Vietnam, the Viet Cong guerrillas were eroding the ground beneath South Vietnam's American-backed government. Village by village, road by road, these jungle-wise rebels were waging a war of ambush and mining: They darted out of tunnels to head off patrols, buried exploding booby traps beneath the mud floors of huts, and hid razor-sharp bamboo sticks in holes.

Groups of 11th graders read the original passage on the Vietnam War or one of the revisions written by the three teams. They then wrote essays which were evaluated in terms of the percentage of the information in the text that was recalled. The results were that the text linguists' revisions produced a 2% gain in information while the composition instructors' revisions produced a 2% loss. In profound contrast, the *Time/Life* editors' revisions produced a 40% gain. Informed of their postor showing and given a second chance to revise the text, the text linguists and composition instructions did better; they produced gains in recall averaging 16% and 21% respectively, while the *Time/Life* editors held their ground at 37%.

The points that should be made about interestingness and readability are essentially the same as the points about prior knowledge and readability. First, interestingness is probably a more potent predictor of text comprehensibility than the surface features of language embodied in readability formulas. Second, readability formulas probably get some of their predictive power because the word difficulty measure is an indirect indicator of interestingness. Third, there are almost certainly interactions between the topics individual readers are interested in and the stylistic features that please them with the topics and styles of texts; therefore, again, it is dangerous to try to predict individual performance using an aggregate statistical model.

CONCLUSION

In this chapter, we have surveyed the problems arising from treating word and sentence complexity as direct causes of difficulty in comprehension, and have noted the far greater influence on comprehension of text and reader properties not measured by formulas. In this chapter, we have looked critically at readability formulas from several perspectives. In doing so, we have been concerned with how close readability formulas come to being accurate and informative predictors of comprehension, when specific readers read a specific text. In most research on readability to date, very high correlations are reported between the predictions of formulas based on text features such as word complexity and sentence length and measures of comprehension associated with reading ability. We suggest that these high correlations are the by-product of using an inappropriate statistical model which aggregates texts and readers, and gives an exaggerated impression of the contribution of linguistic factors in the text to ease or difficulty of comprehension. We propose instead that both texts and readers are more appropriately treated as random factors. This approach, will lessen the correlations of text properties and predicted grade level, and will also give a more accurate picture of what *causes* a text to be difficult to understand.

The presence of long sentences and complex words in a text in some way reflects or is correlated with complexities of subject matter, but need not directly cause a text to be difficult. While these factors may impede comprehension for some readers who have difficulty segmenting words and parsing sentences or who have limited working memory capacity, these very same factors also provide the reader with explicit information about the composition of a word or the relations between sentences.

Recent research in reading and the perception of language has made use of more sensitive measures of comprehension than those which were previously used, either for overall comprehension of whole texts, or for the processing of specific parts of a sentence in working memory. These new measures have made it possible to see in more detail what factors interact when a reader interprets a text. Some of these interactions hold between different linguistic features, and some between the properties of the text and the properties of the reader. Certain kinds of sentences or complex words may be difficult for readers with less processing capacity available in working memory than people usually have. Readers without adequate background knowledge for a text find it much harder to read and understand than readers who have the right background knowledge. A text whose content and way of presenting information are boring to the reader is less well understood than a text which falls within a particular reader's interests.

Clearly while texts differ in the complexity of the language they are written in, so too do readers differ in decoding and parsing skills, background knowledge, and interests. Since reading and understanding a text requires the interaction of a reader with the text, using knowledge and skills that the reader possesses, it is not surprising that there are many factors about readers and texts which cannot be described in terms of a readability formula of the traditional kind. Still less can formulas of this type serve as the basis for a useful model for text understanding. What makes a text easy or difficult for individual readers is the topic of further research which very urgently needs to be done. Because of the highly interactive nature of language understanding, we are confident that it will not prove possible to incorporate the results of this research into procedures of appraising the comprehensibility of texts that look like traditional readability formulas. And we do not think that the goal of such research should be the production of new formulas, since the ultimate purpose of assessing comprehensibility is to understand what makes a given text understandable for particular readers. If texts must be changed so that the intended readers can understand them, we want to be able to identify what the barriers are and what improvements actually increase comprehension. If the goal is not to alter the text, we want to be able to convey to the readers how best to approach a text and to deal most efficiently with its complexities.

REFERENCES

Anderson, R. C., & Freebody, P. (1981). Vocabulary knowledge. In J. T. Guthrie (Ed.), *Reading comprehension and education*. Newark, DE: International Reading Association.

Anderson, R. C., & Freebody, P. (1983). Reading comprehension and the assessment and acquisition of word knowledge. In B. Hutson (Ed.), *Advances in reading/language research*. Greenwich, CT: JAI Press.

Anderson, R. C., Mason, J., & Shirey, L. (1984). The reading group: An experimental analysis of a labyrinth. *Reading Research Quarterly, 20*(1), 6–38.

Anderson, R. C., Reynolds, R. E., Schallert, D. L., & Goetz, E. T. (1977). Frameworks for comprehending discourse. *American Educational Research Journal, 14*, 367–382.

Anderson, R. C., Shirey, L., Wilson, P., & Fielding, L. (1986). Interestingness of children's reading material. In R. Snow & M. Farr (Eds.), *Aptitude learning and instruction* (Vol. 4). Hillsdale, NJ: Lawrence Erlbaum Associates.

Asher, S. R. (1979). Influence of topic interest on black children's and white children's reading comprehension. *Child Development, 50*, 686–690.

Asher, S. R. (1980). Topic interest and children's reading comprehension. In R. Spiro, B. Bruce, & W. Brewer (Eds.), *Theoretical issues in reading comprehension.* Hillsdale, NJ: Lawrence Erlbaum Associates.

Asher, S. R., & Geraci, R. L. (1980). *Topic interest, external incentive and reading comprehension.* Unpublished manuscript, University of Illinois, Urbana-Champaign.

Asher, S. R., Hymel, S., & Wigfield, A. (1978). Influence of topic interest on children's reading comprehension. *Journal of Reading Behavior, 10,* 35–47.

Asher, S. R., & Markell, R. A. (1974). Sex differences in comprehension of high- and low-interest reading material. *Journal of Educational Psychology, 66,* 680–687.

Baldwin, R. S., Peleg-Bruckner, Z., & McClintock, A. H. (1985). Effects of topic interest and prior knowledge on reading comprehension. *Reading Research Quarterly, 20,* 497–504.

Beck, I., McCaslin, E., & McKeown, M. (1980). *The rationale and design of a program to teach vocabulary to fourth-grade students.* Pittsburgh: University of Pittsburgh, Learning Research and Development Center.

Beck, I. L., McKeown, M. G., Omanson, R. C., & Pople, M. T. (1984). Improving the comprehensibility of stories: The effects of revisions that improve coherence. *Reading Research Quarterly, 19*(3), 263–277.

Beck, I., Perfetti, C., & McKeown, M. (1982). The effects of long-term vocabulary instruction on lexical access and reading comprehension. *Journal of Educational Psychology, 74,* 506–521.

Berko, J. (1958). The child's learning of English morphology. *Word, 14,* 150–177.

Bettleheim, B. (1976). *The uses of enchantment: The meaning and importance of fairy tales.* New York: Knopf.

Bever, T. G., & Townshend, D. J. (1979). Perceptual mechanisms and formal properties of main and subordinate clauses. In W. E. Cooper & E. C. T. Walker (Eds.), *Sentence processing.* Hillsdale, NJ: Lawrence Erlbaum Associates.

Blom, G. E., Waite, R. R., & Zimet, S. G. (1970). A motivational content analysis of children's primers. In H. Levin & J. P. Williams (Eds.), *Basic studies on reading.* New York: Basic Books.

Bormuth, J. R. (1966). Readability: A new approach. *Reading Research Quarterly, 1,* 79–132.

Botel, M., Dawkins, J., & Granowsky, A. (1973). A syntactic complexity formula. In W. H. MacGinitie (Ed.), *Assessment of problems in reading.* Newark, DE: International Reading Association.

Botel, M., & Granowsky, A. (1972). A formula for measuring syntactic complexity: A directional effort. *Elementary English, 49,* 513–516.

Bransford, J. D., Barclay, J. R., & Franks, J. (1972). Sentence memory: A constructive versus interpretative approach. *Cognitive Psychology, 3,* 193–209.

Bransford, J. D., & Franks, J. (1971). The abstraction of linguistic ideas: A review. *Cognition, 1,* 211–249.

Bruce, B. (1984). A new point of view on children's stories. In R. C. Anderson, J. Osborn, & R. J. Tierney (Eds.), *Learning to read in American schools.* Hillsdale, NJ: Lawrence Erlbaum Associates.

Carroll, J. B., Davies, P., & Richman, B. (1971). *The American Heritage word frequency book.* Boston: Houghton Mifflin.

Cazden, C. (1968). The acquisition of noun and verb inflections. *Child Development, 39,* 433–448.

Chall, J. S. (1958). *Readability: An appraisal of research and application.* Columbus, OH: Bureau of Educational Research, Ohio State University.

Chall, J. S. (1984). Readability and prose comprehension continuities and discontinuities. In J. Flood (Ed.), *Understanding reading comprehension. Cognition, language and the structure of prose.* Newark, DE: International Reading Association.

Charrow, R. P., & Charrow, V. R. (1979). Making legal language understandable: A psycholinguistic study of jury instructions. *Columbia Law Review, 79*(7), 1306–1374.

Clark, H. H., & Haviland, S. E. (1977). Comprehension and the given-new contract. In R. O. Freedle (Ed.), *Discourse production and comprehension.* Norwood, NJ: Ablex.

Davison, A. (1984). Syntactic markedness and the definition of sentence topic. *Language, 60*(4), 797–846.

Davison, A., & Kantor, R. N. (1982). On the failure of readability formulas to define readable texts: A case study from adaptations. *Reading Research Quarterly, 17*, 187–209.

Davison, A., & Lutz, R. (1984). Syntactic complexity and discourse context. In D. R. Dowty, L. Karttunen, & A. M. Zwicky (Eds.), *Natural language processing: Psychological, computational and theoretical perspectives.* Cambridge, England: Cambridge University Press.

Davison, A., Wilson, P., & Hermon, G. (1985). *Effects of syntactic connectives and organizing cues on text comprehension.* Champaign, IL: Center for the Study of Reading.

Dawkins, J. (1975). *Syntax and readability.* Newark, DE: International Reading Association.

Frazier, L. (1984). Syntactic complexity. In D. R. Dowty, L. Karttunen & A. M. Zwicky (Eds.), *Natural language parsing: Psychological, computational and theoretical perspectives.* Cambridge, England: Cambridge University Press.

Frazier, L., & Fodor, J. D. (1978). The sausage machine: A new two-stage parsing model. *Cognition, 6*, 291–325.

Frazier, L., & Rayner, K. (1982). Making and correcting errors during sentence comprehension: Eye movements in the analysis of structurally ambiguous sentences. *Cognitive Psychology, 14*, 178–210.

Freebody, P., & Anderson, R. C. (1983a). Effects on text comprehension of differing proportions and locations of difficult vocabulary. *Journal of Reading Behavior, 15*(3), 19–39.

Freebody, P., & Anderson, R. C. (1983b). Effects of vocabulary difficulty, text cohesion, and schema availability on reading comprehension. *Reading Research Quarterly, 18*, 277–294.

Glucksberg, S., Trabasso, T., & Wald, J. (1973). Linguistic structures and mental operations. *Cognitive Psychology, 5*, 338–370.

Graves, M. F., & Slater, W. H. (1986). Could textbooks be better written and would it make a difference? *American Educator, 10*(1), 36–42.

Gray, W. S., & Leary, B. E. (1935). *What makes a book readable?* Chicago: University of Chicago Press.

Green, G. M., & Laff, M. O. (1980). *Five-year-olds' recognition of authorship by literary style* (Tech. Rep. No. 181). Urbana: University of Illinois, Center for the Study of Reading.

Hamburger, H., & Crain, S. (1981). Relative acquisition. In S. Kuczaj (Ed.), *Language development: Syntax and semantics.* Hillsdale, NJ: Lawrence Erlbaum Associates.

Irwin, J. W. (1980). The effects of explicitness and clause order on the comprehension of reversible causal relationships. *Reading Research Quarterly, 15*, 477–488.

Irwin, J. W., & Pulver, C. J. (1984). Effects of explicitness, clause order and reversibility on children's comprehension of causal relationships. *Journal of Educational Psychology, 76*(3), 399–407.

Jarvella, R. (1971). Syntactic processing of connected speech. *Journal of Verbal Learning and Verbal Behavior, 10*, 409–416.

Jenkins, J. R., Pany, D., & Schreck, J. (1978). *Vocabulary and reading comprehension: Instructional effects* (Tech. Rep. No. 100). Urbana: University of Illinois, Center for the Study of Reading. (ERIC Document Reproduction Service No. ED 160 999).

Jose, P., & Brewer, W. F. (1983). *The development of story liking: Character identification, suspense, and outcome resolution* (Tech. Rep. No. 291). Urbana: University of Illinois, Center for the Study of Reading.

Kemper, S. (in press-a). Imitation of complex grammatical constructions by elderly adults. *Applied Psycholinguistics.*

Kemper, S. (in press-b). Geriatric psycholinguistics: Syntactic limitations of oral and written language. In L. Light & D. Burke (Eds.), *Language and memory in old age.* Cambridge, England: Cambridge University Press.

Klare, G. M. (1963). *The measurement of readability.* Ames: Iowa State University Press.

52   ANDERSON AND DAVISON

Klare, G. R. (1984). Readability. In P. D. Pearson, R. Barr, M. Kamil, & P. Mosenthal (Eds.), *Handbook of reading research*. New York: Longman.

Kynette, D., & Kemper, S. (in press). Aging and the loss of grammatical forms. *Language and Communication*.

Lipson, M. Y. (1983). The influence of religious affiliation on children's memory for text information. *Reading Research Quarterly, 18*, 448–457.

Marslen-Wilson, W. R. (1975). The limited compatibility of linguistic and functional explanations. In R. E. Grossman, L. J. San, & T. J. Vance (Eds.), *Papers from the Parasession on Functionalism* (pp. 409–420). Chicago: University of Chicago, Chicago Linguistic Society.

Marslen-Wilson, W. R., Tyler, K., & Seidenberg, M. (1980). Sentence processing and the clause boundary. In W. J. M. Levelt & G. B. Flores D'Arcais (Eds.), *Studies in the perception of language*. New York: Wiley.

McKeown, M. G., Beck, I. L., Omanson, R. C., & Perfetti, C. A. (1983). The effects of long-term vocabulary instruction on reading comprehension. *Journal of Reading Behavior, 15*, 3–18.

Nagy, W. E., & Anderson, R. C. (1984). How many words are there in printed school English? *Reading Research Quarterly, 14*, 304–330.

Nagy, W. E., Herman, P. A., & Anderson, R. C. (1985). *Learning word meanings from context: How broadly generalizable?* (Tech. Rep. No. 347). Urbana: University of Illinois, Center for the Study of Reading.

Olson, D. R., & Filby, N. (1972). On the comprehension of active and passive sentences. *Cognitive Psychology, 3*, 361–381.

Pearson, P. D. (1974–75). The effects of grammatical complexity on children's comprehension, recall, and conception of certain semantic relations. *Reading Research Quarterly, 10*, 155–192.

Pearson, P. D., Hansen, J., & Gordon, C. (1979). The effect of background knowledge on young children's comprehension of explicit and implicit information. *Journal of Reading Behavior, 11*, 201–210.

Perfetti, C. A., & Lesgold, A. M. (1977). Discourse comprehension and sources of individual differences. In M. Just & P. Carpenter (Eds.), *Cognitive processes in comprehension*. Hillsdale, NJ: Lawrence Erlbaum Associates.

Reynolds, R. E., Taylor, M. A., Steffensen, M. S., Shirey, L. L., & Anderson, R. C. (1982). Cultural schemata and reading comprehension. *Reading Research Quarterly, 17*, 353–632.

Rodriguez, N., & Hansen, L. H. (1975). Performance of readability formulas under conditions of restricted ability level and restricted difficulty of materials. *Journal of Experimental Education, 44*, 8–14.

Sheldon, A. (1974). The role of parallel function in the acquisition of relative clauses in English. *Journal of Verbal Learning and Verbal Behavior, 13*, 272–281.

Spilich, G. J., Vesonder, G. T., Chiesi, H. L., & Voss, J. F. (1979). Text processing of domain related information for individuals with high and low domain knowledge. *Journal of Verbal Learning and Verbal Behavior, 18*, 275–290.

Spiro, R. J., Bruce, B. C., & Brewer, W. F. (Eds.). (1980). *Theoretical issues in reading comprehension*. Hillsdale, NJ: Lawrence Erlbaum Associates.

Steffensen, M. S., Joag-dev, C., & Anderson, R. C. (1979). A cross-cultural perspective on reading comprehension. *Reading Research Quarterly, 15*, 10–29.

Sticht, T., Armijo, L., Weitzman, R., Koffman, N., Roberson, K., Chang, F., & Moracco, J. (1986). *Progress Report*. U.S. Naval Post-graduate school.

Tanenhaus, M. K., & Carlson, G. N. (1985). Processing anaphors. *Papers from the 1985 NELS meeting*. Amherst, MA: Graduate Linguistics Students Association, University of Massachusetts.

Thorndike, E. L. (1921). *The teacher's word book*. New York: Teacher's College, Columbia University.

Tyler, A. (1986). *Acquisition and use of English derivational morphology: Some experimental investigations*. Unpublished doctoral dissertation, University of Iowa.

Tyler, A., & Nagy, W. (1985). *The role of derivational suffixes in sentence comprehension* (Tech. Rep. No. 357). Urbana: University of Illinois, Center for the Study of Reading.

Tyler, A., & Nagy, W. (1986, April). *The acquisition of English derivational morphology: Implications for models of the lexicon.* Paper presented at the Milwaukee Morphology Meeting/Fifteenth Annual UWM Linguistics Symposium, Milwaukee, WI.

Vogel, M., & Washburne, C. (1928). An objective method of determining grade placement of children's reading material. *Elementary School Journal, 28,* 373–381.

Yngve, V. H. A. (1960). A model and an hypothesis for language structure. *Proceedings of the American Philosophical Society, 104,* 444–466.

3 Cognitive Approaches to Assessing the Readability of Text

Eva L. Baker
University of California, Los Angeles

Nancy K. Atwood
Army Research Institute

Thomas M. Duffy
Carnegie-Mellon University

There was, and perhaps still is, a belief that computerization will lead to the "paperless" society and thus to a dramatic reduction in the requirement for reading. However, as virtually anyone who has entered the age of computers can attest, that prediction thus far has proved to be a wild fantasy. Not only isn't there a decrease in the volume of paper, there is a significant increase both in paper consumption and in reading. Indeed, as we move from a manufacturing-based economy to an economy based on the delivery of services, we see an increase in the amount and the variety of reading demanded. Thus the goal underlying the initial development of readability formulas, matching readers to text, is even more important today. We must ensure that the text is a useful tool, that is, that people can obtain the information which is necessary to carry out professional and other day-to-day activities. We need a mechanism for matching a text to an audience—not only in the selection of a text for an audience but also in guiding the initial design of the text.

Readability formulas and the accompanying readable writing guidelines were designed to provide just such a matching of text to audience (Flesch 1948, 1949; Klare 1963, 1975). A "formula" is actually a regression equation used to predict comprehension. Thus, characteristics of the text are measured and entered into a regression equation to determine the "best" predictor function. In using the formula it is only necessary to measure the predictor variables (word and sentence length factors for most formulas) and enter them into the calculations to obtain the comprehension measure (typically a reading skill requirement). Clearly, a readability formula so developed is an empirical tool. There is complete agreement that the predictor variables are empirically determined and thus do not necessarily represent causative factors.

While readability formulas are empirical devices, they are based on some model of the reading process (Duffy, 1985a). For example, all of the decisions involved in developing and applying a formula are based on some model of the reading process. Predictors are sampled from the set of variables thought to be causally related to comprehension (e.g., word familiarity) or to serve as proxy measures for such variables (e.g., word length). The universe sampled (and by implication the universe not sampled) reflects concepts of the determinants of comprehension. The test used to assess comprehension of the passages provides a definition of what is meant by comprehension. And the index of skill requirements, what the formula predicts, provides an indication of the skill requirements for reading.

There is also a model of the reading process implicit in the application of readability formulas (Duffy, 1985a). For example, the extent to which one is willing to apply a given formula to different audiences, different varieties of texts, and different reading tasks indicates the degree to which reading is viewed as a homogeneous process. When a text is identified as "too difficult," the variables in the formula indicate the kind of simplification which must occur, that is, the variables which must be attended to in the revision process. While the text is never written to the formula, the simplification must be based on the class of variables underlying the predictors.

There are well over 100 readability formulas in popular use today (Klare, 1979) and all of those formulas are based on the same underlying model of the reading process. It is the limitations and faulty assumptions of that model which are the basis of most of the criticism of readability formulas. The model is basically the traditional model of reading which is the basis of most reading instruction. In this model reading is seen as a relatively passive activity in which the reader decodes the text to obtain the meaning (Duffy, in press). Thus it is a bottom up model in common parlance. The decoding is at the level of sentences and of words. Therefore, "reading" can be defined in terms of the skills necessary to decode words and sentences. These skills are not dependent on content knowledge except as reflected in the knowledge of specific vocabulary. Thus skill training is independent of the content domain of the text; instruction is, in general, directed toward reading ability. Furthermore, the level of skill, i.e., the level of general reading ability, applies equally in all content domains.

The application of this model to the analysis of text leads to two primary effects. First, since reading is viewed as decoding words and sentences, the difficulty of the text must be indexed in terms of word and sentence characteristics. Thus even the most complex of the popular readability formulas (e.g., Bormuth, 1969) sampled only syntactic and lexical features to identify the "best" predictors. Second, since reading is viewed as a general process independent of domain knowledge, the formulas have wide applicability. The formulas are applied regardless of the comprehension task (e.g., job related reading, learning in a class, finding facts), regardless of the subject matter expertise of the audience, and regardless of the nature of the text (narrative, expository, technical) (Duffy, 1985a).

Our understanding of the reading process has grown considerably beyond the simple decoding model. Reading is not simply finding the meaning in the text, but rather, meaning is generated based on the text representation and world knowledge. The reader draws from long-term memory to build a coherent structure. Understanding is based on the information goals of the reader, his or her knowledge of the subject matter, and the representation of the information in the text. Thus there is a top down imposition or construction of meaning along with the bottom up decoding of the text (Spiro, Bruce, & Brewer, 1980; Wittrock, 1982).

The importance of this top down process has been illustrated in numerous studies. Perhaps the classic example is a study by Bransford and Johnson (1972) in which a paragraph concerning moving things about made no sense and was very difficult to remember until a title, *washing clothes*, was provided. The title provided a link to prior knowledge; it provided access to a schema or structure for interpreting activities involving the washing of clothes. The text remained the same, yet there was dramatic change in comprehension. Clearly, this was a result that the readability formula score could not predict. Indeed, how would one calculate the readability?

The use of prior knowledge in the form of schemas for organizing and interpreting text is a major construct in current theories of reading. Kieras (1985) has argued that, in addition to subject domain or content relevant schemas, readers employ text structure schemas to interpret text. Content schemas are organizational structures for a content domain—an organization of slots in which facts are to be inserted. The text schema is an organizational structure for texts independent of content. Kieras proposes that there are common text schemas which specify where in a passage specific content is likely to appear. These text schemas are especially important in the comprehension of technical material where the reader frequently has limited knowledge of the content domain.

Text schemas basically reflect that readers learn how to *use* a text. If a new text has the same structure, their text schema will yield positive transfer. However, if a new presentation involves a new structure, the negative transfer of text schemas could well counteract any content or readability based on improvements in the text. The effects of this text schema have been hypothesized to account for the failure of several major revision efforts to improve the usability of a technical manual (Duffy, Curran, & Sass, 1983).

Pichert and Anderson (1977) have demonstrated the importance of the goal in reading on the contents and organization of memory. In one study, readers read the description of a house either from the perspective of a burgler or from the perspective of a home buyer. The characteristics of the house that were retained were a function of the particular perspective of the reader. The burglar organized recall and remembered things appropriate to planning a burglary while the home buyer remembered features of the house. While not a part of the Pichert and Anderson study, the paragraph could have been written to support one or the other interpretation (see, e.g., Frase, 1977). Thus, the readability of the text would depend on the degree to which the organizational structure of the text was consistent with the information goals of the reader. This issue has been of critical concern in the design of technical text as reflected in the discussion of functional vs. topical organizational structures (Duffy, 1985a). The topic organization may be adequate if the comprehension task is learning about a particular component, but a functional organization is essential to using the text to work on the equipment.

These studies demonstrate the active process of meaning generation involved in reading. Prior knowledge, the goal in reading, and the interrelationship of text units all play a critical role in comprehension. Traditional readability formulas do not account for these factors in the reading process. As a consequence, the formulas are theoretically inappropriate and uninteresting. At a more practical level, they simply provide an inadequate prediction of comprehension and inadequate guidance for revision. In fact, the revision guidance may simply be incorrect. For example, simplifying sentences with the intent of improving comprehension may in fact reduce comprehension through an increased requirement for anaphora and an increased separation of the anaphora and referent in the processing of the text (Duffy & Kabance, 1982; Pearson, 1974–1975).

The inadequacy of the predictions arising from traditional readability formulas is not simply a matter of providing an increment in the precision of prediction. Rather, new approaches are required to account for dramatic shifts in the usability of a text when the organization of the sentences, the subject matter knowledge of the user, or the comprehension task is changed. Users of traditional formulas may well be rejecting texts which an audience of subject matter experts could readily use or accepting texts with which the audience of new learners will have considerable difficulty.

There have been several recent attempts to develop text analysis schemes more appropriate to the active processing model of reading. The best known of these are the approaches of Miller and Kintsch (1980) and Meyer (1975). In the Miller and Kintsch model, text is analyzed into propositions and it is these propositions which are used to build a meaning structure. An initial text structure or schema is imposed based on the initial propositions. That structure is expanded, modified, or abandoned as the reader attempts to interpret successive propositions in terms of it. Frequency of occurrence of propositions and the limits of short-term memory in holding sequences of propositions play important roles in determining comprehensibility.

Meyer's (1975) approach is also based on a propositional analysis of the text and the identification of the coherence relations between the propositions. From her theoretical perspective, the reader builds a hierarchical structure of propositions. Propositions higher in the structure or supporting the higher order propositions will be better recalled. Meyer's analysis identifies the structure imposed by the author. However, she recognizes that readers may or may not adopt that structure. Failure to adopt the authors' structure may be due to inadequate signaling of the structure by the author, lack of skill on the part of the reader, or a difference in goals (information requirements) between the reader and writer.

While the Meyer and Miller and Kintsch models account for semantic relations between sentences and address the reader's limitations in processing, the analyses are independent of the reader's knowledge and goals. Thus they fail, as it would seem any text analysis system must fail, to provide a generalizable methodology for adequately indexing the readability of a text for a particular audience. Miller and Kintsch (1980) propose that their model recognizes readability as "an interaction between the text and the reader's prose processing capabilities, rather than as some innate property of text." However, traditional readability approaches also presume an active decoder with prose processing capabilities. The Miller and Kintsch model simply extends beyond sentence boundaries and includes semantic relations in the text. However, neither model identifies differential processing strategies as a function of different reading goals. All text is assumed to be processed in the same way. Furthermore, processing is presumed to proceed sentence by sentence or proposition by proposition from the beginning of the text to the end. Finally, while Miller and Kintsch identify world knowledge as an important variable in comprehension, they have not yet incorporated it into their analysis approach. In essence the approach cannot account for the findings of Bransford and Johnson (1972), Pichert and Anderson (1977), or Osborne and Wittrock (1983); thus, readability does in fact remain inherent in the text.

Indeed any text analysis scheme that excludes the reader and the reading task will by necessity provide an inadequate account of the reading process and inadequate predictions of the usability of the text. Reading in the real world is not the free recall of 250 or 2000 word passages nor is it the ability to fill in words deleted from a text. It is mysterious to us why one would suppose that the processes or strategies in carrying out these types of tasks should at all resemble the process and strategies of using text in real world situations. If the processes differ, then we may well expect the relevant text features to differ.

There is sufficient evidence that assessment of the ability of the audience to use the text and assessment of how they use the text in some meaningful task, provides valuable information as to both the reading process and the assessment of readability. Indeed such an analysis process has become a standard in problem-solving research (Ericsson & Simon, 1980) as a means of understanding the problem-solving process. At the practical level, it would also seem that actual testing of the ability and processes of specific audiences to use text in a meaningful way is essential to effective prediction.

The alternative to actual testing is either the use of prediction formulas or the application of the judgment of expert writers. We have already discussed the inadequacies of prediction formulas. The judgment of expert writers does not fare much better. Carver (1974) and Wright (1985) have found that experienced writers cannot predict the readability of text. Swaney, Janik, Bond, and Hayes (1981) had expert writers revise four different consumer contracts to make them more usable by the intended audience. Comprehension was then assessed by asking representatives of that audience to use a contract to answer specific application questions. That is, scenarios of ways in which the contract would actually be used were created. The results indicated that the expert revision resulted in improved "readability" of one document, decreased "readability" of another, and produced no change in the other two. However, when the writers had the data available from user testing, including transcripts of the users verbalizations (they were instructed to think out loud while they answered the questions), they were able to improve significantly the readability of the documents.

It has long been a contention that text must be evaluated through testing with a segment of the audience (Redish, Felker & Rose, 1981). Readability approaches were developed primarily as an attempt to sidestep the effort involved in such testing, though it also represents an approach to cataloging relevant comprehension factors (e.g., Amarin & Jones, 1982). However, the approach has failed to represent adequately the comprehension tasks, and thus the relevant processing variables, as well as to capture the important role of world knowledge in interpreting text. Thus we would argue that a more fruitful approach to both prediction and understanding would be to develop effective strategies for audience testing using real scenarios. This approach has become standard in the evaluation of procedural information at the Communications Design Center at Carnegie-Mellon University. When computer manuals are written, the procedural information is tested by asking users to think out loud while performing the task described in the document. An analysis of the users' strategies for interpreting and using the text is fed back into the revision process.

In the remainder of this chapter we present data on the use of scenarios to assess the readability of more general, technical text. The text presented the theory of operation (functional description) of a radar receiver. The comprehension goal in using this type of text is not to learn and remember as much as possible. Rather it seems to have three uses: (1) as simply a reference point for facts about the system; (2) as a source for building a representation of the system; and (3) as a means of providing more detailed information on the functioning of a component. We focused on assessing the latter two comprehension goals. Thus we asked subjects to read a segment of text and then to use that information to describe to a colleague how the particular component functioned. We measured the extent to which the subjects summarized in terms of key information units and the gist of the segment. We assessed the effects of the text on subjects' development of a functional representation of the system by asking them to provide a graphic representation of the functional relationships. The graphic representation was collected as a pretest and a postest.

The research also looked at the effects of traditional simplification strategies and of world knowledge on these comprehension measures. We used two versions of the text: an original and a revision based on meeting a variety of readability indices. World knowledge was manipulated by varying the expertise of the users. Expertise was defined in terms of both system knowledge and knowledge of other systems.

Thus, while the research had only limited scope and generalizability, it was designed to provide information related to the following research questions:

1. What were the syntactic and semantic characteristics of the original and revised versions of technical text?

2. How did the original and revised versions of technical text influence the verbal summaries of subjects?

3. What was the effect of different levels of world knowledge on subjects' summaries?

4. What differences were there in subjects' summaries of main ideas and specific information?

5. How did text version and world knowledge influence subjects' summaries of main ideas and specific information?

6. What was the relationship between subjects' graphic representations of the system and text version, world knowledge, and verbal summaries?

STUDY PROCEDURES

Subjects

Eighteen naval fire control technicians served as subjects in the experiment. Subjects were selected to represent three groups of technicians who differed in their world knowledge as indicated by the amount and nature of their experience: (1) expert technicians who were trained and assigned to the electronic system containing the radar receiver described by the technical text (the NATO Seasparrow system[1]); (2) novice technicians who were not trained in school on the NATO Seasparrow system (NSS) but were assigned to the system for on-the-job training; and (3) expert technicians who were trained and assigned to another system other than the NATO Seasparrow system.

Subjects were selected from ships in port at a major naval seaport during the

---

[1]NATO refers to the North Atlantic Treaty Organization. Member countries jointly supported the development of the Seasparrow system.

2-month period in which data collection for the study was conducted. Technicians were identified as experts or novices on the Seasparrow or another system based on the report of their commanding officer. Their classification was verified by inspecting Navy personnel records to determine whether they had attended school training on the NATO Seasparrow system, the length of their on-the-job training, and the specific system to which they were assigned. The personnel records verified the commanding officer's classifications.

Personnel records indicated that six of the subjects had attended NATO Seasparrow School and had an average of 24 months of on-the-job training on the NATO Seasparrow system ("Experienced NSS Technicians"). Six subjects had not attended NATO Seasparrow School and had an average of 15 months of on-the-job training on the NATO Seasparrow system ("Novice NSS Technicians"). The remaining six subjects had not attended NATO Seasparrow School and had no on-the-job training on the NATO Seasparrow system, but had received formal school training and on-the-job training on another system ("Experienced non-NSS Technicians").

Text Versions

Two versions of a section of technical text were used in the study. The text was drawn from a section of the technical manual for the NATO Seasparrow system that is intended to provide a general functional description of the system. One part of this section, that describing the air designate mode of the radar receiver system, was selected for use in the study. This part was selected because it was judged as representative of the type and range of information typically presented in functional system descriptions by a naval subject matter expert.

The text was divided into 25 segments judged to reflect discrete sets of information. This segmentation was made to facilitate the experimental process so that protocols could be collected from each subject after he had read each segment.

One version of the text was the "original" version of the published text taken directly from the technical manual initially prepared by the contractor. This text was prepared according to standard military specifications for technical manuals. The second version was a "revised" version subsequently prepared by the contractor in accordance with guidelines intended to simplify the readability of the text as assessed by standard readability equations. Generally, the guidelines directed the contractor to examine the prose for long or complex sentences, use of the passive voice, vague and ambiguous terms, and the use of unnecessary technical words. More specifically, the contractor was advised that the revised version should meet the following criteria: (1) an overall grade level of 10.0 as measured by the Kincaid Readability Formula; (2) no segment with a grade level exceeding 13.0 as measured by the Kincaid formula; (3) no sentence greater than 30 words in length; (4) all sentences in the active voice; (5) no sentence that

TABLE 3.1
Parallel Segments of the Original and Revised Text

ORIGINAL VERSION

Air Designate Status. During this function, all COMPUTER
COMPLEX DIGITAL COMPUTER functions are sequenced from the ready
mode to the air designate mode status. The status change is reported to the digital and analog EDS by the EDS repeatback function
as the DIGITAL and ANALOG EDS REPEATBACK DATA consisting of the RADAR
A/B MODE STATUS signal. The air designate status is also reported
over the 30-bit A/B DOC DATA word which is routed via the SDC OUTPUT
CHANNELS and the RADAR A/B RSC DOC TRANSFER CIRCUIT (A9). The decoded IND WORD 1 content is provided to the AIR MODE CIRCUIT as the
AIR MODE signal and to the DESIGNATE MODE CIRCUIT as the DESIGNATE
signal. The AIR MODE CIRCUIT produces an AIR MODE status signal
which is distributed as the AIR MODE signal and provided to the FOC
STATUS IND CIRCUIT where it is displayed. The RSC DESIGNATE MODE
CIRCUIT produces a DESIGNATE MODE status signal which is distributed
as the DESIGNATE MODE signals provided to the RADIATE CONT CIRCUIT of
the radar radiate circuit function, and provided to the FOC STATUS
IND CIRCUIT where it is displayed.

REVISED VERSION

Air Designate Status. The air designate function sequences all
digital computer functions from ready mode to air designate mode.
This status change is reported to the digital and analog EDS. The
RADAR A/B MODE STATUS signal (B3) is applied as DIGITAL EDS REPEAT-
BACK DATA signals to the digital EDS. The RADAR A/B MODE STATUS
signal is also applied as ANALOG EDS REPEATBACK DATA signals to the
analog EDS via the SCD output channel circuitry. The air designate
status is also reported to the RSC via the DOC transfer circuit (A9)
as part of the RSC A/B DOC DATA signal (A4). The AIR MODE and DESIG-
NATE MODE signals are decoded from the IND WORD 1 signal (A9) and
applied to the air and designate mode circuits respectively. The air
mode circuit produces an AID MODE signal which is applied to the FOC
status and circuit where it is displayed. The AIR MODE signal is also
distributed to logic circuitry within the RSC. The designate mode
circuit (A10) produces a DESIGNATE MODE signal. The DESIGNATE MODE
signal is applied to the radiate control circuit (B11), and to the FOC
status indicator circuit where it is displayed on the FOC.

---

begins with a preposition; and (6) all simple sentences with no more than two
phrases. Samples of parallel segments of the original and revised versions of the
text are shown in Table 3.1.

Experimental Procedures

All subjects participated in the study in individual sessions. They were told that
they would be reading segments of text taken from the NATO Seasparrow
Technical Manual and asked to tell how they would explain the material to one of
their technician colleagues. Subjects were asked to imagine someone they
worked with who was just learning the system and actually picture themselves
explaining the passages to him. Subjects were asked to identify the name of
someone on their ship to whom they could imagine making these explanations.

Before beginning to read the text, subjects were provided a sheet of paper identifying four pieces of hardware on the NATO Seasparrow system. They were asked to draw a schematic diagram on the given sheet indicating the major hardware components and their interconnections.

After completing the schematic drawing, subjects were provided with one of the text versions and the 7-page schematic drawing from the technical manual. They were asked to read each segment and to use the schematic as they wished. After reading and studying each segment, subjects were asked to explain aloud what they had read to the "buddy" whom they had identified earlier. The sessions were tape-recorded for subsequent analysis and the experimenter recorded the time spent reading and studying, use of the schematic, and the time spent explaining. Finally, subjects were asked to make another schematic drawing of the system hardware and interconnections on a new sheet of paper (with the same identified hardware).

RESULTS

The results of the study can be organized around analyses of three sources of data: the technical prose, transcripts of the verbal protocols of subjects audiotaped during the experiment, and the schematic drawings of subjects.

Three segments were sampled for analysis of the prose and the corresponding protocols. These segments were judged by two electrical engineering experts as low, moderate, and more difficult in technical complexity, respectively. Furthermore, they occurred after the warm-up phase of the experiment during which subjects were getting accustomed to the procedure of speaking aloud, but before fatigue set in.

The following sections present the results emerging from the analyses of the three primary data sources. Analyses of the prose are described first, followed by a discussion of the protocol and schematic analyses.

Prose Analysis

First, the syntactic characteristics of the sampled prose segments were analyzed to determine the extent to which the guidelines were adhered to in the text revision. Second, the semantic characteristics of the two versions of text were examined to explore their comparability in meaning.

Syntactic Analysis.   The syntax of the sampled segments was analyzed using the Writer's Workbench program developed by Bell Laboratories. This computer program provides information on a variety of syntactic indicators including readability level, sentence length, sentence types, verb usage, and sentence beginners.

TABLE 3.2
Syntactic Characteristics of Original (O) and Revised (R) Text

Syntactic Indicator	Segment					
	4		5		7	
	O	R	O	R	O	R
Kincaid Readability Level	13.7	10.8	14.9	10.2	16.0	12.3
Average Sentence Length (in words)	27.0	19.5	27.3	17.1	29.3	21.0
Sentence Type:						
% Simple	43	60	36	67	50	89
% Complex	29	40	18	0	38	0
% Compound-Complex	29	0	27	7	0	0
% Compound	0	0	18	27	13	11
Passive Verbs	56	67	48	48	55	60
Sentences Beginning with a Preposition	14	0	9	0	13	0

Table 3.2 summarizes the results for the original and revised versions of the three sampled segments. These findings indicate that in general the revised text was simplified according to the guidelines provided to the contractor. The readability levels of the original versions were reduced 3 to 4 grade-levels in the revised versions as measured by the Kincaid readability formula. Sentence length was substantially reduced and the percentage of simple sentences was increased in the revised compared to the original versions. As directed, the contractor did modify sentences beginning with a preposition in the revised versions; however, the percentage of passive verbs was not systematically reduced.

In sum, the syntax of the revised version was simplified from the original version. However, passive verb constructions were frequent in both versions.

Semantic Analysis. The semantic content of the sampled segments of prose was analyzed using two sets of procedures. First, the electrical engineering experts identified the "gist" units or main ideas, and the information units represented by the content. In addition, they rated the information units on a number of dimensions, such as hierarchical level and type of topic. Second, a propositional analysis of the prose content was undertaken using the system developed by Kieras for use with technical text (Bovair & Kieras, 1981).

Turning first to the analyses of the subject matter experts, one of the electrical engineering experts formulated gist units to represent the macrostructure of the text and information units to represent its microstructure. The gist units were developed after Pearson and Camperell (1981). One gist unit was prepared for each segment of the original and revised text. Each gist unit consisted of a one sentence summary of the main idea of the text segment. Thus, each gist unit provided an overview of the text segment and roughly approximated terms such as key episode, theme, main plot, and top-level discourse structure used by other writers.

Information units were devised using the guidelines and criteria of Van Matre et al. (1975). Each information unit consisted of a simple sentence that expressed a single fact. In rewriting the text into information units, the electrical engineering expert (EEE) was guided by the following criteria:

1. Rewrite compound sentences as a group of simple sentences.
2. Reconstruct compound subjects, verbs, and objects as a group of simple sentences expressing a single fact per sentence.
3. Rewrite series of phrases as simple sentences that express a single fact per sentence.
4. Treat compound nouns representing a single term as a single word rather than as a noun preceded by a group of modifiers.
5. Use the active voice where possible.

Part A of Table 3.3 summarizes the results of the initial analyses of the subject matter expert. Each version of the sampled segments contained the same number of gist units. Further, the gist units were identical for each pair of segments, suggesting that the revision did not alter the overall nature or amount of information presented.

The original and revised versions did differ in the number of information units that they contained. While both versions of segment 4 were equivalent on this dimension, the revised version of segment 5 contained more information units than the original version. This pattern was reversed for segment 7. However, the revised versions did contain more sentences than the original versions. Thus, when a measure of idea density was constructed (a ratio of the number of information units to the number of sentences), the density of the revised versions was lower than that of their respective original versions.

Subsequently, the second subject matter expert examined the nature of the information units by rating each one on hierarchical level and salience as well as identifying the type of topic presented. Part B of Table 3.3 summarizes the results of this analysis.

Generally, the information units in the revised versions tended to present ideas at a higher hierarchical level (i.e., main ideas rather than supporting details) and with greater salience to the overall passage. Further, information units in the revised versions tended to address the overall system or the interrelationship between the signal and the hardware to a greater extent than those in the corresponding original version.

Table 3.4 summarizes the results of the propositional analyses of the sampled

TABLE 3.3
Semantic Analysis of Prose Using Information and Gist Units

Semantic Indicator	4		5		7	
	O^a	R^a	O^a	R^a	O^a	R^a
A. Summary of Initial Analysis						
Number of Gist Units	3	3	5	5	2	2
Number of Information Units	24	24	26	34	27	20
Number of Sentences	6	10	10	15	8	9
Density	4.0	2.4	2.6	2.3	3.4	2.2
B. Nature of Information Units						
Hierarchical Level^b	2.11	1.83	1.96	1.70	2.30	1.75
Topic – % System	15.8	16.7	23.1	39.4	29.6	25.0
% Signal	21.1	29.2	11.5	18.2	18.5	5.0
% Hardware	21.1	0	38.5	12.1	11.1	10.0
% Signal + Hardware	42.0	54.1	19.2	30.3	22.2	40.0
% Signal + System	0	0	3.85	0	14.8	10.0
% System + Hardware	0	0	3.85	0	3.8	10.0
Salience^a	1.79	1.33	1.42	1.52	1.93	1.30

[a]Where O = Original and R = Revised
[b]Rated on a 3-point scale where 1 = high and 3 = low

TABLE 3.4
Propositional Analysis of Original (O) and Revised (R) Text (After Kieras)

Measure	4 O Mean	4 O SD	4 R Mean	4 R SD	5 O Mean	5 O SD	5 R Mean	5 R SD	7 R Mean	7 R SD	7 O Mean	7 O SD
1. Propositions per sentence	1.17	1.60	4.70	1.77	8.80	4.59	5.87	2.10	8.63	4.31	5.00	1.58
2. By type per sentence:												
verb-based	2.83	1.47	1.60	1.07	3.70	1.77	2.47	1.41	2.88	1.55	1.67	0.71
modifiers	1.83	1.83	1.60	1.58	2.60	2.88	1.93	1.44	3.38	2.07	1.44	1.13
prepositions	2.67	0.82	2.00	1.15	2.30	1.34	2.27	3.61	2.75	1.67	1.78	1.09
3. Embedded propositions per sentence	2.50	1.05	2.00	1.25	2.80	3.33	1.40	1.59	3.38	2.83	2.00	0.87
4. Propositions with missing subject per sentence	1.50	1.05	1.10	1.10	1.60	2.72	0.80	1.15	0.63	0.74	0.67	0.71

segments. The propositional analyses constitute a more fine-grained examination of the text microstructure. As can be seen in Table 3.4, the revised versions contained fewer propositions per sentence than the original versions. Furthermore, there was less variability on this dimension in the revised versions. When the type of propositions per sentence was examined, (i.e., verb-based, modifiers, or prepositional), the revised versions tended to show a reduction in verb-based propositions (and to a lesser extent, modifiers) compared to the original versions. Further, when embedded propositions (propositions referring to other propositions within the same sentence) were examined, their incidence was also reduced in the revised versions. Finally, the number of propositions with missing subjects, e.g., passive constructions, was slightly reduced in the revised versions in two of the sampled segments.

Thus, the results of both sets of analyses suggest that the original and revised versions of the sampled segments were equivalent in the overall amount and nature of the information provided. However, the sentences in the revised versions were simpler in their semantic content. They were lower in idea density, and higher in hierarchical level and salience. Further, they tended to concern the overall system or the relationship between signal and hardware. The revised versions also showed fewer propositions per sentence and less embedding of propositions within sentences than the original versions.

Protocol Analysis

Subjects' verbal protocols were used to investigate reader interaction with the text. These reader responses to the scenario of explaining the passage to a buddy were intended as an alternative to standard syntactic and semantic approaches to assessing readability. Procedures for scoring the protocols and obtaining reliability estimates for the scoring are described first. Then analyses of information unit summaries, gist unit summaries, and their relationship to individual differences among subjects are presented.

Scoring Rules and Reliability. Transcripts of the verbal protocols of subjects explaining aloud the material were used to examine subjects' summaries of both gist and information units. Since the gist and information units contained multiple propositions and partial summary was possible, rating scales were developed to assess the degree to which they were represented (rather than a binary yes/no judgment). Somewhat different procedures were used for scoring the gist and information units. A 5-point scale was used to score the gist units and scoring was conducted liberally, based on the literal statements in the transcripts as well as inferences that followed from what they had said. During training, the two scorers were able to reach a high level of agreement (in fact 100%) using these procedures. (See Table 3.5.)

For the information units, a more stringent policy was adopted that required

TABLE 3.5
Reliability Estimates for Protocol Scoring

Type of Unit	N	Percentage Agreement	Mean Discrepancy Over All Items	Mean Discrepancy Over Items With Disagreements
I. Actual Scoring				
Information Units (3-point scale)	155	90.87	0.12	1.05
Gist Units (5-poing scale)	20	67.23	0.51	1.33
Other (Frequency Counts)	38	88.73	0.11	1.00
II: Final Training Segment				
Information Units (3-point scale)	28	85.71	0.81	1.25
Gist Units (5-point scale)	3	100.00	0.0	0.0
Other (Frequency Counts)	6	100.00	0.0	0.0

the same wording or synonyms in the transcripts. The two scorers were able to score the information units reliably using a 3-point scale where 1 = little or no inclusion, 2 = partial inclusion, and 3 = full or almost full inclusion. Their level of agreement was about 86% on the final training segment. (See Table 3.5.)

In addition, the scorers identified the frequency of connecting statements (with previous text segments and between the text and the schematic), elaborations beyond the text (system-specific or general electronics), and meta-statements about the audience or the summary task. During training, a 100% level of agreement was attained by the two scorers.

Table 3.5 also summarizes the reliability of scoring for the actual scoring. As shown in the table, high reliability was maintained on the information units and the other frequency counts. Interrater agreement fell on the gist units to 67%; however, disagreements were generally only one point off on a 5-point scale.

Summary of Information Units. Subjects' summaries of the information units contained in the text were examined using two strategies. First, the relationship of subject experience and text version (the two primary independent variables in the study) on the *amount* of summary of information units was examined using two-way analyses of variance. Second, the influence of these variables on the *type* of information units summarized was examined.

The results of the first set of analyses are summarized in Table 3.6. Separate

TABLE 3.6

Influence of Experience and Text on Information Unit Summary (3-Point Scale) of Original (O) and Revised (R) Text

Segment 4

a. ANOVA

Source	df	SS	F
E	2	2.7089	17.23****
T	1	2.0842	26.53****
EXT	2	2.1082	13.41****
Error	12	0.9433	

***p<.001

b. Cell Means

	O	R	
Exp. Non-NSS	1.22	2.86	2.04
Exp. NSS	1.25	1.57	1.41
Novice NSS	1.07	1.15	1.11
	1.18	1.86	1.52

c. Graphic Display

Segment 5

a. ANOVA

Source	df	SS	F
E	2	2.6099	22.93***
T	1	1.5744	27.66***
EXT	2	1.4349	12.61***
Error	12	0.6830	

***p<.001

b. Cell Means

	O	R	
Exp. Non-NSS	1.53	2.87	2.20
Exp. NSS	1.35	1.78	1.57
Novice NSS	1.29	1.28	1.29
	1.39	1.98	1.69

c. Graphic Display

Segment 7

a. ANOVA

Source	df	SS	F
E	2	1.4726	13.35***
T	1	2.3835	43.22***
EXT	2	0.6627	6.01**
Error	12	0.6618	

**p<.01
***p<.001

b. Cell Means

	O	R	
Exp. Non-NSS	1.32	2.55	1.94
Exp. NSS	1.26	1.92	1.59
Novice NSS	1.09	1.38	1.23
	1.22	1.95	1.59

c. Graphic Display

analyses were conducted for each text segment with amount of summary measured by subjects' average summary ratings over all information units in the segment. The main effects for experience (E) and text (T) as well as their interaction (EXT) were statistically significant for all three sampled segments. When the cell means were graphed and examined using Scheffe's test for post-hoc comparisons (Kirk, 1982), a similar pattern emerged in all three cases. The experienced non-NSS technicians showed significantly greater information unit summary with the revised compared to the original text. Further, with the revised text the experienced non-NSS technicians performed significantly above the experienced and novice NSS technicians. The three experience groups did not differ significantly with the original version, nor did the experienced and novice NSS technicians differ from each other with the revised version.

The second set of analyses examined the *type* of information units summarized based on ratings and categorizations made by one of the subject matter experts. These included hierarchical level of the information unit, salience of the unit to the overall gist of the segment, and type of topic. The first two types were measured on a 3-point rating scale where 1 = high and 3 = low, while the last was based on a category system of six possible topics or combinations of topics.

Separate analyses were conducted for each text segment. Each analysis included two between-subjects variables (experience and text) and one within-subjects variable (type of information unit). The dependent measures for each subject were average comprehension ratings for information units at each level or category of the scale being examined (e.g., hierarchical levels 1, 2, 3).

Table 3.7 summarizes the results for hierarchical level and Table 3.8 for topic. (No significant differences were obtained for the salience ratings, so the results are not presented here.)

As shown in Table 3.7, the between-subjects portion of the analyses replicated the effects of experience level, text version, and their interaction described earlier. The within-subjects portion revealed a significant main effect for hierarchical level for segments 5 and 7. Post-hoc comparisons among the marginal means using Scheffe's test indicated that subjects tended to show more summary of the units rated high in hierarchical level (i.e., main ideas) compared to those rated lower in hierarchical level (i.e., supporting details).

As displayed in Table 3.8, the effects of experience level, text version, and their interaction were again replicated as expected. In addition, statistically significant interactions between topic and text were obtained for segments 5 and 7. (A main effect for topic with segment 7 was also obtained.) Post-hoc comparisons of the means for the topic by text interaction were conducted using Tukey's HSD test (Kirk, 1982).

The pattern of results was somewhat different for segments 5 and 7. With segment 7, system-related topics tended to be summarized more than more specific topics, particularly with the revised version. With segment 5, there was greater summary of hardware with the revised version compared to the original text.

TABLE 3.7

Influence of Hierarchical Level on Information Unit Summary

Segment 4

a. ANOVA

Source	df	SS	F
E	2	6.2881	5.63**
T	1	6.8152	12.20**
ExT	2	5.2440	4.70**
Error	12	6.7014	
HL	2	1.2825	2.95
HLxE	4	1.8232	2.10
HLxT	2	0.3600	0.83
HlxExT	4	5.2196	
Error	24	5.2196	

**$p < .01$

b. Marginal Means for HL

HL1	1.81
HL2	1.44
HL3	1.66

Segment 5

a. ANOVA

Source	df	SS	F
E	2	8.7549	16.15**
T	1	4.0057	14.78**
ExT	2	5.2518	9.69**
Error	12	3.2528	
HL	2	0.7748	4.25*
HLxE	4	0.0633	0.17
HLxT	2	0.6057	3.32
HLxExT	4	0.2721	0.75
Error	24	2.1868	

*$p < .05$
**$p < .01$
***$p < .001$

b. Marginal Means for HL

HL1	1.83
HL2	1.67
HL3	1.53

Segment 7

a. ANOVA

Source	df	SS	F
E	2	5.9826	19.29***
T	1	6.8603	44.23***
ExT	2	2.8030	0.94**
Error	12	1.8613	
HL	2	2.4432	9.46***
HLxE	4	0.9288	1.80
HLxT	3	0.4295	1.66
HLxExT	4	1.2110	2.35
Error	24	3.0979	

**$p < .01$
***$p < .001$

b. Marginal Means for HL

HL1	1.95
HL2	1.48
HL3	1.53

TABLE 3.8
Influence of Topic on Information Unit Summary

Segment 4

a. ANOVA

Source	df	SS	F
E	2	5.8682	7.29**
T	1	5.8246	14.46**
ExT	2	5.4860	6.81**
Error	12	4.8328	
Top	2	1.1753	2.22
TopxE	4	1.1179	1.05
TopxT	2	0.3901	0.74
TopxExT	4	0.4449	0.42
Error	24	6.3601	

$**p<.01$

Segment 5

a. ANOVA

Source	df	SS	F
E	2	9.1671	16.62***
T	1	6.2143	22.53***
ExT	2	5.0573	9.17**
Error	12	3.3096	
Top	3	0.4039	1.43
TopxE	6	0.8806	1.55
TopxT	3	1.3642	4.82**
TopxExT	6	1.3800	2.44
Error	36	3.3993	

$*p<.05$
$**p<.01$
$***p<.001$

b. Means for TopxT Interaction

	O	R
System	1.56	1.98
Signal	1.59	1.85
Hardware	1.32	2.31
Signal & Hardware	1.27	1.96

Segment 7

a. ANOVA

Source	df	SS	F
E	2	7.9206	21.867***
T	1	19.3661	107.06***
ExT	2	4.1333	4.42**
Error	12	2.1708	
Top	5	5.7686	5.90***
TopxE	10	2.8106	1.44
TopxT	5	4.6316	4.74***
TopxExT	10	1.1552	0.59
Error	60	11.7261	

$*p<.05$
$**p<.01$
$***p<.001$

b. Means for TopxT Interaction

	O	R
System	1.46	2.07
Signal	1.16	1.56
Hardware	1.07	1.72
Signal & Hardware	1.00	1.68
System & Signal	1.33	2.39
System & Hardware	1.00	2.67

TABLE 3.9
Influence of Experience and Text on Gist Unit Summary (5-Point Scale)

Segment 4

a. ANOVA

Source	df	SS	F
E	2	10.7160	3.91*
T	1	2.0000	1.46
EXT	2	2.3704	0.86
Error	12	16.4444	

*p<.05

b. Cell Means

	O	R	
Exp. Non-NSS	3.22	4.77	4.00
Exp. NSS	3.11	2.89	3.00
Novice NSS	1.78	2.44	2.11
	2.70	3.37	3.04

c. Graphic Display

Segment 5

a. ANOVA

Source	df	SS	F
E	2	10.0844	9.22**
T	1	7.2200	13.21**
EXT	2	8.0133	7.33**
Error	12	6.5600	

**p<.01

b. Cell Means

	O	R	
Exp. Non-NSS	1.87	4.80	3.33
Exp. NSS	1.80	3.00	2.40
Novice NSS	1.67	1.33	1.50
	1.78	3.04	2.41

c. Graphic Display

Segment 7

a. ANOVA

Source	df	SS	F
E	2	7.1111	4.13*
T	1	7.3472	8.53**
EXT	2	1.4444	0.84
Error	12	10.3333	

*p<.05
**p<.01

b. Cell Means

	O	R	
Exp. Non-NSS	3.00	4.83	3.92
Exp. NSS	3.67	4.17	3.92
Novice NSS	1.83	3.33	2.58
	2.83	4.11	3.47

c. Graphic Display

Summary of Gist Units. The influence of experience and text version on subjects' overall summary of gist units was also examined using two-way analyses of variance. Again, analyses were conducted separately for each segment where gist unit summary was measured by average gist unit summary ratings for each segment. A somewhat complicated pattern of results emerged, as shown in Table 3.9. For segment 5, a similar pattern of results occurred as described above for amount of information unit summary. Both experienced non-NSS and NSS technicians showed significantly greater gist unit summary with the revised compared to the original text version. The novice NSS technicians did not show significant differences in performance with the original and revised versions and they performed significantly below the two groups of experienced technicians on the revised version. For segment 7, all three experience groups showed greater gist summary with the revised compared to the original version. In addition, the two experienced groups (non-NSS and NSS) showed significantly greater gist comprehension than the novice NSS technicians. For segment 4, only a main effect for experience was obtained, suggesting that the groups were ordered on degree of gist summary as follows: experienced non-NSS technicians, experienced NSS technicians, and novice NSS technicians.

A similar analysis was conducted for the frequency of connectives, elaborations, and meta-statements. No statistically significant effects were isolated for experience or text. In fact, the frequency of such statements was generally quite low. The most frequent type of statement was system-specific elaborations which averaged 1.39 per segment (s = 2.89).

Relation to other Individual Difference Measures. The relationship of information and gist unit summary to time spent reading and studying, use of the provided schematic diagrams, and individual differences among subjects as measured by their Armed Forces Qualification Test scores (AFQT) and their Armed Services Vocational Aptitude Battery (ASVAB) scores was examined. No significant relationships were identified.

In sum, the revised text version contributed to greater summary of information units for the experienced non-NSS and NSS technicians but did not appear to facilitate the information unit summary of the novice NSS technicians. There was also some evidence that subjects tended to comprehend more global ideas rather than supporting details, particularly with the revised text.

Schematic Analysis

The schematic drawings prepared by subjects before and after reading the text were scored using a system developed by one of the subject matter experts. The scoring system produced two subscores and a total score. The first subscore was concerned with the functional topology or nodes of the drawing, e.g., the functional boxes such as the Computer Complex. The nodal hierarchies were additive and weighted in a geometric fashion by level of specificity to emphasize the level of knowledge. Thus, a person could earn a score of 1, 2, 4, 8, or 16 for the computer complex, for example, depending on the level of detail. The second subscore concerned the signal flow or connections between nodes. One point was assigned for a connection between boxes, two points for the direction of the path, and four points if the connection was named. The scoring system also contained a penalty for incorrect nodes and signals such that points were subtracted for errors drawn. The total score was simply the sum of the function and signal subscores.

Because the subscore distributions were highly skewed, the first step in the analysis was to truncate the distributions and to transform the original scores to a 5-point scale. This transformation was accomplished by examining the frequency distributions of the subscores and dividing them at naturally occurring breaks between score values.

Analysis of the pretest drawings indicated a significant main effect for experience on both the function subscore and the signal subscore (see Table 3.10). Post-hoc comparisons between means using Scheffe's method revealed that, on

TABLE 3.10
Relationship of Experience and Text
to Pretest Schematic Drawings

A. Function Subscore

1. ANOVA

Source	df	SS	F
E	2	12.6627	8.19**
T	1	3.1405	4.06
EXT	2	1.2261	0.79
Error	11	8.5000	

$**p<.01$

2.
Experience Group	Means
Exp. Non-NSS	2.17
Exp. NSS	4.17
Novice NSS	3.60

B. Signal Subscore

1. ANOVA

Source	df	SS	F
E	2	9.3000	5.48**
T	1	0.9444	1.11
EXT	2	4.4333	2.61
Error	11	9.3333	

$**p<.01$

2.
Experience Group	Means
Exp. Non-NSS	1.50
Exp. NSS	3.00
Novice NSS	1.40

TABLE 3.11
Relationship of Experience and Text
to Posttest Schematic Drawings

A. Function Subscore

1. ANOVA

Source	df	SS	F
E	2	9.9353	4.15*
T	1	0.1381	0.12
EXT	2	0.9953	0.42
Error	11	13.1667	

$*p<.05$

2. Experience Group — Means

	Means
Exp. Non-NSS	2.50
Exp. NSS	4.00
Novice NSS	4.20

B. Signal Subscore

1. ANOVA

Source	df	SS	F
E	2	10.2510	3.28*
T	1	2.5621	1.64
EXT	2	4.1379	1.33
Error	11	17.1667	

$*p<.07$

2. Experience Group — Means

	Means
Exp. Non-NSS	2.33
Exp. NSS	3.33
Novice NSS	1.40

the function subscore, the experienced and novice NSS technicians performed significantly above the experienced non-NSS technicians. On the signal subscore, the experienced NSS technicians showed significantly higher performance than either of the other two groups.

Table 3.11 presents an analysis of the posttest schematic drawings by experience and text version. There was a significant main effect for experience on the function subscores. Post-hoc comparisons among means using Scheffe's method showed that, as in the analyses of the pretest drawings, both the experienced and novice NSS technicians performed higher on this dimension than the non-NSS technicians.

The main effect for experience on the signal subscores approached statistical significance $(p<.07)$; and the pattern of means was somewhat different than at the pretest. In this case, the experienced NSS technicians performed significantly higher than the novice NSS technicians as at pretest. However, the performance of the experienced non-NSS technicians was not significantly different from the experienced NSS technicians.

Finally, pretest and posttest scores were compared for each of the three experience groups using t-tests for dependent groups. While no statistically significant differences were observed, examination of the means suggests that the novice NSS technicians tended to show more improvement on the function subscore from pretest to posttest, while the experienced non-NSS technicians tended to show improvement on the signal subscore.

In sum, the NSS technicians exhibited greater understanding of the functional hardware in their schematic drawings than the non-NSS technicians, as would be expected based on their direct experience with the NSS system. Further, experienced NSS technicians showed a greater understanding of the signal paths at pretest than the other two groups. However, the experienced non-NSS technicians improved at posttest such that their signal performance was not significantly different from the experienced NSS technicians.

DISCUSSION

This research examined the potential use of scenarios simulating a real world task to assess the readability of general technical text. The scenario consisted of asking subjects to read a segment of text and to explain to a colleague how the particular component described in the passage functioned. Subjects' summaries were assessed based on the extent to which the gist of the passage was represented in their summaries as well as specific information units.

Two experimental variations were conducted to examine their effects on subjects' summaries in response to the scenario. The first variation involved the text with an original version and a revised version that was simplified using traditional readability indices. The second variation centered on the world knowledge that subjects brought to the task, with three groups of subjects differing in their amount and type of experience. Finally, subjects' graphic representations of their system as indicated by schematic drawings were examined to determine the influence of the text and subjects' world knowledge on functional understandings of the system.

Results supported the initial distinctions drawn between text versions and experience groups. The revised version was indeed syntactically simpler on a number of dimensions such as readability level, sentence length, and sentence structure. Furthermore, while the overall semantic content or gist of corresponding segments remained comparable, the revised version was lower in density of ideas and ideas presented were higher in hierarchical level and salience than the original version.

Further, analyses for the pretest schematic drawings supported that there were preexisting differences among the three groups of technicians. NSS technicians showed greater functional knowledge in their drawings than non-NSS technicians, while experienced NSS technicians showed greater signal knowledge than either of the other two groups.

Analyses of the verbal summaries suggest that the revised version had the greatest facilitating effects for experienced non-NSS technicians. Technicians in this group showed performance superior to both experienced and novice NSS technicians in analyses of both the amount and types of information summarized.

One might speculate that the simpler revised version of the text allowed the experienced non-NSS technicians to apply their general world knowledge about electronic systems and technical manuals in order to extract the information necessary to understand the specific operations of the Seasparrow System. Such an explanation aligns with work by Rumelhart and Ortony (1977), which suggests that efficient learners call up schema corresponding to the particular type of discourse and instantiate the schema based on what is read. The experienced non-NSS technicians were familiar with technical manuals generally, thus, they may have had a well-developed text scheme for this type of technical manual. Furthermore, they were familiar with electronic systems and may have had a content schema as well. The simplifications in the revised version may have facilitated the ability of the experienced non-NSS technicians to instantiate their preexisting content schema with specific facts related to the Seasparrow System.

One might further speculate that the hands-on experience of the experienced NSS technicians actually interfered with their instantiation of facts from the text into their content schema. In several cases, members of this group noted that the text was incomplete or inaccurate (e.g., "it doesn't really work that way"). Meyer (1983) reported a similar phenomenon in which readers disagreed with an author's message, rejected his schema, and substituted their own schema with instantiations based on information outside the text.

The analyses of the verbal protocols also suggested that main ideas rather than supporting details tended to be summarized. This finding replicates the work of Meyer (1975) and others who have shown that height in the content structure is the best predictor of information recalled.

Analyses of the posttest schematic drawings revealed the same effects for experience as the pretest drawings. Changes in performance from pretest to posttest suggest that technicians with different types and amounts of experience may be extracting different types of information from the text. Novice NSS technicians tended to show improved functional understanding of the system while technicians experienced in systems other than the Seasparrow System showed improvements in signal knowledge.

The study reported here was exploratory and the results should be cautiously interpreted. However, there are indications that the use of scenarios and verbal summaries from subjects may provide valuable insights into the readability of text. Some advantages of the approach are that it can be used to establish a task environment that more closely parallels reading demands in the real world than much of the prior readability research, that it views the reader as an active processor of text extracting meaning and incorporating meaning into preexisting cognitive structures, and that it yields rich data on what and how subjects use information contained in text.

Additional research is needed to clarify and operationalize the concept of readability. However, as this work and other research suggests, emerging concepts of readability must take into account the interaction of a reader (preexisting world knowledge, content and text schemas, goals for reading, for example) and the text (its syntactic and semantic characteristics). The use of task scenarios and verbal protocols may provide one means of learning more about this interaction so that guidance can be developed to make specific types of text more "readable" for particular types of readers.

Methodologically, the study illustrates a larger connection between the analytic schemes for assessing readability and for emerging procedures for assessing written productions. Although the relationship between reading and writing ability has received popular support of historical proportions, the demonstration of such a relationship depends on the adaptation of common frameworks and comparable procedures for analyzing text. The cognitive vs. the communicative uses of writing suggest that writing is a way to clarify and then to demonstrate the clarity of conceptual understandings as evidence of the comprehensibility of written text. Present applied development in writing-from-reading (Quellmalz, 1984) demonstrates these interrelationships.

Yet, writing assessment itself has grown (as have concepts of readability) more sophisticated and has moved toward functional organization and semantic analysis. Newer scoring processes for writing depend less on the convention of syntax and more on what meaning and purpose is inherent in the text. Relatively simple procedures and rigorous training programs are available to teach the assessment of writing reliably (Quellmalz & Burry, 1983). These are presently being applied in the ongoing international comparison of written composition supported by the IEA (Baker, 1982) and may well contribute to the task of protocol analysis. The analysis of oral protocols as indicators of the readability of text will undoubtedly remain of research rather than of applied interest in education and training settings (until computerized speech analysis is perfected). Yet, scholars interested in either oral or written text analysis must begin to profit from the conceptual framework and research processes used by one another. Parallel effort need not go unacknowledged, and the analysis of language understanding can only benefit.

REFERENCES

Amirin, M. R., & Jones, B. F. (1982). Toward a new definition of readability. *Educational Psychologist, 17,* 13–30.

Baker, E. (1982). The specification of writing tasks, *Evaluation in Education, 5,* 291–295.

Bormuth, J. R. (1969). *Development of readability analyses* (Contract #OEG-3-7-070053-0326). Washington, D.C.: U.S. Office of Education.

Bovair, S., & Kieras, D. E. (1981). *A guide to propositional analysis for research on technical prose* (Technical Report #8). San Diego, CA: NPRDC.

Bransford, J. D., & Johnson, M. K. (1972). Contextual prerequisites for understanding: Some investigations of comprehension and recall. *Journal of Verbal Learning and Verbal Behavior, 11,* 717–726.

Carver, R. P. (1974, September). *Measuring the reading difficulty levels of Navy training manuals* (Tech. Rep.). Washington, D.C.: Office of Naval Research, (NTIS No. AD 780 448/7).

Duffy, T. M. (1985a). Readability formulas: What's the use? In T. Duffy & R. Waller (Eds.), *Designing usable texts.* New York: Academic Press.

Duffy, T. M. (1985b). Preparing technical manuals: Specifications and guidelines. In D. Jonassen (Ed.), *The technology of text. Vol II.* Englewood Cliffs, NJ: Educational Technology Publications.

Duffy, T. M. (in press). Literacy instruction in the Armed Forces. *Armed Forces and Society.*

Duffy, T. M., Curran, T. & Sass, D. (1983). Document design for technical job tasks: An evaluation. *Human Factors, 25,* 153–160.

Duffy, T. M., & Kabance, P. (1982). Testing a readable writing approach to text revision. *Journal of Educational Psychology, 74,* 733–748.

Ericcson, K. A., & Simon, H. A. (1980). Verbal reports as data. *Psychological Review, 87,* 215–251.

Flesch, R. F. (1948). A new readability yardstick. *Journal of Applied Psychology, 32,* 221–233.

Flesch, R. F. (1949). *The art of readable writing.* New York: Harper.

Frase, L. (1977). Purpose in reading. In J. T. Guthrie (Ed.), *Cognition, curriculum, and composition.* Newark, DE: International Reading Association.

Kieras, D. (1985). Thematic processes in the comprehension of technical prose. In B. Britton & J. Black (Eds.), *Understanding expository prose.* Hillsdale, NJ: Lawrence Erlbaum Associates.

Kieras, D. E., Tibbits, M., & Bovair, S. (1984). *How experts and nonexperts operate electronic equipment from instructions* (Technical Report #14). Arlington, VA: Office of Naval Research.

Kirk, R. E. (1982). *Experimental design* (2nd edition). Belmont, CA: Brooks/Cole.

Klare, G. R. (1963). *The measurement of readability.* Ames: Iowa State University Press.

Klare, G. R. (1975). *A manual for readable writing.* Glen Burnie, MD: REM Company.

Klare, G. R. (1979). *Readability standards for Army-wide publications* (Evaluation Report 79-1). Fort Benjamin Harrison, IN: U.S. Army Administrative Center.

Meyer, B. J. F. (1984). Text dimension and cognitive processing. In H. Mandl, N. Stein, & T. Trabasso (Eds.), *Learning and comprehending text.* Hillsdale, NJ: Lawrence Erlbaum Associates.

Meyer, B. J., & Rice, G. E. (1983). *Interaction of text variables and processing strategies for young, middle-aged, and older expert readers* (Research Report #12). Tempe, AZ: Department of Educational Psychology, Arizona State University.

Miller, J. R., & Kintsch, W. (1980). Readability and recall of short prose passages: A theoretical analysis. *Journal of Experimental Psychology: Human Learning and Memory, 6,* 335–354.

Osborne, R., & Wittrock, M. (1983). Learning science: A generative process. *Science Education, 67,* 489–508.

Pearson, P. D. (1974–1975). The effects of grammatical complexity on children's comprehension, recall, and conception of certain semantic relations. *Reading Research Quarterly, 10,* 155–192.

Pearson, P. D., & Camperell, K. (1981). Comprehension of text structures. In J. T. Guthrie (Ed.), *Comprehension and teaching: Research reviews.* Newark, DE: International Reading Association.

Pichert, J. W., & Anderson, J. C. (1977). Taking different perspectives on a story. *Journal of Educational Psychology, 69,* 309–315.

Quellmalz, E. S. (1984). *A system for analyzing functional writing: An example of research in service of policy and instruction.* Paper presented at the Annual Meeting of the American Educational Research Association, New Orleans.

Quellmalz, E. S., & Burry, J. (1983). *Analytic scales for assessing students' expository and narrative writing skills* (CSE Resource Paper No. 5). Los Angeles: UCLA Center for the Study of Evaluation.

Redish, J. C., Felker, D., & Rose, A. (1982). Evaluating the effects of document design principles. *Information Design Journal, 2/3/4,* 236–243.

Rumelhart, D., & Ortony, A. (1977). The representation of knowledge in memory. In R. C. Anderson, R. J. Spiro, & W. E. Montague (Eds.), *Schooling and the acquisition of knowledge.* Hillsdale, NJ: Lawrence Erlbaum Associates.

Spiro, R., Bruce, B., & Brewer, W. (Eds.). (1980). *Theoretical issues in reading comprehension.* Hillsdale, NJ: Lawrence Erlbaum Associates.

Swaney, J., Janik, C., Bond, S., & Hayes, J. R. (1981, June). *Editing for comprehension: Improving the process through reading protocols* (DDP-TR #14). Pittsburgh, PA: The Communications Design Center, Carnegie-Mellon University.

Van Matre, N. H. et al. (1975). *Learning from lecture: Investigation of study strategies involving note-taking.* San Diego, CA: NPRDC.

Wittrock, M. (1982). *Generative reading comprehension.* Los Angeles: University of California.

Wright, P. (1985). Editing: Policies and processes. In T. Duffy and R. Waller (Eds.), *Designing usable texts.* New York: Academic Press.

4

Readability vs. Comprehensibility: A Case Study in Improving a Real Document

Veda Charrow
Document Design Center, American Institutes for Research

This paper describes a study of the comprehensibility of automobile recall letters which was conducted for the National Highway Traffic Administration (NHTSA). Linguists and other scholars in the area of writing and readability may find it interesting and useful for three reasons:

First, it is a study that pits the predictions of readability formulas against the results of a sensitive measure of comprehensibility.

Second, it is a study of the comprehensibility of adult, real-world documents, not just school textbooks.

Third, it lends further support and validity to research-based guidelines for clear writing and graphics.

NHTSA asked us to conduct this study as part of an effort to increase the response rate to automobile recall letters, which is unsatisfactorily low. One reason for the poor response rate, according to a report by the General Accounting Office (GAO, 1982) which addressed this problem, is that the reading level of recall letters is too high. GAO based this conclusion on an analysis of the readability of 11 typical recall letters and on the Adult Performance Level Study which was conducted at the University of Texas at Austin in 1975. According to the Adult Performance Level Study, 54% of U.S. adults read at or below the 11th grade level. And according to the GAO's readability tests of the 11 letters, using the Fry and Flesch readability formulas (Flesch, 1949), most of the letters were at the college reading level (12.4 years to 16.4 years). Hence, the reading level of the recall letters as measured by these formulas is much higher than the reported reading ability of the majority of U.S. adults.

In addition to improving the "readability" of the letters, the GAO report suggested using organization and highlighting techniques to make recall letters easier to understand:

Letters informing owners of a recall are written at a higher reading level than the reading level of most adults and generally fail to highlight important information. We believe more owners would respond to a recall if these letters were easier to read and if key information were highlighted. (p. 27)

Unfortunately, none of the GAO report's findings and recommendations were based on *empirically derived* evidence. Readability formulas provide, at best, second-hand information about how well people actually understand a text. They do not provide any valid information about how much, and what precisely, readers understand in a text (Charrow, 1979; Redish, 1979). Similarly, the GAO report gave no scientific basis for the recommendations regarding highlighting information in recall letters. In fact, several of their recommendations are contradicted by scientific research on what is most legible.[1] In short, although some of the GAO's recommendations may have been worthwhile, the only way of knowing whether and to what extent they are valid is by empirically testing the recall letters on a sample of real car owners. In 1982 and early 1983, we set up and conducted just such a study.

MATERIALS

Materials were a typical recall letter and two rewritten versions—one rewritten to fit a readability formula and one rewritten according to the Document Design Center's guidelines for organization, language, and graphics. (See Appendix A for the three versions of the letter.) To find the original letter we reviewed a large number of real recall letters and chose one that typified the language, organization, and layout of all of them. We made sure that the letter had enough content and dealt with a serious enough problem that it would be useful for testing various aspects of comprehension and several different potential comprehension problems.

When we had chosen the letter, we simply changed the name of the manufacturer, the names of the car models, and the engine number. NHTSA staff reviewed our choice to ensure that the letter was, indeed, typical of recall letters.

To create the two rewritten versions of the recall letter, we waited until we had tested the original letter and had done a preliminary analysis of the results. We created the Readability Letter by rewriting the original letter—shortening sentences and using shorter words. We did this because we have found that in the majority of cases, when people in business and government are required to meet a readability standard, they simply write to "fit the formula." Thus, we subdivided long sentences into shorter sentences. (We did not use sentence fragments.) Occasionally, we removed introductory phrases to make a sentence

---

[1]For example, research has shown that text in all capitals—such as the text of the boxed notice recommended by the GAO report—is much harder to read than text in lower-case letters (Tinker, 1965).

shorter, if we could do so without interfering with the meaning. We also replaced many of the long words in the original letter with shorter synonyms.

We created the Guidelines Letter by looking carefully at the organization, language, and layout of the original letter, and at the results from the test of the original letter. On the basis of the test results and AIR's guidelines for clearer writing, we rewrote the original letter in the following ways: We reorganized it to make the progression of ideas more logical. We provided a context, in the form of a NOTICE statement at the top of the letter and an introductory sentence in the first paragraph. We eliminated redundancy by cutting out several repetitive sentences. We made the tone of the sentences more personal. We eliminated complex grammatical constructions such as passives and nominalizations. We changed several vocabulary items. Finally, we used graphic devices such as a box at the top and headings throughout to highlight information.

In addition to the letters themselves, we created three other sets of test materials:

1. A multiple-choice test consisting of 8 questions, based on eight major content areas in the original recall letter. Each question was typed on a separate 5″ × 8″ card, so that the questions could be randomly ordered.

2. An opinion questionnaire consisting of 4 questions with 5-point rating scales, asking for subjects' opinions or attitudes regarding various aspects of recall letters.

3. A demographic questionnaire consisting of 7 questions about the subjects themselves.

(See Appendix B for a copy of one complete set of these materials.)

SUBJECTS

Subjects were 56 people who had brought their cars in for servicing at various automotive centers in the Washington, D.C. area. The subjects were randomly assigned to three groups, and each group received only one version of the letter.

The subjects were 39 males and 17 females, whose mean age was 44.2 and whose mean education level was 14.2 years. The mean age when they acquired their first car was 22.5.

These demographic characteristics were distributed across the three groups as follows:

TABLE 4.1
Demographic Characteristics of the Three Groups of Subjects

Group	N	Mean Age	(s.d.)	Mean Education	(s.d.)	First Car	(s.d.)	M	F
Original	19	39.7	(10.8)	14.9	(1.9)	21.3	(4.6)	13	6
Readability	18	46.3	(15.2)	14.2	(1.9)	23.7	(10.9)	12	6
Guidelines	19	46.7	(14.2)	13.5	(2.4)	22.4	(9.6)	14	5

Note. None of the differences among the groups was statistically significant.

As it happened, the largest difference among groups was in the educational level of the Guidelines group. Although this difference was not statistically significant, the Guidelines group, in general, had a slightly lower educational level than the other two groups. They were also slightly older than the other two groups. On the basis of this, we might expect slightly (but perhaps not significantly) worse performance in the tasks by the Guidelines group—unless the Guidelines letter itself was written in a way that improved comprehension.

METHODOLOGY

The methodology combined paraphrase testing and multiple-choice questions.

In the paraphrase methodology, a subject reads a piece of the text and then explains it in his or her own words onto audio tape. For this study, we divided the recall letters into roughly equal-sized paragraphs. The paragraphs were separated by several spaces and a flap of paper slightly larger than the paragraph was taped over each paragraph, so that the reader could read one paragraph at a time, cover it with the flap, and then paraphrase. We felt that paraphrase testing would be the appropriate primary measure for several reasons. First, it measures readers' comprehension, not "readability." Second, unlike a multiple-choice test, it can pinpoint precisely what and how subjects are understanding or misunderstanding in a given piece of the text. The paraphrase methodology can be used to find specific differences between subjects' understanding of two or more versions of a text; this, in turn, can allow the researcher to determine which words or sentence structures in the text are causing comprehension problems for readers. Multiple-choice questions might then be used to confirm some of the results of the paraphrase test.

PROCEDURE

A researcher from the Document Design Center approached a prospective subject in the waiting room of the service center. The researcher briefly explained that he or she was conducting a study of recall letters for NHTSA, and asked the prospective subject if he or she had 20–30 minutes to participate in the study. If the subject agreed, the researcher took the subject to an empty office and the two sat down at opposite sides of a desk. The researcher gave the subject a copy of the instruction sheet and asked the subject to read along as the researcher read the instructions aloud. The subject was then given a practice paragraph to read and paraphrase and the researcher answered any questions that the subject might have about the task.

The researcher then gave the subject one version of the letter, turned on the tape recorder, and asked the subject to read the first paragraph, cover it with the flap, and then paraphrase it. The subject followed the same procedure for all the paragraphs in the letter. When the subject finished paraphrasing the letter, the researcher turned off the tape recorder and shuffled the eight objective question cards to put them in random order. The subject read the first card and indicated which answer he or she thought was the correct one on the answer sheet. The subject followed this procedure for all eight multiple-choice questions. When that was done, the subject filled in the four rating scales in the Opinion Questionnaire and then completed one of the three versions of the Demographic Questionnaire. That ended the task.

SCORING

Each subject's paraphrases were transcribed. A subject's paraphrase was then compared to the letter that he or she had paraphrased, to determine what the subject had understood, misunderstood, or omitted. The scoring was done in the following way:

First, we broke down the content of each letter into "idea units," each of which corresponded to one "idea"—clause, phrase, modifier. Thus, for example, the first paragraph of the Original Letter was broken down into these 16 idea-units:

001   This notice is sent to you
002   in accordance with the requirements
003   of the National Traffic and Motor Vehicle Safety Act.
004   Swift Motors has determined
005   that a defect . . . exists
006   which relates to motor vehicle safety
007   on some 1981 Pembrooks
008   and (on some 1981) Monteveros
009   equipped with the HK2000 engine
010   These vehicles were assembled
011   with the incorrect
012   accelerator cable bracket
013   which under certain conditions
014   could allow the Cruise Control servo rod
015   to bind on
016   the accelerator cable bracket

Two raters then independently scored several subjects' paraphrases, noting, for each idea-unit in the letter, whether the subject had paraphrased it correctly, made an error, or omitted it. The raters then compared their ratings and found that the interrater agreement was almost 90%. At that point, the raters resolved the differences in their ratings, and the scoring was continued by only one rater, who periodically checked with the other rater to resolve any questions. This procedure was followed for all three groups of subjects.

In addition, the results from the multiple-choice test and the Opinion Questionnaires were tallied.

Data Analysis and Results

The data from the paraphrase task, the multiple-choice questions, and the Opinion Questionnaire (rating scales) were analyzed by computer. For the paraphrase data, we used analyses of variance (ANOVAs) to find differences among groups in their overall scores of items correct, wrong, or omitted (full measure) and differences among groups in items correct, wrong, or omitted for those items in all three letters that could be considered particularly important for car owners (importance measure).

We also looked at those idea-units in one or another of the letters that appeared to be causing problems for three or more subjects and compared them to the corresponding idea-units in the other letters.

For the objective, multiple-choice questions, we used ANOVAs and analyses of covariance (ANCOVAs) to find any differences among groups in their scores on each question, or any differences in scores that could be attributed to other factors, such as education.

For the Opinion Questionnaire, we looked for differences among groups in their ratings on the four rating scales.

We also looked for information from the subjects' paraphrases and comments to provide answers to questions that we did not directly ask. Thus, for example, we did not ask subjects who they thought had sent the letter they were paraphrasing, but several subjects in each group volunteered that information.

In all three letters, we examined those idea-units and sentences where subjects omitted the most information or made the most errors. We looked for organization, sentence structures, vocabulary, layout, or concepts that might be responsible for subjects' omissions and poor comprehension.

RESULTS

The Paraphrase Task and Objective Questions. The most telling statistical results are for the overall scores, comparing items correct, wrong, or omitted for each group of subjects. All three groups had similar scores for the proportion of items omitted and the proportion correct. However, as Table 4.2 shows, subjects who paraphrased the Original Letter and the Readability Letter made a higher proportion of errors than the subjects who paraphrased the Guidelines Letter.

This difference between the Guidelines group and each of the other two

TABLE 4.2
Items Wrong for the Three Groups

	Number Wrong	Proportion Wrong	N
Original	5.3	.0483	19
Readability	4.6	.0461	18
Guidelines	3.6	.0325	19

groups was statistically significant, which is what one would predict if the Guidelines Letter is more understandable than the other two letters.

Looking at some individual important items, we found other significant differences among the three groups—almost all of them showing significantly better comprehension on the part of the Guidelines group.

In the items describing what is mechanically wrong with the car, 48% of the Guidelines group showed they knew that the defect was a *wrong* part, as opposed to only 5% of the Original group and 17% of the Readability Group. (Some subjects erroneously believed that the problem was a *defective* part.)

Significantly more of the Guidelines group (63%) than of the Original group (21%) or the Readability group (22%) mentioned that *the company* had found the problem/defect in the car.

Modifying the wording of one item also produced significantly better results for the Guidelines group. The "Cruise Control servo rod" referred to in the first paragraph of the Original and Readability Letters is a noun string—several nouns in a row—that linguistic theory would predict to be difficult for people to understand and remember. Breaking up the noun string into "the servo rod for the Cruise Control mechanism" should produce better results. This is what we did in the Guidelines Letter, and, in fact, the Guidelines group made significantly fewer errors on this item (5%) than either the Original (37%) or the Readability group (33%).

Aside from these items, however, the technical explanation of the defect (incorrect accelerator cable bracket; Cruise Control servo rod possibly binding on accelerator cable bracket) was generally not well understood by subjects in any of the three groups. Subjects generally did not know the names of the parts and did not understand the nature of the possible malfunction.

Most subjects in all groups understood that the repair work would be done free of charge. This finding from the paraphrase task was confirmed by the results from Question 5 of the Objective Questions, which all the subjects answered correctly. The Guidelines group, however, was significantly more likely to omit mentioning the need to allow additional time for normal service procedures beyond the 15-minute repair time.

Another difference between the Guidelines Letter and the other two is in the item explaining *when* to contact the Swiftmobile dealer to make an appointment to bring the car in. The Original and Readability groups—whose letters said "on or after January 5, 1983"—made more errors on this item (27% and 17%, respectively) than the Guidelines group (0)—whose letter said "any time after January 4, 1983." The difference between the Original and the Guidelines group is statistically significant.

Another item of interest in the paraphrase task is the reference to the Owner Identification Card. In the Original and Readability Letters, the first reference to "the enclosed Owner Identification Card" is followed two sentences later by a reference to "this postage-paid card," while in the Guidelines Letter the card is first referred to as "the enclosed postage-paid card" and the second reference is to "the card." This difference in wording made a difference in the clarity of the concepts. Six subjects in the Original group (32%) made errors on the second reference to the card and five subjects in the Readability group (28%) made errors; they thought the second reference was to a *different* card. Only one subject in the Guidelines group (5%) made an error on this item. The difference between the Guidelines group and the Original group is statistically significant.

In the paragraph dealing with whom one should notify if the dealer does not fix the car as he should, approximately the same proportion of subjects in all three groups correctly indicated that the customer should notify the Swiftmobile Zone Office (Original = 53%; Readability = 56%; Guidelines = 68%). However, everyone in the Original group and 89% of the Readability group mentioned calling the Administrator of NHTSA, while only nine (47%—significantly fewer) of the Guidelines group indicated this (and most of these were the same people who would notify the Zone Office). What this means is that there are a great many subjects in both the Original and Readability groups who believe (erroneously) that they should call NHTSA *without first having called* the manufacturer's Zone Office. This constitutes a serious misunderstanding of the letter.

The answers to Objective Question 6 ("If Murray Rosen took his 1981 Swiftmobile to his dealer to get the problem fixed and the next day he found that his car still had the same problem, what should he do?") did not shed much light on whether subjects were misunderstanding the Original and Readability letters. All three groups scored very poorly on this question, but the most common wrong answer was (a) "take it back to his Swiftmobile dealer." However, four of the 18 Readability subjects did incorrectly choose (b) "contact the NHTSA Administrator" as opposed to two subjects each in the Original and Guidelines groups. This could be an additional small indication that the Readability Letter may be providing misleading information.

An interesting finding emerged not from the data itself but from comments that subjects made during the paraphrase task. This had to do with subjects' perceptions of where the recall letter was coming from. For the Original Letter, six of the 19 subjects stated, at some point in their paraphrase, where the letter had come from. Four of these subjects thought that the letter came from the government, not from the manufacturer.

For the Readability Letter, one of the 18 subjects stated whom the letter was from, and correctly identified Swift Motor Company.

For the Guidelines Letter, eight of the 19 subjects mentioned whom they thought the letter was from, and all eight correctly identified the sender of the letter as the car manufacturer.

Thus, the Original Letter appears to be misguiding some readers, which does not appear to be the case with the Guidelines Letter. (The paraphrase transcripts for the Readability Letter do not provide enough information.) The introductory sentence in the Original Letter may be the culprit. Subjects may have assumed that a first sentence that says "This notice is sent to you in accordance with the requirements of the National Traffic and Motor Vehicle Safety Act" is really saying "This notice is being sent to you by a government agency." In fact, the passive construction "is sent to you" may also be misleading to some readers. It appears to create a logical expectation that the next proper noun is the entity doing the sending, the "National something or other," which looks like a government agency. In the Readability Letter, the entire phrase "is sent to you in accordance with the requirements" is rewritten as "is required by." This appears to be less ambiguous and less misleading; it does not create an expectation of who the sender is. And, of course, in the Guidelines Letter, the reference to the Act is put at the end of the letter, where it is least misleading, and where it does not receive an inappropriate focus or create any expectation regarding who the sender is. Interestingly, a number of subjects in all three groups interpreted the statement about the National Traffic and Motor Vehicle Safety Act as saying, essentially, that "we're only sending you this recall letter because we're forced by law to do so"—which was not the purpose of that statement.

The Objective Questions.   Results from the Objective Questions are presented in Table 4.3.

There were no statistically significant differences among the three groups in six of the eight objective questions. For questions 2 and 8, however, there were statistically significant differences. In question 2 ("Harry Smith of New York City is having problems with his 1981 Swiftmobile Montevero. Which one of the following problems is covered by the recall letter?"), the Guidelines Letter produced the largest proportion of wrong answers. On further examination, using an analysis of covariance (ANCOVA), we found that education level was responsible for a statistically significant difference in subjects' performance regardless of which letter they had read. The letters themselves were responsible for a marginally significant difference. On examining the most frequent wrong answer given by the Guidelines group, a possible explanation emerged. Most of the wrong answers in the Guidelines group were answer (c) "throttle does not return to idle position when transmission gear selector is shifted to 'l'." In the Guidelines Letter, information about the throttle not returning to the idle position is stated twice, in different words, as opposed to only once in the other two

TABLE 4.3
Scores on the Objective Questions

		Mean Proportion Correct	Standard Deviation
Question 1	original	.53	.51
	readability	.56	.51
	guidelines	.63	.50
Question 2	original	.89	.32
	readability	.88	.32
	guidelines	.58	.51
Question 3	original	1.0	-
	readability	1.0	-
	guidelines	.89	.32
Question 4	original	.68	.48
	readability	.83	.38
	guidelines	.68	.48
Question 5	original	1.0	-
	readability	1.0	-
	guidelines	1.0	-
Question 6	original	.32	.48
	readability	.17	.38
	guidelines	.21	.42
Question 7	original	.16	.37
	readability	.33	.49
	guidelines	.37	.50
Question 8	original	.89	.31
	readability	.78	.43
	guidelines	.79	.41

letters. This repetition would tend to give undue prominence to that particular piece of information; it would stand out in people's minds, even if they did not understand it completely. We suggest that this is what happened in Question 2.

In Question 8 ("If Tom Jefferson traded his 1981 Swiftmobile Montevero a month before receiving this letter, what should he do?"), all of the significant difference is accounted for by differences in education. In other words, people with lower education were more likely to give the wrong answer to this question. (The most common wrong answers here were (a) "send the letter on to the new owner" and (d) "complete and return the enclosed postage-paid card to the new owner.")

The Opinion Questionnaire. Results for the rating scales in the Opinion Questionnaire are interesting in that, for each question, there were no statistically significant differences among the three groups. Following are the mean scores for each question:

Question 1. "If you received a letter like this along with all your other mail, how likely would you be to read it?"

The average response was between 1 and 2 on a 5-point scale where 1 was very likely and 5 was very unlikely. In other words, all the subjects indicated that they would be very likely to read the letter.

Question 2. "How easy or difficult was this letter to read and understand?"

The average response to this question was around 2 on a 5-point scale where 1 was very easy and 5 was very difficult. Here again, subjects in all three groups indicated that their letters were relatively easy to read and understand. (Of course, no group saw the other groups' letters, and so they had no basis for comparison.)

Question 3. "If you received a letter like this about your car, how likely would you be to take it to the car dealer for inspection and/or servicing?"

The average response to this question was a little over 1 on a 5-point scale where 1 was very likely and 5 was very unlikely. All subjects in all three groups indicated that they would be fairly likely or very likely to bring their car in in response to a recall letter such as the one they had paraphrased.

Question 4. "If this recall letter had to do with a seat belt that didn't close properly, how likely would you be to take your car in for inspection and/or servicing?"

The average response to this question was between 2 and 2.5 on a 5-point scale where 1 was very likely and 5 was very unlikely. For this question, as for Question 3, the results of subjects in the three groups are almost identical.

However, there was a highly significant difference between the overall score for Question 3 and the overall score for Question 4. In Question 4, unlike Question 3, subjects would only be somewhat likely to bring their cars in if the problem had to do with a malfunctioning seat belt rather than a mechanical problem involving the accelerator and the throttle. Apparently, the perceived gravity of the defect would affect compliance on a real recall.

CONCLUSIONS AND RECOMMENDATIONS

The results of our study indicate that people tend to misunderstand certain important ideas in typical recall letters. Rewriting the recall letter to fit a readability formula does improve its score on a readability formula—in this case from a score of 41 ("difficult") on the Original Letter to a score of 73 ("fairly easy") on the Readability Letter, using the Flesch formula. However, it does not improve subjects' understanding of the letter. Rewriting the letter following research-based guidelines for document design may also improve the letter's score on a readability formula (to a score of 70 ["standard" to "fairly easy"] using the Flesch formula), but it also produces significantly fewer errors—significantly better comprehension than for either the Original or the Readability Letter.

Providing a context in the form of a notice at the top of the letter and an introductory sentence explaining the purpose of the letter may also be helpful. Certainly, potentially misleading statements such as the first sentence in the

Original Letter ("This notice is sent to you in accordance with the requirements of the National Traffic and Motor Vehicle Safety Act") do not belong at the beginning of the letter. Given the fact that a number of subjects in all three groups interpreted that sentence or its equivalent somewhat cynically, it may be that the statement is better left out.

The technical explanation of what is wrong with the car went over most subjects' heads in all three letters. However, it is probably worth keeping in a recall letter for those car owners who do understand auto mechanics and for identifying the problem to the auto dealer. The explanation of the mechanical implications of the defect is tricky: The explanation in the Original and Readability Letters "If binding occurs, it could prevent . . ." was not well understood, but amplifying the explanation in the Guidelines Letter did not improve comprehension and, from the results of Question 2 in the Objective Questions, appeared to mislead a number of subjects.

It may be necessary to find better ways of explaining the mechanical implications of a defect to lay people, or it may be better not to explain them at all.

As for the safety implications, most subjects in all three groups understood that the defect could result in a crash. However, as Questions 3 and 4 in the Opinion Questionnaire (rating scales) indicated, many people may not be willing to respond to a recall where the perceived safety implications are not particularly grave.

In the paragraph covering what to do before the defect has been repaired if the car's speed does not decrease when it should, performance on all three letters was similar: in general, most subjects remembered most of what they should do. However, given the nature of the paraphrase task, where each paragraph is given the same amount of prominence and importance, it is unclear whether car owners reading a recall letter through once or twice would remember what to do in case of an emergency. Instructional research tends to show that having informative headings, as the Guidelines Letter does, would probably increase the likelihood that a reader would focus on, and remember, this important piece of information (Allen, 1970; Ausubel & Fitzgerald, 1961, 1962).

In the paragraph telling when to make an appointment with the dealer, a number of subjects in the Original and Readability Letters were confused by the words "*on or after* January 5, 1983." Changing this to "any time after January 4, 1983" in the Guidelines Letter seemed to solve that problem. In general, the fewer time periods a person sees, the less confusing it appears to be.

In case of problems with the dealer, subjects in the Original and Readability groups were far more likely to make the mistake of thinking they were supposed to contact the Administrator of NHTSA without first contacting the Swiftmobile Zone Office than subjects in the Guidelines group. Again, this could be a result of the informative headings—and consequently a more reassuring tone—in the Guidelines Letter. Perhaps, too, the placement of the paragraph has an effect. In the Original and Readability Letters, this paragraph comes *before* any reference to the Owner Identification Card and how this will help the dealer repair the defect. In the Guidelines Letter, this paragraph comes after the reference to the card, and also very near the end of the letter. Contacting NHTSA may thus look more like a "last resort" than it does in the Original and Readability Letters.

The paragraph about the enclosed postage-paid card caused a fair amount of confusion for subjects in the Original and Readability groups. Because of the wording of the Original and Readability Letters, it looked to many subjects as though the letter was referring to two different cards. The rewrite in the Guidelines Letter made it much clearer that the same card was being referred to.

In general, following the Document Design Center's guidelines for organization, language, and graphics produced significantly better results than using the recall letter in its original form or rewriting it according to the parameters of a readability formula. This was in spite of the fact that the Guidelines group had a somewhat lower educational level than the other two groups.

Guidelines for Writing Better Recall Letters

Based on our findings in this study, we suggested the following guidelines for producing more understandable recall letters:

Provide a Context.   An opening statement, such as the one in the Guidelines Letter, immediately tells the reader what the letter is about and sets the stage for what is to follow:

This is a recall letter. We have found a problem with some 1981 Swiftmobile Pembrooks and Monteveros with the HK2000 engine. The defect could result in a crash if it is not fixed. This letter tells you how to have your car checked and, if necessary, fixed—FREE of charge.

The reader does not have to read part way through the letter to know what the letter is for. Furthermore, the type of opening paragraph we used in the Guidelines Letter provides a "roadmap" for the rest of the letter.

A notice at the top, such as the boxed notice in our Guidelines Letter, also helps provide a context, but may not be absolutely necessary for all recall letters.

Put the Information in Logical Order.   It is important for readers' understanding to create a logical sequence to the information in a letter. Readers have certain expectations based on their experience and on the early paragraphs in a letter. If a writer violates these expectations, he or she will mislead readers, as readers of the Original Letter were misled by the reference in the first sentence to the National Traffic and Motor Vehicle Safety Act.

Write Informative Headings.   The informative headings we used make the organization of the letter clear to the reader. An informative heading is not a single noun or string of nouns. We used questions that car owners would be likely to ask; questions, statements, or question-like statements make informative headings.

e.g., *What is the defect?*
OR *A description of the defect*
OR *What the defect is*

Do Not Use Impersonal or Difficult Grammatical Constructions.   The Original (and Readability) Letters contain many sentences that use the passive voice and nominalizations (nouns created from verb clauses). These constructions tend to be impersonal and to sound bureaucratic. They often lack information about *who* is doing the action in the sentence. (Research shows that they can also cause comprehension problems for readers.) We recommend using active sentences and verb constructions with explicit actors instead.

1. *Use active sentences.* For example, we changed the following passives to an active form:

Passive	Active
These vehicles *were assembled*	Certain 1981 Pembrooks and
when the accelerator pedal *is released*	Monteveros *have*
until it *is corrected* by a Swiftmobile dealer	when you *take* your foot *off* the gas pedal
	until a Swiftmobile dealer *has fixed* it

2. *Use verbs, not nouns made out of verbs.* We changed the following nominalizations (nouns created from verbs) into verbs with subjects:

Nominalization (Noun)	Verb Clause
if *binding* occurs	If these parts *stick or bind* together
This could result in a *loss* of *vehicle control*	The car *could go out of control*
a *vehicle crash* could occur	(the car could) *crash*
to have this *correction* performed	to have your car . . . *fixed*
presentation of this card to your dealer	*give* it to your dealer
in making the necessary *correction* to your vehicle	*fix* your car

Changing passives and nominalizations to active sentences with explicit and preferably human actors and real actions (as opposed to "filler" verbs such as those in the nominalization examples above) also tends to make the letter more personal. This personal tone may be useful in impressing upon car owners the very real dangers of the defect.

Do Not Use Noun Strings.   Long strings made up of noun, noun, noun, etc., are difficult for readers to read and understand. In general, unless a noun string is the title of a program or agency, it can be broken down into smaller chunks joined by prepositions. "Unstringing" noun strings usually improves readers' comprehension, as when we changed "Cruise Control servo rod" in the Original Letter to "servo rod for the Cruise Control mechanism" in our Guidelines Letter. Similarly, even short strings such as "vehicle control" and "vehicle crash" read better when they are unstrung (e.g., "control over your car") or simply shortened (e.g., "crash").

Avoid or Explain Technical Terms, Vague Terms, and Unfamiliar Words.   Technical terms are difficult for people who are unfamiliar with them, especially if the context does not help clarify the terms. The lower the education level of the reader, the more difficult technical terms will be. We have found that poor readers often give up if they encounter too many technical terms or unfamiliar words. The subjects in all three groups in our study were probably better educated than average, and yet they had difficulty with the mechanical terms used to explain the problem because they were unfamiliar with those terms.

We changed	vehicle	to	car
	remedy	to	fix
	engine speed . . .		
	decrease	to	car . . . slow down
	arrange an		
	appointment	to	make an appointment
	correct	to	fix
	release the		
	accelerator pedal	to	take your foot off the gas
	operate the vehicle	to	drive the car
	additional time	to	time
	at no charge to you	to	free (of charge)
	telephone	to	phone
	making the necessary		
	correction	to	fix your car
	assist	to	help
	in the shortest		
	possible time	to	as quickly as possible

We also explained some terms by using the term and a synonym in the same context:

Original	*Guidelines*
defect	problem; defect
inspect	inspect; check
modify	modify; change; replace
bind	bind; stick

Leave Out Unnecessary Words.   We eliminated some redundant constructions in the Original Letter (these were phrases or clauses that repeated information that appeared in the previous, subsequent, or even the same sentence).

    e.g., without prior warning

        in this event

        To prevent the possibility of this occurring on your vehicle

        this service will be performed

After consulting with NHTSA staff, we changed at least one vague phrase in the Original Letter to a more informative one. We changed—"process your vehicle"—to the somewhat more informative "the dealer's normal service procedures."

One thing we would not recommend doing is giving a technical explanation of a technical phrase. In the Guidelines Letter, we tried to clarify "it could keep the throttle from closing" by adding the parenthetical explanation "(That means the throttle doesn't return to the 'idle' position)." Unfortunately, the explanation was too short and too technical and appeared to cause confusion for the Guidelines subjects later when they were answering Objective Question number 2. We suggest either providing a longer, more detailed explanation—perhaps with diagrams—or leaving out the explanation altogether.

Use Layout to Make the Letter Legible.   To make a recall letter more inviting and more legible for its readers, there are graphic devices that a writer can use even if his or her only tools are a typewriter and a ruler and pen. Use layout— such as headings, white space, (occasional) underlining, or a box—to:

    break up long paragraphs
    highlight important information
    rest the reader's eyes

A box at the top, containing crucial information, can sometimes be useful for getting readers' attention. However, the text in the box should *not* be in all caps (capital letters), as that makes it less readable.

Informative headings, underlined (again, not all caps) break up otherwise dense text, call attention to important information, and show the letter's organization to readers.

Lists, indented and set off by numbers or "bullets" (lowercase "o," filled in—•) make it clear to the reader how many tasks are involved in a given procedure,

    e.g., • shift the transmission gear selector to "1"
          • pull safely off the road, and
          • shut off the engine.

White space, in the form of frequent paragraphing, indenting addresses within the text, and using a ragged right margin, helps rest readers' eyes and also carries them easily from one section to the next.

Underlining or all caps can be useful, but not if they are overdone and not if both are used together. Underlining a single word (or two or three words) or putting a word in all caps (e.g., FREE) makes the word stand out. However, underlining a whole sentence or paragraph or putting it in all caps makes it harder to read. In particular, if you have used underlining for headings, an underlined sentence following or preceding a heading will be interpreted as a heading, and not as a piece of important information. Never use underlining *and* all caps together.

Conclusion

This study underlines the problems with using readability formulas both as gauges of the difficulty of prose and as criteria for rewriting documents. A formula would have predicted that both of the rewritten versions of the recall letter—the Guidelines and the Readability versions—would have been equally easy to read and equally informative to the audience. (The Readability Letter should have been slightly easier.) In fact, the inherent problems in organization, layout, context, and sentence structure of the Original Letter could not be detected by the readability formula and could not be remedied by rewriting to fit the parameters of a formula. And although the readability score of the more comprehensible Guidelines Letter was relatively high, it was lower than that of the Readability Letter. A readability formula could not have predicted that subjects would make so many fewer errors on the Guidelines Letter.

As a sidelight, the study also underlines some of the drawbacks of multiple-choice tests as criterion measures for comprehension. Our multiple-choice test, although carefully constructed, did not shed much light on what the subjects did and did not understand. The more sensitive paraphrase test appears to be an ideal measure for testing the comprehensibility of text.

ACKNOWLEDGMENT

The author wishes to thank the following people for helping to collect and analyze the data: Brad Allen, Sally Dillow, Myra Erhardt, Ingrid Heinsohn, Carol Manning, and Frances Pickering. The author also wishes to thank Dr. Janice Redish for overseeing the project and reviewing the report.

REFERENCES

Allen, K. (1970). Some effects of advance organizers and level of question on the learning and retention of written social studies materials. *Journal of Educational Psychology, 61,* 333–339.

Ausubel, D., & Fitzgerald, D. (1961). The role of discriminability in meaningful verbal learning and retention. *Journal of Educational Psychology, 52,* 266–274.

Ausubel, D., & Fitzgerald, D. (1962). Organizer, general background and antecedent learning variables in sequential verbal learning. *Journal of Educational Psychology, 53,* 243–249.

Charrow, V. (1979). *Let the rewriter beware.* Washington, D.C.: The Document Design Center, American Institutes for Research.

Flesch, R. (1949). *The art of readable writing.* New York: Harper & Row.

General Accounting Office (1982). *Changes to the motor vehicle recall program could reduce potential safety hazards.* Report to the Secretary of Transportation. Washington, D.C.: GAO.

Redish, J. C. (1979). *Readability.* Washington, D.C.: The Document Design Center, American Institutes for Research.

Tinker, M. (1965). *Bases for effective reading.* Minneapolis: University of Minnesota Press.

Appendix A

The Instruction Sheet
The three versions of the recall letter

INSTRUCTION SHEET

Thank you for agreeing to participate in a study of automobile recall letters sponsored by the National Highway Traffic Safety Administration (NHTSA). The study should take 20–30 minutes, and will be completely confidential. We will not record any information that could be used to identify you at a later date. We will need some personal information, such as your age and education, but we will group this information together with the information from other participants and use it for statistical purposes only.

As you may know, a recall letter is a letter from an automobile manufacturer, such as Ford, Toyota, etc., notifying a car owner that there is some specific thing wrong with the car, asking the owner to have it fixed, and telling him or her how to go about doing so.

The National Highway Traffic Safety Administration at the Department of Transportation would like to find out whether recall letters do what they are supposed to do. In order to find this out, we would like you to read this letter, section by section, and then paraphrase each section—in other words, explain, in your own words, what each section means after you've read it. I'm going to tape record what you say on this tape recorder. After you have finished paraphrasing the letter, I'll ask you a few questions about it. Remember, the study is confidential; no one will know who you are.

THE THREE VERSIONS OF THE RECALL LETTER

ORIGINAL LETTER

SWIFTMOBILE MOTOR CAR DIVISION
Swift Motors

January 1983

Dear Swiftmobile Owner:

This notice is sent to you in accordance with the requirements of the National Traffic and Motor Vehicle Safety Act. Swift Motors has determined that a defect which relates to motor vehicle safety exists on some 1981 Pembrooks and Monteveros equipped with the HK2000 engine. These vehicles were assembled with the incorrect accelerator cable bracket which under certain conditions could allow the Cruise Control servo rod to bind on the accelerator cable bracket.

If binding occurs, it could prevent the throttle from returning to the closed (idle) position when the accelerator pedal is released. In this event, engine speed may not decrease to a level anticipated by the operator. This could result in a loss of vehicle control and a vehicle crash could occur without prior warning.

To prevent the possibility of this occurring on your vehicle, please contact your Swiftmobile dealer on or after the date shown below to arrange an appointment to have this condition corrected. Your dealer will inspect and, if necessary modify, the accelerator cable bracket. This service will be performed at no charge to you.

Until this service has been completed, you should be alert for any occurrence of the vehicle's speed not decreasing after you have released the accelerator pedal. Should this condition occur, you should immediately shift the transmission gear selector to "1" and then drive safely to the side of the road and shut off the engine. You should *not* restart the engine or attempt to operate the vehicle until it is corrected by a Swiftmobile dealer.

Instructions for making this correction have been sent to your dealer. Please contact your dealer on or after January 5, 1983 to arrange a mutually satisfactory service date to have this correction performed. The labor time necessary to perform this correction is approximately fifteen minutes. Please allow additional time for your dealer to process your vehicle.

If you take your vehicle to your dealer on the agreed service date and they do not remedy this condition without charge on that date or within five days, you should contact your nearest Swiftmobile Zone Office either in person or by telephone for assistance. The locations and telephone numbers of zone offices are listed in your Owner's Manual. If your dealer or Swift Motors fails or is unable to remedy this condition without charge within a reasonable time, you may wish to notify the Administrator, National Highway Traffic Safety Administration, 400 Seventh Street, SW, Washington, D.C. 20590.

The enclosed Owner Identification Card identifies your vehicle. Presentation of this card to your dealer will assist in making the necessary correction to your vehicle in the shortest possible time. If you have sold or traded your vehicle, please let us know by completing this postage-paid card and returning it to us. We are sorry to cause you this inconvenience; however, we have taken this action in the interest of your safety and continued satisfaction with our products.

Swiftmobile Motor Car Division
Swift Motors Corporation

READABILITY LETTER

SWIFTMOBILE MOTOR CAR DIVISION
Swift Motors

January 1983

Dear Swiftmobile Owner:

This notice is required by the National Traffic and Motor Vehicle Safety Act. Swift Motors has found a safety defect on some 1981 Pembrooks and Monteveros. These cars have the HK2000 engine. These cars were put together with the wrong accelerator cable bracket. The Cruise Control servo rod could bind on the accelerator cable bracket.

This could stop the throttle from returning to idle when the gas pedal is released. Engine speed may not decrease as much as expected. Loss of car control could result. The car could crash without warning.

To keep this from happening to your car, call your Swiftmobile dealer on or after the date shown below. Arrange an appointment to have your car fixed. Your dealer will inspect your car. If necessary, he will change the accelerator cable bracket. This service will be done free.

Until this service has been done, be alert for any time the car does not slow down after the gas pedal has been released. Should this happen, at once shift the transmission gear selector to "1." Drive safely to the side of the road. Shut off the engine. Do *not* restart the engine. Do not try to drive the car until it is fixed by a Swiftmobile dealer.

Instructions for fixing your car have been sent to your dealer. Please contact your dealer on or after January 5, 1983. Arrange a mutually agreeable service date to have your car fixed. The time needed to fix your car is about fifteen minutes. Please allow more time for your dealer to process your car.

If you take your car to your dealer on the agreed service date and he does not fix it free within five days, contact your nearest Swiftmobile Zone Office. Go in person or phone for help. The addresses and phone numbers of zone offices are in your Owner's Manual. If your dealer or Swift Motors fails or is unable to fix your car free within a reasonable time, you may contact the Administrator, National Highway Traffic Safety Administration, 400 Seventh Street, SW, Washington, D.C. 20590.

The enclosed Owner Identification Card identifies your car. Giving this card to your dealer will help him fix your car in the shortest possible time. If you sold or traded your car, fill in this postage-paid card. Return it to us. We are sorry to bother you. We have sent this letter in the interest of your safety and continued satisfaction with our products.

Swiftmobile Motor Car Division
Swift Motors Corporation

GUIDELINES LETTER

SWIFTMOBILE MOTOR CAR DIVISION
Swift Motors

January 1983

NOTICE

Your 1981 Swiftmobile
may have a safety defect

Dear Swiftmobile Owner:

This is a recall letter. We have found a problem with some 1981 Swiftmobile Pembrooks and Monteveros with the HK2000 engine. The defect could result in a crash if it is not fixed. This letter tells you how to have your car checked and, if necessary, fixed—FREE of charge.

What is the defect?

Certain 1981 Pembrooks and Monteveros have the wrong part—an incorrect accelerator cable bracket. Under certain conditions, another part, the servo rod for the Cruise Control mechanism, could stick on the accelerator cable bracket.

If these parts stick or bind together, it could keep the throttle from closing when you take your foot off the gas pedal. (That means the throttle doesn't return to the 'idle" position.)

What could happen?

The engine might not slow down as much as you expect it to. The car could go out of control and crash.

What problem should you look for while driving?

While driving, if your car does not slow down after you have taken your foot off the gas, do the following:

• shift the transmission gear selector to "1,"
• pull safely off the road, and
• shut off the engine.

Do *not* restart the engine or try to drive the car until a Swiftmobile dealer has fixed it.

What should you do to get your car fixed?

Any time after January 4, 1983, please make an appointment with your Swiftmobile dealer to have your car inspected and, if necessary, fixed—free. Your dealer may have to modify or replace the accelerator cable bracket. It takes

108

about 15 minutes to fix your car, but you should allow time for the dealer's normal service procedures.

The enclosed postage-paid card identifies your car. Give it to your dealer when your car is inspected. It will help him fix your car as quickly as possible. If you have sold or traded your car, please fill in the card and mail it to us.

What if you have problems with your dealer?

The defect should be fixed—*at no cost*—on your appointment date or within five (5) days after your appointment date.

If it is not, you should contact the nearest Swiftmobile Zone Office in person or by phone. The address and phone number are in your Owner's Manual.

If the dealer or Zone Office does not or cannot fix the defect free of charge, or in a reasonable time, you can notify:

> The Administrator
> National Highway Traffic Safety Administration (NHTSA)
> Washington, D.C. 20590

We are sorry to inconvenience you, but we care about your safety and want you to be satisfied with our products. This notice is required by the National Traffic and Motor Vehicle Safety Act.

> Swiftmobile Motor Car Division
> Swift Motors Corporation

Appendix B

Listing of the Multiple-Choice Questions
Opinion Questionnaire
Demographic Questionnaire

LISTING OF THE OBJECTIVE (MULTIPLE-CHOICE) QUESTIONS

1. Mary O'Brien owns a 1981 Montevero with a V-6 HK2000 engine and a 1981 Pembrook with a V-8 HK1200 engine. The recall letter

   a) applies to just the 1981 Montevero with V-6 HK2000 engine.
   b) applies to just the 1981 Pembrook with V-8 HK1200 engine.
   c) applies to both of Mary O'Brien's cars.
   d) applies to neither of Mary O'Brien's cars.

2. Harry Smith of New York City is having problems with his 1981 Swiftmobile Montevero. Which one of the following problems is covered by the recall letter?

   a) engine speed doesn't increase after driver puts foot on accelerator
   b) engine speed doesn't decrease after driver takes foot off the gas
   c) throttle does not return to idle position when transmission gear selector is shifted to "1"
   d) vehicle goes out of control when driver puts foot on accelerator at high speeds

3. Let's say you own a 1981 Swiftmobile Pembrook that is covered by the recall letter, but you have noticed absolutely nothing wrong with your car. According to the recall letter, what should you do?

   a) make an appointment with a Swiftmobile dealer to get the car inspected
   b) make an appointment with a Swiftmobile dealer only if you notice something wrong
   c) make a call to the Administrator, National Highway Traffic Safety Administration
   d) make an inspection appointment with the local gas station that you normally patronize

4. Your neighbor, Helen, owns a 1981 Swiftmobile covered by the recall letter. If she is driving down a highway, takes her foot off the accelerator at a crossroads and finds that the car does not respond, what should she do?

   a) tap the brake pedal lightly and pull off the road
   b) apply the emergency brake gradually and drive safely to the side of the road
   c) shift into first gear and pull off the road
   d) shift into neutral and drive carefully to the side of the road

5. You receive this recall letter and take your 1981 Swiftmobile to your dealer. When the repairs are done, you receive a bill with a $10 inspection charge and a $15 repair charge.

a) You should pay only the $10 inspection charge.
b) You should pay only the $15 repair charge.
c) You should pay both charges.
d) You should pay neither charge.

6. If Murray Rosen took his 1981 Swiftmobile to his dealer to get the problem fixed and the next day found that his car still had the same problem, what should he do?

a) take it back to his Swiftmobile dealer
b) contact the National Highway Traffic Safety Administrator
c) take it to another Swiftmobile dealer
d) contact the nearest Swiftmobile Zone Office

7. What problem with the 1981 Swiftmobile does the recall letter deal with?

a) cruise control servo bracket may bind to accelerator cable
b) cruise control servo rod may not return to "idle" position
c) car has wrong accelerator cable bracket
d) car has incorrect cruise control servo rod

8. If Tom Jefferson traded his 1981 Swiftmobile Montevero a month before receiving this letter, what should he do?

a) send the letter on to the new owner
b) nothing
c) complete and return the enclosed postage-paid card to Swift Motors Corporation
d) complete and return the enclosed postage-paid car to the new owner

OPINION QUESTIONNAIRE

Directions:

Answer the questions below by putting an "X" in the *space* that best reflects your opinion. For example:

always |_____|_____|_____|_____| never

1. If you received a letter like this along with all your other mail, how likely would you be to read it?

very likely |_____|_____|_____|_____| very unlikely

2. How easy or difficult was this letter to read and understand?

very easy |_____|_____|_____|_____| very difficult

3. If you received a letter like this about your car, how likely would you be to take it to the car dealer for inspection and/or servicing?

very likely |_____|_____|_____|_____| very unlikely

4. If this recall letter had to do with a seat belt that didn't close properly, how likely would you be to take your car to the dealer for inspection and/or servicing?

very likely |_____|_____|_____|_____| very unlikely

DEMOGRAPHIC QUESTIONNAIRE

1. Sex _____ M _____ F
2. Age_____
3. Occupation_____
4. Education (circle highest grade completed)

primary and secondary

1 2 3 4 5 6 7 8 9 10 11 12

college   graduate school

13 14 15 16   17+

What degree(s) have you received? _____

_____

5. When did you first buy your own car?_____
6. a. Have you ever received a recall letter?
   b. How many?
   c. What did you do?

THE THREE VERSIONS OF DEMOGRAPHIC QUESTIONNAIRE QUESTION #7

A. Have you ever participated in a study before?
B. Have you ever owned a car that you considered to be a lemon? What make and year was it?
C. Have you ever served in the military?

5 Preferences for and Comprehension of Original and Readability-adapted Materials

Georgia M. Green
Margaret S. Olsen
University of Illinois

Fifty-eight 2nd-graders participated in a study designed to provide a basis for answering two questions:

1. Do children prefer original, unadapted stories which may have longer sentences and more vocabulary items than are permitted by readability formulae for their grade level? Or do they prefer adaptations of those stories which meet the formulae's criteria for their grade level? Critics (e.g., Green, 1982) have argued that the adaptation procedures make the stories less interesting, less exciting and less coherent, and may hinder motivating children to read more. What do the children think?

2. Are the adapted materials, which according to readability formulae are closer to the children's grade level, really easier to understand?

There was a strong tendency for the original stories to be preferred to adaptations of them, especially among the less able and the average readers. There was no significant difference in the comprehension scores between the originals and the adaptations. These findings have implications for instructional practice: Since children seem to find original materials written for them to be more interesting and no more difficult to understand than adaptations, there is no educationally valid motive for continuing to adapt otherwise suitable texts to meet the demands of readability formulae.

1. INTRODUCTION

The question of the advisability of adapting literary texts[1] to improve their readability according to some formula or other has a long history, throughout which it has generated strong opinions. For example, Claire Huchet Bishop, writing in 1935 about Thorndike's adaptations of classics states:

> The "removal of obstacles" seems to be, today, the chief concern of educators. They fail to make a distinction between obstacles artificially created for so-called building-up of mind and natural obstacles which are inevitable, necessary and inspiring, if one is going to live at all.
>
> In music, in a work of art, there is something called style, that very creation which makes it impossible for two artists to treat the same subject in the same manner and is the *raison d'etre* of the piece. What could be more brutal or unintelligent than the modification of a masterpiece which destroys the essence of the spirit of the work? The so-called obstacles are absolutely one with the work and the slightest change of a sentence, a word, or a comparison cannot but destroy the beauty of style. Thus, refusing to be bound by literary tradition and removing difficulties from the work achieve nothing but the most dried-up and limited kind of education. It is pathetic and contrary to life to be confronted only with what one can understand, and children who read the title-page of the Thorndike edition—"edited to fit the interest and abilities of young readers"—will very likely lay the book aside, because if there is anything a child dislikes, or any one at any age for that matter, it is to have something handed to him and announced as being specially prepared to meet his understanding. Because, in everything, real obstacles, which are a part of a rich experience within the scope of one's own abilities, are a source of joy. (Bishop, 1935, pp. 204–205)

Objections along these lines are still made today (see, for example, Bruce, 1984; Green, 1984), for with few exceptions, the publishers of instructional materials (e.g., basal readers) continue to rely almost exclusively on adapted texts. The purpose of the research reported here is to address directly the issues that those objections raise.

Effects and Expected Consequences of Adapting Texts to Reduce Their Readability Scores

The means used to lower the readability score for a text are discussed at some length in Davison and Kantor (1982). Since the primary factors in computing the scores are word frequency or word length (which vary together pretty much, since frequent words tend to be short), and sentence length, the techniques for

---

[1] By *literary texts* we mean not just works adjudged by critics to have special merit, but any story written just to be a story, and not, for example, intended specifically for use in a reading instruction program.

reducing the readability score involve (1) substituting shorter or more frequently used (or sometimes, more phonetically regular) words for words which the original author chose; (2) deleting words and phrases, both to remove "difficult" words, and to reduce sentence length; and (3) breaking up compound and complex sentences into series of simple sentences—generally this requires deletion of subordinating conjunctions (*because, after, so . . .*), which connect clauses by stating or implying specific relations among the propositions they represent. Occasionally, passages in the original are completely reworked and summarized in the adaptation, but the more mechanical techniques of altering texts are far more common.

All four of these methods of adaptation change the character of the texts adapted. Most of them, in making sentences shorter and vocabulary "simpler," have the effect of making the adapted text less specific and less connected. One would expect that as a consequence, the stories would be less vivid, less clear about relations among events (including causes and motivations), and as a result, less interesting, less engaging, and more difficult to comprehend than the author intended. Indeed, Schlager (1978) reports that children much prefer to read about individuals (human or otherwise) that appear to be like them: to have the point of view, attitudes, reactions, emotions, etc. that a 7-to-12-year-old would be likely to have. If the image an adapted story presents of a character gives only vague information about that character's situation, feelings, and motivations, we can expect it not to evoke an image of a sentient and animated being that feels and reacts as a child believes people do. Thus we can expect a story adapted this way not to be as appealing as an original, which presents a more vivid picture of the character and his or her situation, feelings, and motivations for action.

One might be skeptical that beginning readers could discriminate between two versions of the same story, but work with very young children (Green, 1982a, 1984; Green & Laff, 1980) indicates that many are quite sensitive to various aspects of literary style, and can identify the author of an unfamiliar story if they have heard other stories by the same person. Thus, it does not seem unreasonable to expect that 2nd-graders might be able to make rational preference judgments on two different versions of the same story.

Adapting stories to lower readability scores has a number of effects. First of all, when a complex sentence is subdivided into a series of simple sentences, the subordinating conjunction that connected the clauses gets left out; to leave it in, just putting a period before it, would result in an incomplete sentence, and paraphrasing it with something like *This was because* or *The reason they did that was so that* would not be as effective in shortening sentences. For example, in the following sentences from the beginning of one of the stories used in our study, the second sentence in the original (*The Secret Hiding Place*) is broken up into two sentences, and the reader must infer that the REASON the big hippos were eager for Little Hippo to wake up was that they got a thrill out of taking care of him.

(1) Little Hippo was the pet of the heard. Every morning the big hippos waited for him to wake up so they could take care of him.
[SHP-original: 26 words, 13 words/sentence, 11% not on Dale List of 769 Easy Words]

Every morning was the same for Little Hippo. All the big hippos would wait for him to get up. They wanted to take care of him.
[LH-adaptation: 26 words, 9 words/sentence, 5.5% not on Dale list]

It wasn't just that the big hippos liked Little Hippo. If readers fail to make this inference, it will not be so clear later why the big hippos' taking care of him bugs Little Hippo so much.

When a short, common word is substituted for a longer, less frequently used word, the common word is almost certain to be less specific than the word the author chose, and thus cannot convey the precise shade of meaning she or he intended. The passage in which the substitution is performed is made vague, and consequently, as with deletion of connecting words, intended inferences are less likely to be drawn. Description is made less accurate, and incorrect (unintended) inferences may then, and therefore, be drawn. As a result of substitution, the passage has less detail, and again as with deletion of connecting words, the reader has fewer clues as to the situation the characters are in, and the possible motivations for them to act as they do; situations and events are less likely to engage the reader's interest, and the characters appear flat, lifeless, and unrealistic. This is exemplified in another passage from *The Secret Hiding Place* and its adaptation:

(2) One morning Little Hippo felt cross. "I don't want lily pads and corn," he grumbled. "I wish the hippos wouldn't watch everything I do."
[SHP-orig. 24 words, 16% not on Dale list]

One morning Little Hippo said to himself, "I don't want anyone to bring me food. I don't want anyone to take care of me.
[LH-adap. 24 words, 8% not on Dale list]

In this case, *food* is substituted for *lily pads and corn; said to himself* for *felt cross* and *grumbled;* and *take care of me* for *watch everything I do.* This decreases the percentage of longer and less frequent words, but it exaggerates the effect of the alteration cited in (1), especially the latter two substitutions. In the original, Little Hippos is represented as feeling a desire for autonomy (to choose his own breakfast) and privacy—feelings quite familiar to children. In the adaptation, he sounds quite irrational, rejecting food and care IN GENERAL. What child would identify with that?

Deleting words and phrases reduces even more dramatically the detail in a story which allows a reader to understand the relations among characters and events, and to make the identification with a character that will make her WANT to go on reading to "find out what happens to" the character. This reduction of detail is clearly demonstrated in the following passages from *Benjy's Dog House*, the other story used in our study.

(3) One day Father said, "Benjy's not a puppy anymore. I think it's about time he slept outside. Let's make that old apple barrel into a dog house."
[BDH-orig. 27 words, 9 words/sentence, 26% not on Dale list]

One day Father said, "Benjy is not a puppy anymore. I think it's time he went outside to sleep. Let's make him a dog house."
[BDH-adapt. 25 words, 8.3 words/sentence, 20% not on Dale list]

The image of Benjy's dog house that this passage conjures up is quite different depending upon whether one reads the original or the adapted version. The original goes on to detail how the dog house was established, decorated, and furnished, while the adaptation merely declares that it was constructed:

(4) Father brought the barrel out of the cellar. Jimmy put bricks on either side to keep it from rolling, and Linda painted it. Then mother put a blanket inside, and the dog house was finished.
[BDH-or. 35 words, 11.7 words/sentence, 20% not on Dale list]

So Benjy's family made a dog house for him.
[BDH-ad. 9 words, 9 words/sentence, 11% not on Dale list]

Finally, the original makes a point of noting the dog Benjy's failure to react positively to the dog house, while the adaptation leaves out that aspect of the story entirely.

(5) Everybody stood around admiring it—everybody, that is, except Benjy.
[BDH-or. 10 words, 30% not on Dale list.]
[BDH-AD. 0 words.]

The reader of the original knows just what Benjy's dog house looks like, and how Benjy feels about it. The reader of the adaptation knows that he has a dog house. The gist of the rest of the story is that Benjy can't sleep in the dog house, and when he finds another place to spend the night, the family is mortified, and allows him to sleep on the children's beds, as he used to. In the original, we are given a graphic description of what happens to the old dog house, so that the reader can understand how Benjy could know that he would never have to sleep in it again. In the adaptation, it just says that Benjy knew it, but the reader can see no justification for such a belief on Benjy's part.

(6) A few days later, Jimmy and Linda made Benjy's dog house into a strawberry barrel. They made holes in the barrel, filled it with earth, and planted strawber-

ry plants in the holes. Benjy watched happily. Now he knew for sure he'd
never have to sleep in that old barrel again!
[BDH-or. 51 words, 13 words/sentence, 16% not on Dale list]

Benjy knew he would never have to sleep outside again.
[BDH-ad. 10 words, all on Dale list]

Naturally, summarizing also has the effect of reducing detail, and, predictably, deletes information from which inferences were intended to be drawn about
relations among events and characters, and motives, as illustrated in this passage
from the hippo story.

(7) And every morning the big hippos pushed and bumped each other, hurrying to
bring Little Hippo his breakfast of lily pads and corn. Big Charles said, "Put
the lily pads here and the corn there." Then they all settled down to watch
Little Hippo eat.
[SHP-or. 45 words, 15 words/sentence, 15.6% not on Dale list]

After Little Hippo was up, he was never by himself. Someone was always
around to take care of him.
If Little Hippo wanted food, Big Charles would see that he got it.
"Little Hippo wants food," Big Charles would call. "Bring it over here.
The big hippos would do just that. Then they would wait for Little Hippo to
eat.
[LH-ad. 61 words, 8.7 words/sentence, 3% not on Dale list]

In the original, Big Charles appears as a benevolent dictator, running the show,
while the other hippos are falling over each other fawning on Little Hippo. In the
adaptation, we see only that Big Charles has organized the other hippos to care
for Little Hippo as he sees fit, and they are obedient and watchful. Again, the
original gives us hints as to why Little Hippo wants so much to get away, while
the adaptation makes this desire seem capricious. It is easy to identify with the
Little Hippo of the original, less so with the one in the basal.

Thus, a major effect of adapting stories to meet readability formulae is to
make those stories less specific, and give less information about relations among
events and about characters' motivations for their attitudes and actions. Given
that, readers can be expected to identify less strongly with the characters in the
adaptations than in originals, and to the extent that identification is an important
factor in motivating readers, they can be expected to prefer originals to
adaptations.

We have already mentioned Schlager's evidence (based on content analysis of
Newbery Award books with the highest and lowest circulation) that children in
middle childhood prefer stories about individuals who perceive the world as they
do. Bower (1978) reports experimental evidence that mature readers identify
with the characters whose mood most resembles their own, and that they have

better recall for stories when they have some indication of the main characters' goals and plans. Bettleheim and Zelan (1981) report that 1st and 2nd graders they interviewed were unhappy with the books they read in school because the characters didn't seem real:

> They said they read only because they had to, and that on their own they would never choose such "junk." "It's all impossible," one of them said. When he was asked why, answers came from around the room: "The children aren't real!" "They aren't angry!" When one child exclaimed, "They aren't anything!" all agreed that there was nothing more to be said." (1981, p. 27)

Of course, vocabulary and syntax do affect the ease with which a text is read, but sentence length probably does not, although sentences whose difficulty can be traced to unusual or archaic syntactic constructions do tend to be longer than sentences that do not contain such constructions. [There, that was 47 words; was it so hard?] In any case, we do not expect 8-year-olds to sit down and read through *Oliver Twist,* no matter how much they may identify with Oliver. Indeed, Grover (1976) has shown that readability is a fairly good predictor (along with text length, relative number of illustrations, illustration style, genre, theme, and setting) of what books 2nd graders check out of the school library. But we are not really concerned with differences on the order of the difference between *Oliver Twist* (Fry and Spache scores: roughly 12th grade) and some 2nd grade basal, but differences on the order of one or two grade levels, as this is the average amount of reduction when trade books are adapted for use in basal readers.

The question is: Is it really necessary to replace more specific words with short vague words just because they are on some list of "easy" words (e.g., the Dale List of 769 Easy Words or the Dale-Chall list of 3000 Common Words—cf. Davison and Kantor 1982 for discussion) and will therefore lower the readability score? As it happens, 10% of the 100 most frequent words in first graders' vocabulary according to Moe, Hopkins, and Rush (1982) are not even on the Dale list, and 24% of the 644 words which each constituted .02% or more of their entire corpus (a 286,108 word running oral language sample) are not on the Dale list either. Since the 329 children interviewed by Moe et al. used over 6000 distinct words, we can suppose that a 1st grader will have active mastery of at least 5000 words. If this is so, then by limiting the vocabulary in a story to just a few more words than are on the Dale list, the limits are set way below what is necessary to ensure comprehension. It may be distracting (if it's not just boring) to have a general word in place of a more specific word which the context would lead one to expect, and if the specific word is in fact in the child's vocabulary, then the substitution is also arbitrary and pointless. Having a text that consists entirely of words that a child can be expected to decode because:

1. they have previously been taught as sight words;
2. they have been "prepared" by the teacher—pronounced; defined and exemplified, for the sole purpose of reading the passage at hand; or
3. phonics rules have been taught that will completely determine the correct translation of print into sound.

is of value only if the criterion for being able to read is defined as the ability to read aloud with no mispronunciations. It is in fact possible to read silently and understand a text while having wildly incorrect beliefs about how certain words are pronounced. We have seen a child read *ocean liner* as "ocean linner", yet understand perfectly that what was being referred to was a large ocean-going ship. Almost everyone can remember finding out that they have had an incorrect image of the pronunciation of some word (like *misled,* or *determined*) that they have been understanding, maybe even writing for years.

Furthermore, the ability to learn new words from context is an important reading skill. Johnson (1979) defends not preparing all of the vocabulary a child will encounter in a text:

> In general, it is better to leave the words alone and let the children encounter them within the meaningful flow of language. When an unknown word prevents them from understanding something in which they are interested, they will ask. Two reasons support this rather cavalier approach:
>
> 1. Struggling to understand a word encountered in the flow of meaningful language is the usual, normal, and natural way that children acquire new vocabulary.
>
> 2. It gives the children practice in doing what they must do when they encounter unfamiliar words in their private reading. No one will have "prepared the vocabulary" for them and there may not even be an adult to answer questions. The only resources they have are their own abilities and the context. (p. 41)

Indeed, if children come to expect that they will know how to pronounce and understand every word in every text that they are asked to read, they will be cruelly handicapped when they reach junior high school and discover that they are expected to be able to understand new words from the context, or use a dictionary, or ask someone. They will feel frustrated, ill-prepared, and cheated, or perhaps, quite unjustifiably, stupid.

Bettleheim and Zelan's interviews (1981) indicate that children do in fact object to the language of their readers, as well as to the characterizations:

> Many told us that their teachers must have faked an interest in the stories, or that they must think children are not very smart.
>
> Fourth- and fifth-graders who had left the beginners' books behind described their resentments to us quite clearly. One rather quiet boy, who preferred to read or work

by himself and rarely participated in class, spoke up all on his own and with deep feeling. He had felt so ashamed to say the things written in primers that he could not bring himself to do it. And although he now liked reading a lot, he said, he still had a hard time reading aloud. (p. 27)

Previous Studies

We are aware of a handful of studies of children's preferences in reading material. Some of this focuses on what kinds of illustrations children prefer (e.g., Lam, 1969). Other studies, such as Schlager's, and Grover's, approach the issue from the point of view of analyzing the books that children have freely picked. We know of no work that directly addresses the issue of preferences for and comprehension of readability-adapted material: Do children prefer to have their reading material adapted to meet the arbitrary criteria of a readability formula in such a way that it will yield a score supposed to be appropriate to their status on the educational ladder, or do they prefer the texts as the original author wrote them? And regardless of their preferences, how does their comprehension of the originals compare with their comprehension of the adaptations?

2. EXPERIMENTAL RESULTS

Subjects

Fifty-eight 2nd-graders from a public school in Rantoul, Illinois, who represented a cross-section of race, sex, and ability, participated in the study, which was carried out in November, 1982. Each child participated in both a preference interview and a comprehension task.

Materials

Two original children's books which had been adapted by basal reader publishers were used. Text characteristics of the two stories are indicated in Table 5.1.

TABLE 5.1
Properties of the Texts Used in the Preferences and Comprehension Studies

Title	Version	Publisher	Length[a]	Fry	Spache
The Secret Hiding Place (SHP) by Rainey Beckett	original	Collins-World 1960	812	3	3+
Little Hippo (LH)	adaptation	Laidlaw 1976[b] Toothless Dragon	738	1	2.2
Benjy's Dog House (BDH-or.) by Margaret Bloy Graham	original	Harper & Row 1973	823	2	3
Benjy's Dog House (BDH-ad.)	adaptation	Harper & Row 1977 Wings & Wishes	633	1	2+

[a]In words.
[b]A different adaptation appears in Houghton-Mifflin Secrets·

TABLE 5.2
Format Properties of Materials on Which Preference Ratings Were Made

Story-Version	Line Length	Number of Lines	Characters per inch	Number of pages	Percentage of Story
SHP-or.	75	37	12	1	39%
LH-ad.	59	43	10	1	38%
BDH-or.	53	48	10	1.3	49%
BHD-ad.	53	32	10	1	43%

For the comprehension task, all of the stories were retyped in the same format (roman characters, 10 to the inch, double-spaced, 55-space line) so that typographical and format differences between the versions would not affect attention and thus, possibly comprehension. The original version was identified by an orange border around the title; the basal version by a blue border, mainly to reduce the possibility of error in administering this task.

For the preferences task, all of the stories were retyped in two parts, the first filling roughly a single-spaced page, with spaces between paragraphs, and the break coming at a natural break in the story. We wanted to keep format and typographical differences between the two versions of a story to a minimum, but our experience in piloting an experiment of this sort indicated that children were quite sensitive to the number of pages they were asked to read, so we did our best to keep the first part to a single page, even if this meant using elite (12 characters per inch) type rather than pica (10 characters per inch), and wider margins on some pages than others. In one case the story still overflowed, and was presented as a page and a third. The original version was on yellow paper and the adaptation on green paper, to make it as easy as possible for the subjects to identify which version they preferred. Format properties of the preference materials are summarized in Table 5.2.

The adaptations in SHP/LH involve vocabulary and syntax. Several presumably unfamiliar words (e.g., *rhinoceros, zebra, leopard, chameleon, cave*) are removed, mostly by deletion of the episode involving the item which the word names, or by substitution of a more familiar word (*house* for *cave; friend* for *chameleon*). In addition, a number of sentences with subordinate clauses are broken up into two independent sentences, as illustrated earlier in example (1).

The adaptations in BDH are mostly at the discourse level, rather than the word level or the sentence level: 190 words of details and whole episodes are simply deleted. The most obvious effect of this is to make the story shorter, but it also has the effect of reducing characterization and obscuring the motivations for the characters' actions.

Procedures

Both the preference task and the comprehension task were carried out as individual oral interviews, after the administration of a vocabulary test (from the WRAT) which we used to identify groups of low-. medium-, and high-ability readers. The comprehension task involved the story which was not used in the preference task. The preference interview was always done first, as experience in piloting these materials indicated that if the preference task was done after the comprehension task, some children would insist on comparing the preference story with the comprehension story, instead of comparing the two versions of the preference story.

The preference interview was conducted as follows. The children were given the two versions of the first half of their preference story, randomized for version order. They were asked to read the two versions in succession, aloud or silently, as they liked. They were told that if there were words they didn't know, they could ask the interviewer, and she would just tell them. When the child had finished both versions, a brief questionnaire about preferences was administered orally. Then the children were invited to read the rest of whichever version of the preference story they selected, and their choice was noted.

For the comprehension task, the children were asked to read to themselves, unless they preferred to read aloud. A comprehension questionnaire was then administered, again orally, covering what we considered to be the important points in the story, and also certain questions from the teachers' guide to the basal reader containing the adapted version. These latter we didn't consider necessarily important to understanding the story (e.g., for BDH: What kind of dog was Benjy?); they were to help in assessing which version was more likely to provide a reader with the ability to answer the questions which the publisher of the basal reader considered important. The comprehension questions thus differed a bit between stories.

Some of the questions could be answered on the basis of information contained in a single sentence in the text read. For example, the answer to LH question 1 (Why did the big hippos always wait for Little Hippo to get up in the morning?) is to be found in a single sentence from SHP: "Every morning the big hippos waited for him to wake up so they could take care of him." In some other cases, the question could be answered entirely on the basis of information explicit in the text, but that information might be spread out over several sentences. For instance, the answer to BDH question 9 (Why did the baker let Benjy in?) is explicit in the text, but takes up 3 sentences in BDH-ad.:

"Come on in," said the baker. "My cat ran away weeks ago. I have really missed her."

We refer to the first kind of question as a sentence-meaning question, the second kind as a paragraph-meaning question. Still other questions require the reader to

TABLE 5.3
Comprehension Question Types, By Story and Version

Story	Number of Questions	Percentage Sentence-Meaning		Percentage Paragraph-Meaning		Percentage Inference	
		N	%	N	%	N	%
SHP-or.	14	3	21	6	43	5	36
LH-ad.	14	1	7	5	36	6	43
BDH-or.	22	11	50	3	14	8	36
BDH-ad.	22	11	50	3	14	8	36

not only understand what is explicit in the text, but make substantial inferences from it.[2] One example (of many) is BDH question 16 (What made Benjy sick that night?). Answering this question involves making the correct inferences from the following text (from BDH-or.)

> Meat pies! He ate one. It tasted so good . . . that he ate another one, and another, and another till all the meat pies were gone!

> Then he curled up to go to sleep. But in a little while . . . Benjy began to have an awful stomach ache.

Another example of an inference question is LH question 8a (Why didn't Little Hippo like being where the lion lived?); the answer must be inferred from a passage like this if the reader read LH-ad.

> Little Hippo was very quiet as he sat in the lion's house. It was like night in there. Little Hippo was afraid to walk around. He was sure that someone was in the house with him.

> "I don't like this hiding place," he said.

The differences are summarized in Table 5.3.

RESULTS

Overview

The preference interview consisted of questions (listed in Table 5.4) which asked for preference opinions (questions 3, 9, 13) or evaluations of story proper-

---

[2]In fact, answering almost any question required making some inferences. For example, to answer LH question 1 from the SHP sentence cited, the reader must know who *he* refers to (the antecedent *Little Hippo* occurs in the previous sentence), and that getting up usually follows waking up. Likewise, to answer to BDH question #9, the reader must infer that the baker invited Benjy in BECAUSE he missed his cat (BECAUSE she ran away).

TABLE 5.4
List of Preference Questions

3. Would you want to [finish] the yellow version, or the green version?

5. Which version do you think is harder to read?

7. So far which one do you think is more interesting?

9. If you were going to choose one of these to read again sometime when you wanted to read a good book, which one would you want to read?

11. So far which one is more exciting?

13. Which version of the story did you like best?

ties (questions 5, 7, 11) we considered likely to be major factors in determining preference ratings, and reasons for those opinions or evaluations. In addition, the choice of version to finish was recorded as a preference opinion.

In no case did more children rank the adapted version above the original than vice versa, either in preference opinion, or in evaluation of interest or excitement, although 36 children evaluated the original as harder, while 18 thought the adaptation was harder. This indicates that finding a text easier was apparently not a sufficient reason to prefer it. There were some inconsistent responses—children who said they liked one version better, but finished the other one. When these are factored out, the preference for the original over the adaptation is even clearer. Preferences are discussed in the following section, along with differences between the stories, and among ability groups.

The comprehension questions mentioned above were open-ended questions (e.g., Why couldn't Benjy sleep in the doghouse? What did the baker give Benjy? Where was Little Hippo's secret hiding place? Who tried to help Little Hippo finding a hiding place?) Consequently, guessing would not be likely to be an effective answering strategy, as it might be with true–false or multiple-choice questions; the percent correct reflects how accurately students' understanding of the story allowed them to answer the questions we asked, and not their guessing. Though the mean percent correct overall was around 55%, this is significantly above chance, given the kinds of questions being asked. The range was 3.5% correct to 82% correct.

Differences in comprehension between versions were not significant. Children reading the original version answered a mean of 55% of the comprehension questions correctly, while children who read the adaptation answered a mean of 56% correctly. Children reading the dog story (BDH) had 63% of the answers correct if they had read the original, 60% correct if they read the adaptation. For the hippo story (SHP/LH), the difference is reversed: The mean percent correct was 47% for children who read the original, 50% if they read the adaptation. There were differences among ability groups, of course, but in different directions. These are most noticeable when the stories are examined separately. This is discussed in the Effect of Ability section (see p. 133).

TABLE 5.5
Overall Preference Ratings

Qn. # Content	Prefer Original		Prefer Adaptation	
	n	%	n	%
3 Want to finish	33	58	23	40
7 Interesting	33	58	24	42
9 Read again	30	53	23	40
11 Exciting	26	46	26	46
13 Like best	33	58	20	35
14 Finished	29	51	25	44

Preferences

As mentioned above, answers to all the preference questions indicated that the original version was preferred to the basal version, though in some cases the differences were not very large. Answers to the preference questions are summarized in Table 5.5.

The original was preferred by a ratio of almost 3 to 2 on the question which asked for rankings when the 2 versions were freshest in the children's minds (#3), and on the question which asked most directly which one they preferred (#13). The original version was considered more interesting, by the same ratio, and in fact, the answers to questions #7 (Which one was more interesting?) and #5 (Which one is harder?) seem to be the best predictors among the evaluation questions (5, 7, 11) of which version they actually finished. Forty-three of the 58 students finished the version they said was more interesting. An equal number finished the version they said was easier. (Thirty-eight finished the version they said was more exciting.)

When the two stories are considered separately, some of the differences are even more striking, as shown in Tables 5.6 and 5.7. The majority of children who preferred the original SHP to the adaptation LH did so by a 3 to 2 ratio, although their evaluations of the two versions don't indicate clearly why, being

TABLE 5.6
Preference Ratings: SHP/LH

Qn. # Content	Original		Adaptation	
	n	%	n	%
3 Which to finish	17	61	11	39
7 Interesting	14	50	14	50
9 Read again	14	50	12	43
11 Exciting	12	43	13	46
13 Like best	14	50	12	43
14 Actually finished	15	54	12	43

TABLE 5.7
Preference Ratings: BDH

Qn. # Content	Original		Adaptation	
	n	%	n	%
3 Want to finish	16	55	12	41
7 Interesting	19	66	10	34
9 Read again	16	55	11	38
11 Exciting	14	48	13	45
13 Like best	19	66	8	28
14 Actually Finished	14	48	13	45

divided pretty evenly between the two versions, as are the other preference questions (9 and 13). A majority, by a ratio of 2 to 1, thought that the original version of BDH was more interesting than the adaptation, and said at the end of the interview that they preferred the original. It is not surprising that they found the original more interesting, since the main difference between the versions is that the original contains details indicating motivations that are left out in the adaptation.

Consistency. As mentioned above, about half of the subjects gave "inconsistent" responses, that is, rated one version higher in one of the preference questions and the other higher on one or more of the others. There are several possible reasons for this. First, the questions were in fact different from each other. It is plausible and rational to say, for example, that you want to finish one version, but if you were going to re-read for pleasure, would choose the other version, and this holds for either choice of version. The basal might be preferred for the immediate task because of its simpler vocabulary, and the original for re-reading because more of the context would be known, and the more difficult words could be more easily guessed. Or the original might be preferred for the moment because it was more interesting, but the basal for reading at home alone because it could be read without assistance. In fact, the reasons the children gave are actually more complicated than this. Some preferred the basal for re-reading because they assumed the re-reading would be done at school, and therefore there wouldn't be much time, and the basal was shorter (i.e., "because in school you have to have a short story"). Others preferred the original for re-reading because it was longer, and they wouldn't be done with it so quickly ("I like pretty long things"). Several others said they preferred to re-read the original because it was harder and they wanted to work on it some more ("because I couldn't understand it," "to keep trying to understand it better").

A second reason for apparently inconsistent answers is that some questions were extremely similar, and subjects may have assumed that the experimenters could not possibly have been asking the same question twice, therefore the question must be rather different from the one it sounds like, so the answer must be the opposite of the answer to that question.

Two more possible reasons turn on what we might consider to be less rational reasons. Four children said they liked one version better than another because they liked the color of the paper it was on better, but this was not a response to questions about why they found one version more interesting or exciting than the other. A few other children may have deliberately distributed the largesse of their preference pronouncements in such a way as to ''be fair'' or ''not hurt the other story's feelings.'' We do not know if any of our subjects actually fall into this latter category, but we have observed this behavior in other children.

Finally, some, perhaps most, of the children who gave ''inconsistent'' responses may simply have been unable to keep straight which story was which. It should be noted that, rather than casting doubt on the validity of the preference research as a whole, the possibility of irrational responses of the sorts described makes only the sets of inconsistent answers suspect.

In light of this, we also present a tabulation, in Table 5.8, of the preference evaluations for children who were consistent in their answers to the questions which directly probed preferences (i.e., questions 3, 9, 13, and 14). Again, the original was preferred to the adaptation by a ratio of more than 3 to 2, overall, and by more than 2 to 1 for the story BDH.

Reasons for Preferences.   We close this section with an informal analysis of the responses given to the open-ended questions (4, 6, 8, 10, and 12). These questions ask the children to give their reason(s) for answering the preceding question (3, 5, 7, 9, 11) as they did. We decided to have these questions open-ended rather than, say, multiple choice (even though that kind of response would have been much easier to evaluate) in order to avoid putting words in the children's mouths or suggesting things that would not have occurred to them on their own. In other words, we wanted to elicit their true impressions as much as possible.

As would be expected of 7-year-olds, many of the children tested were not particularly articulate about their opinions, but even so, the answers clearly indicate that most could and did understand the questions and answered them to

TABLE 5.8
Preference Ratings of Subjects Whose Answers
to Questions 3, 9, 13, 14 were consistent

	Prefer Original		Prefer Adaptation		Total n
Overall	19	63	11	37	30
SHP/LH	8	42	6	55	14
BDH	11	58	5	45	16

the best of their ability. By far the most common justification given for the answer to "Which one would you like to finish?" was "I like it." Eleven children said this about the original version, 5 about the adaptation. Four children preferred the original because it was longer; one preferred the adaptation for that reason. (In fact, the portion of the original of LH/SHP that the children read is 42 words longer than the portion of the adaptation, and the material from the original of BDH is 139 words longer than the adaptation excerpt.) Here, as with most of the other justification questions, n other responses were distributed more or less evenly over 2n to 3n respondents, where n ranges from 7 to 12.

The children agreed that having more detail made a version more interesting. Eight said this about the original, which in fact had more detail; one attributed it to the adaptation.

When asked to justify their answer to "Which one would you like to read again some day?" 5 cited greater length, 6 cited ease of reading, and 5 said "because it is more interesting." In each group, 4 preferred the original.

As indicated above, the children judged the original to be more difficult, by a ratio of 2.5 to 1. Most of the respondents attributed the greater difficulty of WHICHEVER version they found more difficult to "the words" (31 of the 33 who judged the original harder, and 9 of the 13 who judged the adaptation harder). This is not surprising, since more of the words in the original are less likely to have been encountered in print before (e.g., *zebra, chameleon, barrel*), while more of the words in the adaptation are too vague (i.e., *friend* for 'non-hippopotamus friend') or misleading (i.e., *house* for 'dwelling' or 'cave') to enable the reader to pick out an appropriate referent with any degree of certainty or precision.

None of the responses to "What makes it more exciting?" (to justify the answer to "Which one is more exciting?") addresses the question directly. Six children said "It has more detail" (5 preferring the original); 5 children attributed their choice's being more exciting to its being "written better" (all 5 preferred the adaptation).

Predictably, where the adaptation was preferred over the original, the most common reason given for this preference was that the adaptation was shorter. This answer was very common for questions 4 and 10. Most did not elaborate on this theme, but one child showed a fine awareness of exactly what made the original longer than the basal: the child reported preferring the basal (of BDH) because "you don't have to go through that many stores, like the police station." (In the original, Benjy tries to sleep in several places, such as the firehouse and the police station, before ending up at the bakery, but in the basal he goes straight to the bakery.) Thus, this child was aware that the original was longer because it was more detailed. Length again was a common factor mentioned in answer to #10 (Why [would you want to read] that one [again]?), although "It's more exciting" or "I like it better" or "It's better" were also quite common.

In contrast to the child quoted above, a significant number (14) of children said they preferred the original BECAUSE it was longer and/or more detailed, e.g., ''[the original] has more parts than the green one [i.e., the basal],'' ''it [the original] is longer and more of a story,'' ''the green one [basal] doesn't have as much words in it and I like to read a lot.'' Some responses show an acute sensitivity to and appreciation for the extra detail found in the original. For example one child said the original was more exciting (question 12) because of an incident that occurred only in the original: ''because Benjy walked down the street and nobody wanted him but the baker.'' (As was already noted, the basal doesn't mention Benjy's visiting anyone but the baker.) Another child, who consistently preferred the original, listed details not found in the basal in answer to three of the five open-ended questions, e.g., ''he (Little Hippo) was gonna run into a thorn bush and catch stripes from a zebra,''—this incident is deleted in the adaptation. Another reported preferring the original (of LH) because the title of that version (''The Secret Hiding Place'') was more interesting than the title of the adaptation (''Little Hippo''). One can see why: The title of the original refers to two notions (secrets, hiding) that represent an important part of life for a 7-year-old, while *Little Hippo* scarcely refers to one (littleness).

The answers given to #8 and 12 (What makes it more interesting? What is more exciting about it?) deserve some further consideration. Some children appealed to length or reading ease as reasons for one version being more interesting/exciting than the other. Others responded to these questions by mentioning an incident from the story, as mentioned earlier. A few became confused and recalled an incident that occurred *only* in the *other* version (i.e., not in the one which the child had indicated preference for in #7 and 11), or an incident that was equally present in *both* versions.

The responses to these open-ended questions were not amenable to statistical analysis. But certain things are obvious and significant without formal statistics. First of all, in the majority of cases the responses indicate that the children understood the task and answered the questions directly and sincerely. Most answers, although not always articulate, were straightforward and easy to evaluate. Confused and uninformative responses were relatively uncommon, but did occur at least once with each of the open-ended questions. But such responses were much more common with #8 and 12 than with 4, 6, and 10.[3]

---

[3]This is probably due to the nature of these two questions as opposed to the other three. Questions 4 and 10 both ask ''Why do you want to read that one?'', which is essentially the same as asking, ''Why do you like that one better than the other?'' Since most 7-year-olds know what they like and don't like, this is presumably a relatively easy question for the children to answer. The numbers support this claim: of the 56 who answered #4, 37 responded informatively; and of the 53 who answered #10, 40 gave informative responses. Question #6 asked which version was harder—again a fairly straightforward question. It asks for a simple evaluation, which 41 of the 54 children who responded were able to give in a straightforward, informative manner, indicating that they had little difficulty with this question.

But questions 8 and 12 asked for judgments about what makes one version more excit-

In conclusion, the evidence from these open-ended responses indicates that the children understood the task presented to them and did their best to answer informatively. They were uniformly cooperative and straightforward. We found no evidence of any child being facetious or deliberately misleading. The main problem in collecting preference data is the children's inability to articulate their feelings and opinions and/or to make a coherent analysis of the differences between the two versions. But these problems are due much more to the age of the children than to the questions or materials. It is fair to say, then, that these data support our conclusions because they show that the majority of the children knew what they were saying and why when they expressed their preferences for one version over the other.

Effect of Ability.   When the preference ratings were analyzed according to the ability groups of the students (as measured by their WRAT scores), some differences showed up which surprised us, since they contradicted our assumption that good readers would discriminate more between the versions than children who did not read as easily. The students were divided into three groups of roughly equal size. Overall, and for LH/SHP, the preference differences were not significant (though almost always in the direction of the original) as indicated in Table 5.9. For BDH, however, the differences are striking, and significant.

What was surprising to us was that the best readers (as measured by their performance on the WRAT vocabulary screening) were the only ones who, as a group, preferred an adaptation to an original, while the least able group preferred the original over the adaptation by a huge margin.

We have assumed that (1) preferences affect motivation, in particular, that children will be more motivated to read things they like better, and that (2) motivation is more crucial among the less able readers than it is for children who read easily. If this is correct, the fact that the less able readers preferred the original of BDH by 9 to 1 is much more significant than the fact that the best readers preferred the adaptation 5 to 3; it matters less[4] how the best readers felt as they are generally already highly motivated and well-disposed toward reading, and in any case, in this experiment, were reading texts well below their ability. The fact that the least able readers strongly preferred the original provides per-

---

ing/interesting, requiring a more subtle analysis of the differences between the versions, thus calling for more thought and more specific answers. Presumably, therefore, these questions were more difficult to answer. Significantly, 21 subjects who answered #4, 6, and 10 with ease could only say "I don't know" to #8 and 12, or they simply listed an incident and confused the versions or failed to differentiate between them. These children, then, succeeded in saying what they thought was exciting/interesting about the *story*, but made no significant comment about the differences between the versions.

[4]On the other hand, to anyone concerned with teaching literature and appreciation of literary style (cf. Green, 1982a), it must be depressing that the most able students preferred the adaptation to the original.

TABLE 5.9
Responses to "Which Version Did You Like Best?"
By Ability Group, All Subjects

Ability Group	N	Prefer Original N	%	Prefer Adaptation N	%
Overall					
Low	18	13	72	5	28
Med	17	12	71	5	29
High	18	8	44	10	56
LH/SHP					
Low	8	4	50	4	50
Med	8	5	62	3	38
High	10	5	50	5	50
BDH					
Low	10	9	90	1	10
Med	9	7	78	2	22
High	8	3	38	5	62

suasive testimony that we needn't fear discouraging poor readers by giving them texts that aren't edited down to someone's statistically derived conception of their ability. They are more motivated to read integral stories with enough text and language for proper plot and character development than they are to read awkwardly strung together strings of "easy" sentences.

The fact that the children were apparently more sensitive to differences between the versions of BDH than to the differences between the versions of SHP/LH may indicate that the differences in language (vocabulary and sentence length) that characterize the latter are not so salient to them as they are to the readability industry. In any case, there is no evidence that they found the longer sentences and less familiar vocabulary of the original SHP to be a reason to prefer the adaptation.

When only the consistent subjects are included, the differences are even more striking, as indicated in Table 5.10.

Discussion. The low- and average-ability groups still overwhelmingly prefer the original version, while the higher ability group is more equally divided. Perhaps the higher ability students are not as discriminating in their tastes as those for whom reading is more of a struggle. After all, if reading is easy for them, it may not matter too much to them how satisfying any individual book is. For them, just reading is enjoyable. But for children for whom reading is work, the kind of payoff that work yields is much more important; some things will be judged worth reading and will be read, while other things will be judged to be not worth the trouble, and won't get read. For good readers, it's no trouble, and everything gets read. Teachers and librarians will testify that many good readers will read formula fiction and other "junk" as readily as literature.

134

TABLE 5.10
Responses to "Which Version Did You Like Best?"
By Ability Group. (Consistent Subjects)

Ability Group	Prefer Original		Prefer Adaptation	
	n	%	n	%
Overall				
Low	5	71	2	29
Med	9	82	2	18
High	5	42	7	58
LH/SHP				
Low	1	33	2	67
Med	4	80	1	20
High	3	50	3	50
BDH				
Low	4	100	0	0
Med	5	84	1	16
High	2	33	4	67

When ability was measured according to subjects' performance on the comprehension task, the results are a little different. The high ability group preferred the original by a ratio close to 2 to 1 overall, preferring the original of LH/SHP by 3 to 1, and the original of BDH by a small margin, as indicated in Table 5.11. However, taking into consideration all the preference questions asked, the low group tended to prefer the adaptation of BDH, while the medium group overwhelmingly preferred the original, and the high group was close to evely divided. For LH/SHP, there was little consistency within ability groups across

TABLE 5.11
Responses to "Which Version Did You Like Best?"
By Ability Groups

Ability Group	Prefer Original		Prefer Adaptation	
	n	%	n	%
Overall				
Low	6	46	7	54
Med	13	57	10	43
High	11	65	6	35
LH/SHP				
Low	1	20	4	80
Med	5	38	8	62
High	6	75	2	25
BDH				
Low	5	63	3	37
Med	8	80	2	20
High	5	56	4	44

Ability sorted according to comprehension score.

TABLE 5.12
Mean Comprehension Scores, Comparing Versions, Stories,
and Versions Within Story

Group	Number of Subjects	Percentages of Questions Answered Correctly	
Overall	49		55.63
Original	25	55.00	
Adaptation	24	56.29	
SHP/LH	23		48.91
Original	13	47.62	
Adaptation	10	50.60	
BDH	26		61.58
Original	12	63.00	
Adaptation	14	60.36	

TABLE 5.13
Mean Comprehension Scores for Each Ability Group

Group	Number of Subjects	Mean Percentage Correct	
Overall			
Low	14		40.14
Original	6	41.50	
Adaptation	8	39.12	
Med	17		54.29
Original	7	52.10	
Adaptation	10	57.43	
High	18		68.94
Original	9	67.22	
Adaptation	9	70.67	
SHP/LH			
Low			26.50
Original	3	22.00	
Adaptation	3	31.00	
Med			46.25
Original	4	37.25	
Adaptation	4	55.25	
High			66.22
Original	6	67.33	
Adaptation	3	64.00	
BDH			
Low	3		50.37
Original	5	61.00	
Adaptation		44.00	
Med			61.44
Original	6	62.00	
Adaptation	3	60.33	
High			71.67
Original	3	67.00	
Adaptation	6	74.00	

136

questions. One implication of these results may be that it would be premature to make generalizations about the preferences according to "reading ability."

Comprehension

The comprehension data are summarized in Tables 5.12 and 5.13. The difference between versions was not statistically significant. However, students who read BDH answered a greater percentage of questions correctly than the ones who read SHP/LH, and the difference between stories was significant. As might be expected, the high-ability group did better than the medium-ability group, who did better than the low-ability group. The differences among ability groups was significant.

No doubt these means appear quite low (the range was 3.5% correct to 83% correct). Even good readers, reading grade-level adapted material, did not score above 70% correct on SHP/LH. There are (at least) three probable reasons for this. First, the questions may have been harder than the kinds of questions typically asked in assessment procedures; we attempted to ask exclusively questions which would indicate whether the child understood all of the events and relationships necessary to understanding the point of the story. There were no questions about details just for the sake of having questions about details. However, we included questions from the teachers' guide which may have probed details we considered irrelevant.

Second, no questions were asked until the children had read the entire story. Then questions covering the entire story were asked, following the sequence of the story. This means that there are questions which can only be answered correctly if a previous question has been answered correctly. It also means that the material covered is much greater, and the series of questions much longer and more richly structured than is usual for comprehension assessments, whether on standardized tests, or in the course of instruction. This situation is bound to generate lower scores than otherwise might have been obtained.

A question that naturally arises at this point is: Why there is such a striking difference in the comprehension of the two stories? Probably some disparity arises from differences in the stories themselves, as discussed in Section 1. For example, SHP/LH was a relatively inexplicit story—typically inexplicit for both trade picture books (illustrated books meant to be read to children), and primary-level basal reader stories. A certain amount of the story has to be inferred. We were careful not to use texts which required inferences from illustrations to be correctly understood,[5] but there is no doubt that illustrations could have confirmed and reinforced the inferences that were necessary. Relative inexplicitness

---

[5]In fact, we had to add two sentences to the original of SHP to substitute for information that was carried by illustrations. We added *But they were full of hippos, who called out* after *He raced to the flowering trees*, and added *he said. The water was full of hippos, who called* after *"Oh, no . . ."* We also deleted, from a paragraph about where different animals hid, the words *Pottos curled up in trees, and* because even we were distracted by not knowing what pottos were.

of the text is quite likely a major factor in the relative depression of scores, as the scores on BDH, which was much more explicit, were considerably higher. In addition, some of the difference may be attributable to the fact that the mix of question types differed between stories, as indicated in Table 5.3. Thus, 50% of the questions for BDH could be answered correctly just by understanding the meanings of the individual sentences, while only 7% (adaptation) or 21% (original) of the SHP/LH questions had this property. On the other hand, 14% of the BDH questions required the subject to put together the information in an entire paragraph to be answered correctly, while 36% (original) to 43% (adaptation) of the questions for SHP/LH had this property.

Probably the fact of most significance to emerge from these data is that overall, the difference in comprehension between versions is not significant, while there are large and significant differences between texts. (The mean comprehension scores on the level 3 original of BDH was 16 points above the mean comprehension score on the level 3 original of SHP. The comprehension scores on the level 2 adaptations were 10 points apart, and in the same direction.) This means that more global structural and organizational properties of texts (as just described), are significant. But readability formulae do not measure these. At the same time, characterizations based on word length, word frequency, and sentence length fail to predict differences of the sort that are obvious here. It is true that when the result are broken down by ability groups, there are some apparently large differences between versions. However, three other facts make it unreasonable to attribute much to these differences. First, the difference between stories is significant, and striking: differences of 5 to 39 percentage points for 5 of the 6 groups (all except the high ability group that read original versions); the low-ability group reading original versions got 22% correct on SHP, 61% correct on BDH. Yet the poor readers reading the original of BDH did almost as well as the good readers reading SHP (the good readers got an average of 67.33% correct). Second, the differences are in both directions; the high-ability group performed better on comprehension questions when they read the original of SHP/LH than when they read the adaptation, though the opposite was true for the low- and medium-ability groups. With BDH, the results are just the reverse: the low- and medium-ability groups (especially the low-ability group) did better answering questions about the original than about the adaptation, while the high-ability group did worse. (Again this points to a difference between the stories or the questions asked about them.) Third, when the groups are broken down by story version and ability group, they are too small to make meaningful comparisons between cells.

CONCLUSIONS

The study reported here supports the hypotheses of text analysts (e.g., Davison & Kantor 1982; Green, 1984) that

1. Children prefer texts as originally written for children to texts that are adapted from such material to meet the criteria of readability formulae. This is especially true of poor and average readers.

2. Readability-adapted materials are not significantly easier for children to understand than the originals one or two grade levels higher, from which they were adapted.

The differences in word length, word frequency, and sentence length that are the stock in trade of the readability industry and the sacred cows of ignorant legislatures and adoption committees are irrelevant both to comprehensibility of texts and children's preferences.

To the extent that the results reported here are robust and general, they indicate that the pressure on educators, and on the publishers of reading textbooks, to provide materials which conform to the rigid and artificial criteria of readability formulae is misguided, and should be resisted. If editing to readability formulae results in texts that are less interesting and no more difficult than what is already available in bookstores and public libraries, then it is a very risky business, as it is potentially boring to read materials with little or no syntactic or lexical challenge and even less stylistic variation. There is evidence (Green, 1982a; Green & Laff, 1980) that children attend to and appreciate stylistic differences. It would seem to follow that expecting them to read "simplified," style-neutralized, Muzak texts is, to say the least, inconsiderate. At best it is pointless; at worst, it is counterproductive. It wastes valuable time that could be spent in more profitable ways and risks boring the children and conveying to them that there is nothing interesting to be gained from reading books, or even from school. It seems possible that Johnny does not learn to read because there is no thrill in being able to read the adaptations of stories that constitute the reading books. A significant part of the problem of teaching children to read may be motivation: It may be that they would do better on more complex, more difficult, more challenging material, since successfully meeting a challenge is itself a source of pleasure and satisfaction.

Furthermore, having only style-neutralized adapted materials to read also deprives children of an opportunity to learn in a natural way the complexities of syntactic and lexical manipulation (Green, 1982b) that constitute style, and contribute ubiquitously to the task of interpreting text as intended by the author. If children are not exposed to unfamiliar words and syntactic constructions because they are "too hard," how are they supposed to ever learn to deal with them? A child who is not exposed to the wealth of literary usages and devices, and to a variety of writing styles in school, and who does not read much independently, may be seriously handicapped in understanding texts written in styles at variance with the prose of the homogenized texts that have been his primary model of written text.

REFERENCES

Bettelheim, B., & Zelan, K. (1981). Why children don't like to read. *Atlantic Monthly,* Nov., 1981, 25–31.

Bishop, C. H. (1935). An obstacle race. *The Horn Book, 11,* 203–209.

Bower, G. H. (1978). Experiments on story comprehension and recall. *Discourse Processes, 1,* 211–231.

Bruce, B. C. (1984). A new point of view on children's stories. In R. C. Anderson, J. Osborn, & R. J. Tierney (Eds.), *Learning to read in American schools.* Hillsdale, NJ: Lawrence Erlbaum Associates.

Davison, A., & Kantor, R. (1982). On the failure of readability formulas to define readable texts: A case study from adaptations. *Reading Research Quarterly, 17*(2), 187–208.

Green, G. (1982a). Competence for implicit text analysis: Literary style discrimination in five-year-olds. In D. Tannen (Ed.) Analyzing discourse: Text and task. Washington, D.C.: Georgetown University Press.

Green, G. (1982b). Linguistics and the pragmatics of language use. *Poetics, 11,* 54–76.

Green, G. (1984). On the appropriateness of adaptations in primary-level basal readers: Reactions to remarks by Bertram Bruce. In R. C. Anderson, J. Osborn, & R. J. Tierney (Eds.), *Learning to read in American schools.* Hillsdale, NJ: Lawrence Erlbaum Associates.

Green, G., & Laff, M. (1980). *Five-year-olds' recognition of authorship by literary style* (Tech. Rep. No. 181). Urbana, University of Illinois Center for the Study of Reading. (ERIC Document Reproduction Service No. ED 193 615).

Grover, R. J. (1976). *The relationship of readability, content, illustrations, and other formal elements to the library book preferences of 2nd grade children.* Unpublished doctoral dissertation, Indiana University.

Johnson, T. D. (1979). Presenting literature to children. *Children's Literature in Education, 10,* 1:35–43.

Lam, C. D. (1969). Pupil preference for four art styles used in primary reading textbooks. *The Reading Teacher, 23,* 2:137–43.

Moe, A. J., Hopkins, C. J., & Rush, T. (1982). *The vocabulary of 1st-grade children.* Springfield, IL: Charles C. Thomas.

Schlager, N. (1978). Predicting children's choices in literature: A developmental approach. *Children's Literature in Education, 10,* 136–142.

6 Inferential Complexity and the Readability of Texts

Susan Kemper
University of Kansas

Traditional approaches to matching a text to the knowledge and skill of the reader have relied on formulas for determining the "readability" of the text. Two primary indices of readability were commonly used: vocabulary and sentence difficulty. Although many different readability formulas have been devised since the appearance of those of Lorge (1939) and Dale and Chall (1948, 1949), lexical and syntactic variables continue to predominate (e.g., Duffy & Kabance, 1982).

An alternative approach to matching texts and readers can be derived from the knowledge-based approach to text comprehension and memory. In this approach, the reader uses knowledge of possible causal connections as well as known scripts for event sequences and plans for solving problems to understand the text. Research on text comprehension and memory has demonstrated that readers use causal event knowledge to answer questions about texts and to fill in missing details when recalling texts (Black & Bower, 1979, 1980; Bower, Black, & Turner, 1979; Graesser, 1981; Nicholas & Trabasso, 1980; Omanson, Warren, & Trabasso, 1978; Schank, 1975; Schank & Abelson, 1977; Warren, Nicholas, & Trabasso, 1979).

Kemper (1982, 1983, 1984; Kemper, Otalvaro, Estill, & Schadler, 1985) has extended the knowledge-based approach to text comprehension by analyzing texts as causally connected chains of actions, physical states, and mental states. The event chain explains "who did what to whom and why" by describing the causal antecedents and consequences of characters' actions and of natural and social processes. The event-chain analysis of texts is described below; succeeding sections demonstrate how this analysis may be used to evaluate the comprehensibility of texts as an alternative to measuring "readability."

THE EVENT-CHAIN ANALYSIS OF TEXTS

This analysis uses a three-step process for parsing narrative and expository texts. In the first step, a text is segmented into a sequence of clauses. Next, these clauses are classified as describing actions, physical states, or mental states. Finally, a taxonomy of possible causal connections is employed to determine the underlying event chain as a connected sequence of actions, physical states, and mental states.

The event-chain analysis of texts is similar to the analysis schemes of Frederiksen (1975), Norman and Rumelhart (1975), and Turner and Greene (1977). However, the event-chain analysis does not capture the entire meaning of a text; most adjectives, adverbs, quantifiers, and prepositional phrases are ignored. It is derived from the causal inference taxonomies of Schank (1975) and Nicholas and Trabasso (1980). It includes only those aspects of texts directly relevant to determining the underlying causal and temporal organization of the text. This analysis does not include all possible inferences but only those necessary to interconnect actions and states explicitly mentioned in the text. As Nicholas and Trabasso (1980) have suggested, readers must also be able to infer (1) pronominal and nominal references, (2) the location, duration, and time of the occurrence of events, and (3) the significance, normality, and morality of events.

Clause Segmentation

In the event-chain analysis, a text is initially divided into syntactically defined clauses. The analysis identifies both tensed clauses, containing verbs that may be inflected for tense, and untensed clauses, containing uninflected imperative or infinitive verbs. Four tense markers can be used, in general, to identify tensed verbs: *-ed* characteristic of past tense verbs, *-s* that marks third-person, singular present tense verbs, *has* or *have* that signal perfective tense verbs, and *be + -ing* of progressive tense verbs. Irregular verbs such as *caught* or *ran* are those that are not inflected by these markers but are treated functionally the same as tensed verbs.

Tensed and untensed verbs may be found in different types of sentences. Simple sentences contain a single verb and, hence, a single clause, as in (1). Coordinate verb phrases or sentences, as in (2), contain multiple verbs and, hence, multiple clauses connected by conjunctions such as *and, or,* or *but.* Complex sentences contain two or more verbs and clauses; unlike coordinate sentences, the clauses in complex sentences consist of a main or matrix clause and one or more embedded or subordinate clauses. The analysis distinguishes six types of embedded clauses: infinitive phrases, gerundive phrases, noun phrase complements, relative clauses, participial adjectives, and subordinate clauses. Examples of these embedded phrases and clauses are given in (3).

(1) Simple sentences
Bob crashed into the store.
The nurse has worked all night.
He frequently steals second base.
The horse is running away.

(2) Coordinate sentences
Bob crashed into the store and stole the
    diamond necklace.
The nurse worked all night but did not save
    the baby's life.
Either the victim was strangled or
    she died from shock.

(3) Embedded clauses
A. Infinitive phrases
    . . . to marry a rich woman . . .
    . . . to be a thief . . .
    . . . for him to be announced . . .
    . . . for Alice to enter the contest . . .
B. Gerundive phrases
    . . . Bob's marrying a rich woman . . .
    . . . being a thief . . .
    . . . his having been announced . . .
    . . . Alice's entering the contest . . .
C. Noun phrase complements
    . . . that Bob married a rich woman . . .
    . . . that he is a thief . . .
    . . . that he was announced . . .
    . . . that Alice entered the contest . . .
D. Participial adjectives
    . . . married woman . . .
    . . . unannounced man . . .
    . . . running horse . . .
    . . . screaming baby . . .
E. Relative clauses
    . . . the drink that he ordered . . .
    . . . the person who is a thief . . .
    . . . the man who has been announced . . .
    . . . the contest that Alice entered . . .
F. Subordinate clauses
    . . . after he married the rich woman . . .
    . . . because he was a thief . . .
    . . . until she was announced . . .
    . . . when Alice entered the contest . . .

Embedded infinitive clauses, noun phrase complements, and gerundive phrases may occur within noun phrases or verb phrases of any clause (see Postal, 1974, or Rosenbaum, 1967). Participial adjectives and relative clauses may modify any noun within a clause; subordinate clauses may precede or follow the matrix clause. Complex sentences like those in (4) are possible. Each example has two clauses: slash marks segment the sentences into clauses.

(4) Complex sentences
     John wants / to marry a rich woman.
     Being a thief / is exciting.
     That he was announced / surprised everyone.
     Joel believes / that Alice entered the contest.
     The screaming / baby woke up the nurse.
     The drink / that he ordered / cost $2.50.
     Joel laughed / when Alice entered the contest.

The Classification of Clauses

In the second step of the analysis of texts as event chains, each clause is classified as referring to either an action, a physical state, or a mental state. As in the first step, syntactic criteria and procedures are used to classify the clauses. Actions are distinguished from states on the basis of three criteria derived from Chafe (1970) and Miller and Johnson-Laird (1976): (1) Actions can be expressed with verbs in the "progressive" aspect. (2) Verbs denoting actions can be used as answers to questions such as "What happened?" or "What's happening?" (3) Actions can be used in imperative constructions. Actions include processes involving the change of state or condition of objects, as in (5), and the activities of agents, as in (6). The event chain analysis does not distinguish these two subcategories of actions.

(5) Nonagentive processes
     It is raining.
     Kennedy lost the Vice-Presidential nomination.
     The victim died.
     The contest happened last weekend.

(6) Agentive actions
     He killed a walrus.
     The train ran into the cow.
     The old woman kissed the hippie.
     The girl walked over to the flowers.

Clauses that fail the three tests for actions are classified as referring to states. States include both observable physical states and unobservable mental states. Physical states include states of possession, attribution, and specification, as in

(7). Mental states include emotions, cognitions, and intentions, as in (8). States describe enduring, although not permanent, properties or characteristics of agents, objects, and locations.

(7) Physical states: external attributes
     The window is near the door.
     That dress is much too expensive.
     Dogs have four legs.
     The general is a fool.
     There is no reason for his confusion.

(8) Mental states: internal attributes
     John believes the old woman's story.
     Alice loves Henry.
     The nurse relied on the doctor's honesty.
     Cats need respect.
     Mary wants the dress.

Following Fillmore (1968) and Chafe (1970), all clauses with verbs such as *to see* or *to hear*, as in (9a), are classified by a special convention. These verbs involve an *experiencer* rather than an agent. Although they can answer "What's happening" questions, a mental disposition or internal process is described. These unobservable mental processes are paralleled by observable actions, as in (9b). Thus, in this taxonomy by convention, *experiencer* verbs are classified as referring to mental states rather than actions.

(9) A. Unobservable mental processes
         John saw the walrus.
         The little girl heard the sound of
             the ice cream truck.
         The old lady felt the rose.

     B. Observable actions
         John looked at the walrus.
         The little girl listened to the sound of
             the ice cream truck.
         The old lady touched the rose.

Periphrastic causative constructions are also treated by a special convention. Periphrastic causatives involve a verb such as *to cause, to make,* or *to get* and an infinitive, adjectival, participial, or locative complement. Although such sentences have two clauses, the first refers to an unstated action that results in the action or state described by the complement. Only the complement clause is considered to be explicitly stated in the text. Thus, the examples in (10) are treated as single-clause sentences. Each is classified as an action (A), a physical state (PS), or a mental state (MS).

(10) Periphrastic causative constructions
Uncle Sam will make you a man. (PS)
Paul got himself to school. (PS)
John caused Mary to be unhappy. (MS)
The mother made the baby smile. (A)

Truncated passive sentences, as in (11), are also classified by convention. Passive sentences traditionally derive from active sentences that refer to actions. Truncated passives, however, do not explicitly refer to the agent of the action described; they resemble descriptions of states. Truncated passives are treated as predicate adjectives that describe enduring states by Miller and Johnson-Laird (1976). Thus, in this taxonomy by convention, the truncated passives of (11) are classified as referring to either physical (PS) or mental (MS) states.

(11) Truncated passives
The dog was run over. (PS)
The horse has been saddled. (PS)
Alice is surprised. (MS)
The rumor was believed. (MS)
The old lady was kissed. (PS)

Event Chain Construction

A taxonomy of possible causal connections is used to construct the event chain underlying the text. The taxonomy assumes that there are four types of causal connections (Omanson et al., 1978; Schank, 1975; Warren et al., 1979): One event may cause a new physical state—a resultant causal link. (2) One event may cause a new mental state—an initiation link. (3) One event may cause a new action by enabling the action to occur—an enablement link or (4) by providing a psychological motive or reason for the action—a motivational link. New physical states result from agents' actions or from natural and social processes that alter pre-existing physical states. Agents' actions arise from internal intentions, dispositions, and emotions. These mental states are the reasons for characters' actions. Internal states are causally initiated by prior actions or physical states. However, certain physical states or conditions must be fulfilled in order for actions of agents or natural and social processes to be possible. These physical states thus enable the actions to occur; other physical states may prevent or disenable actions.

These four types of causation are constrained by a taxonomy of causation such that an action cannot cause a new action without an intervening physical or mental state, a physical state cannot lead to a new physical state without an intervening action, and mental states cannot cause new mental or physical states without intervening actions. The rules of (12), thus, summarize this causal taxonomy. A complete causal analysis of characters' actions involves specifying the physical states that enable it and result from it and the mental states that provide reasons for the actions or that were initiated by it. Example sentences referring to each type of causation are given in (13).

(12) Causal event taxonomy
      ACTIONS——result in→PHYSICAL STATES
      ACTIONS——initiate→MENTAL STATES
      PHYSICAL STATES——initiate→MENTAL STATES
      PHYSICAL STATES——(dis)enable→ACTIONS
    ✓ MENTAL STATES——reasons for→ACTIONS

(13) A. ACTION——results in→PHYSICAL STATE
          Mary knocked over the bricks. The bricks were
            lying on the ground.
          Joel picked up the grapes from the counter.
            Joel has the grapes.
          The sunlight warmed the wax. The wax was soft.
          It is raining. The grass is wet.

      B. ACTION——initiates→MENTAL STATES
          Suddenly, Bill jumped out from behind a bush.
            Alice saw him.
          Paul dropped the hammer on his toe. His
            toe hurt.
          The hail broke the window. Jenny worried
            about the carpet.
          The train approached the station. The
            passenger heard the whistle.

      C. PHYSICAL STATE——(dis)enable→ACTION
          The passenger was waiting at the station. The
            conductor looked at him.
          The floor got wet. Jenny mopped the floor.
          The alley was dark. Mary bumped into the bricks.
          The grapes were lying on the counter. Joel
            looked at them.

      D. PHYSICAL STATES——initiate→MENTAL STATE
          The street light was out. Alice was scared.
          The carpet got wet. Jenny worried about it.
          The restaurant wasn't closed. Peter
            was delighted.
          A giraffe was beside the silo. The farmer saw it.

      E. MENTAL STATE——reason for→ACTION
          Peter was hungry. He entered the restaurant.
          The farmer saw the giraffe. His eyes bulged out.
          Nancy remembered the story. She told Phil.
          The dog was timid. It hid beneath the bed.

Not all the causal links in the event chain underlying a text are explicitly stated in sentences or clauses. Some must be inferred. The causal taxonomy can be used to guide the inference of unstated causal links. In general, action-action, physical state-physical state, mental state-mental state, and mental state-physical state sequences in a text violate the taxonomy and require obligatory inferred actions or states to fill gaps in the event chain. The examples in (14) illustrate the application of these rules. In each case, the required inference is indicated in parentheses.

(14) A. Action—Action sequences with inferred
          Physical states
          John dropped the hammer. (It was lying on the
              ground) Alice picked it up.
          The volcano erupted. (There was a lot of
              lava) The lava buried the village.
          The trolley rolled down the ramp. (It did
              not rest on the end) It fell
              off the platform.

      B. Action—Action sequences with inferred
          Mental states
          The doctor pointed to the chart. (The nurse
              recognized his request) The nurse handed
              him the chart.
          The train bumped into the cow. (The cow was hurt)
              It bellowed.
          The judge reviewed the testimony. (She
              concluded that the prisoner was innocent) She
              ordered the prisoner's release.

      C. Physical state-Physical state sequences with
          inferred Actions
          The money was in the bank. (Mary wrote a
              check) Mary's check was honored.
          The sun was hot. (The sun warmed the
              butter) The butter melted.
          The donkey was very old. (It died) Its corpse
              is under the tree.

      D. Mental state—Mental state sequences with inferred
          Actions
          John remembered the story. (He told it to
              Nancy) Nancy laughed at it.
          The riddle puzzled William. (Donna explained
              it to him) He didn't understand Donna's
              explanation.
          Jimmy heard the train's whistle. (He looked
              for the train) Then he saw it.

E. Mental state—Physical state sequences with
inferred Actions
Janet remembered the combination. (She tried
it) The safe was opened easily.
The dog was scared. (It whined) Its
whine was mournful.
The children really like chocolate ice cream.
(They ate a gallon of it) One gallon
wasn't enough for them.

Not all sentence sequences referring to successive actions, physical states, or mental states violate the causal taxonomy. The event chain underlying a text need not consist of a simple, linear string of actions and states. Rather, branching chains are characteristic. A single action or state may lead to multiple new actions or states; a single action or state may arise from multiple causes. A sequence of causally connected actions and states may dead-end; the event chain may resume by returning to an earlier action or state and developing a new sequence of events. Parallel causal chains may be present; these chains may arise from a common cause or lead to a common event.

A principle of parsimony guides the reader in recovering the sequence of stated and inferred causal links underlying a text. While many physical and mental states and actions can be inferred, only the minimal number necessary to fully interconnect the text are incorporated as inferred propositions in the analysis of the text. As articulated by Warren et al. (1979), this parsimony principle states:

> In understanding a narrative a listener makes only those inferences [e.g., missing causal connections] relevant to the progress of the narrative . . . relevant inferences establish the information necessary to determine what happened and why. This knowledge is essentially that necessary for comprehension of the event chain. "What happened" refers to physical events and characters' actions or responses; "why" refers to their causes and motivations. Other inferences are made when they become important to this basic thread of the story . . . (p. 44)

PREDICTING COMPREHENSIBILITY

Kemper (1983) assumed that the event-chain analysis of texts forms a model for text comprehension: Readers must segment a text into clauses, identify each clause as referring to an action, physical state, or mental state, and establish the event chain underlying the text by inferring causal connections among the actions, physical states, and mental states. This model of text comprehension predicts that the overall difficulty of a text should reflect how easily readers can establish the causally connected event chain underlying the text. Hence, a primary source of comprehension difficulty is the inferential processing required to construct the causally connected event chain.

Individual differences in reading skill may affect how rapidly and efficiently readers can establish causal connections (Nicholas & Trabasso, 1980; Warren et al., 1979) and differing levels of background knowledge about relevant events may affect how accurately readers can infer missing causal connections (Graesser, 1981; Kemper et al., 1985; Sanford & Garrod, 1981). If so, measuring the inferential complexity of texts will permit the difficulty due to inference load to be adjusted. Causal connections can be deleted from texts, up to a point, to raise their inferential complexity, or added to texts to lower their inferential complexity. Kemper (1983) used multiple regression techniques to obtain the best-fitting regression equation for predicting the inference load of texts that differ in grade level suitability.

Materials

Experimental materials were chosen from among the McCall and Crabbs (1979) *Standard Test Lessons in Reading* consist of a series of short passages designed to evaluate reading and comprehension skills. Grade level norms, based on large-scale field test, are provided for students' performance on eight multiple-choice questions about each passage. The passages span 3rd grade to high school reading levels. Two coders independently parsed the 62 passages selected from this corpus; the coders segmented each passage into clauses and then categorized the clauses as referring to either actions, physical states, or mental states. Using the causal taxonomy described above, the coders constructed the event chain underlying each text. The event chain analysis of a sample text is presented in Table 6.1.

Results

A regression analysis of these passages produced an inference load formula for assessing the inferential complexity of the 62 passages. The dependent variable was the grade level (3rd through 12th) of each passage. There were six independent or predictor variables based on the density of stated and inferred actions, physical states, and mental states. The mean number of actions, physical states, and mental states, both stated and inferred, was obtained from the two coders' analyses. This number was divided by the number of words in the passage to give the density of each type of causal link; these densities were then adjusted to a standard passage length of 100 words. The analysis used the "best subset" approach to regression (Daniel & Wood, 1971). The analysis fitted the six predictor variables to the grade level of each passage. The "best" fitting equation, in terms of C_p and r^2 statistics, had three predictors: stated mental states, inferred mental states, and stated physical states. For this equation, $C_p = 0.92$,

TABLE 6.1

The event chain analysis of a sample passage. Slash marks segment the text into clauses. Each clause is labeled as referring to either an action (A), a physical state (PS), or a mental state (MS). The clauses are serially numbered. The underlying event chain is schematically presented in Fig. 6.1. The inference load of the passage is also calculated.

Rocky

/Elizabeth went to the window A1/ where she sat down A2/ to wait for Rocky. A3/ Rocky was the name PS4/ she had given to a raccoon A5/ who had come to their house every night for the past week. A6/ Each night he had gotten into the garbage PS7/ and spread bits of paper and fruit peelings all over the yard, A8/ which angered Elizabeth's father. MS9/ Rocky always came at night A10/ because, like the owl, the bat, and the mouse, the raccoon is a nocturnal animal. PS11/ These animals wander about at night A12/ and sleep during the day. A13/
/That day her father built a new fence around the garbage cans A14/ and she wondered MS15/ if Rocky would be able PS16/ to get to them. PS17/ She did not have to wait long A18/ to see. MS19/ Very soon, Rocky scurried around the back of the house A20/ and went straight to the new fence A21/ and sniffed. A22/ Next he scratched at the wooden slats A23/ trying MS24/ to climb up, A25/ but there was nothing PS26/ for his curved toes to grab onto. A27/ Discouraged, MS28/ he left A29/ and Elizabeth wondered MS30/ if she would ever see Rocky again. MS31/ She probably would not. MS32/ Because raccoons are shy of humans, MS33/ Rocky did not come A34/ to make friends. PS35/ He only wanted food, MS36/ and since he could no longer get it, AS37/ he would not return. A38/

Calculation of Inference Load

	Number (per 222 words)		Density 100 x (Number/222 words)	
	Stated	Inferred	Stated	Inferred
Actions	21	1	9.46	.45
Physical states	7	3	3.15	1.35
Mental states	10	5	4.50	2.25

Inference load = 8.41 + .54(4.50) - .86(3.15) + .23(2.25) = 8.65 McCall-Crabbs grade level: 7th.

and $r^2 = +.58$, $F(3,56) = 5.44$, $p < .05$. The equation is given in (15) below. It is applied to the example passage in Table 6.1.

(15) Inference load grade = 8.41
+ .54 (density of Stated Mental States)
− .84 (density of Stated Physical States)
− .23 (density of Inferred Mental States).

According to this formula, the grade level suitability of texts depends on how many stated mental states, stated physical states, and inferred mental states occur in the text, relative to the length of the text. Texts with relatively many stated mental or inferred mental states are more difficult than texts with relatively few mental states in their event chains. Texts with relatively many stated physical states are easier than texts with few mental states perhaps because they involve more references to concrete objects and observable events.

Comparison to Readability Formulas

The predictive power of the inference load formula is comparable to that of two well-known readability formulas, the Dale and Chall (1949) and Flesch (1974) formulas. Two coders computed both the inference load score and the Dale-Chall score for 16 additional passages from the McCall and Crabbs (1979) series. The Dale-Chall formula correlated r (16) $= +.63$ with the reported McCall-Crabbs grade levels. The inference load of the passages correlated r (16) $= +.63$ with the reported grade levels. The two formulas, however, are not strongly correlated, r (16) $= +.31$.

The two coders also calculated the Flesch readability score of these passages. The correlation between the inference load and Flesch scores was r (16) $= +.23$. The Flesch score correlated r (16) $= +.57$ with the assigned grade levels while the correlation between grade level and inference load was r (16) $= +.72$.

Thus, the inference load formula and the traditional Dale–Chall and Flesch readability formulas are equivalent in their ability to predict grade-level difficulty. The two types of formula do so on the basis of different, and relatively uncorrelated, aspects of the passages. One interpretation of these results is that the inference load formula directly measures properties of texts which contribute to difficulty, whereas traditional readability formulas measure indirect indices of passage difficulty.

Discussion

Major readability formulas to date have been based on surface aspects of texts. They do predict performance on comprehension tests but there is no obvious explanation as to why measures of sentence and word length should predict comprehension (Hirsch, 1977; Kintsch & Vipond, 1975; Klare, 1974/75). Further, these formulas cannot distinguish a well-structured text from a sequence of randomly ordered sentences.

The event chain model of text comprehension suggests that texts are difficult to comprehend when the reader is required to make too many causal inferences. The densities of stated and inferred mental states and of stated physical states index the inferential complexity of texts; the inference load formula, obtained by Kemper (1983), can be used to predict the grade-level suitability of texts that differ in inference load.

One direct implication of the event chain model of text comprehension is that comprehension is likely to be impaired whenever a reader must infer missing causal connections. Gaps corresponding to such missing causal connections will occur in a text if not all of the actions, physical states, and mental states in the underlying event chain are explicitly stated in the text. At such gaps in text, the reader must infer the missing causal connections in order to link the current action or state with preceding ones. Kemper (1982) demonstrated that readers will detect and fill in such gaps in event chains with actions, physical states, or mental states. The following study was designed to further examine how rapidly readers can fill in the gaps in texts by inferring actions and physical or mental states.

READNG TIMES AND QUESTION-ANSWERING

The event chain model of text comprehension assumes that readers actively segment a text into syntactically defined clauses (Jarvella, 1971) and identify the referent of each clause as either an action, physical state, or mental state. Then, readers construct the event chain underlying the text by using a taxonomy of possible causal antecedents and consequences. This model implies that deleting sentences referring to critical actions, physical states, or mental states should adversely affect comprehension of the event chain: (1) Understanding causally contingent actions or states may be slowed at such gaps in the text. (2) Readers may be unable to complete the causal event chain which may impair how rapidly or accurately they can answer questions about the text.

In this experiment, passages suitable for college readers were prepared in which the immediate causes of actions, physical states, and mental states were either explicitly stated in the text or deleted. Of interest was the comparison of reading times for the target actions or states as well as question-answering latencies and accuracy scores for the causally intact and causally abridged texts.

Method

Twenty native speakers of English participated. All were first year college students who received course credit. Each reported scores on the English subtest of the American College Test of 25 or better.

The study used two 1000 word biographical essays about well-known contemporary scientists. An event-chain analysis of each passage identified 12 critical sentences, four referring to actions, four to physical states, and four to mental states. The three types of sentences were matched in terms of word length so that in isolation, readers understood them equally rapidly (mean = 3.69 sec), all $p > .05$.

There were two versions of each passage. In the intact version, the text included sentences which explicitly referred to the immediate cause of each target action, physical state, or mental state, according to the event chain analysis. In the abridged version, a gap in the text occurred because these sentences were deleted. An extract from one passage is presented in Table 6.2 and Fig. 6.1.

TABLE 6.2

An extract from a passage about Steven Wozniak. Target sentences referring
to an action, a physical state, and a mental state are underlined. The sentences in brackets [ ] were deleted to abridge the event chain. A factual
and an inference question about this extract follow.

Wozniak had an accident with his single-engine airplane at
the Scotts Valley Airport. He had been practicing with two friends
and his fiancee. [The nosewheel collapsed on impact.] Wozniak and
his fiancee were injured. He was lucky [the plane came down near
the run-way]. Hundreds of children were playing at the rink. Wozniak suffered cuts on his face but was considered in good condition
otherwise. [Wozniak had no dizziness or blurry vision.] No one
realized the seriousness of his injuries. Wozniak had hit his head
badly enough to bring on amnesia. Soon he could remember everything
up to the day before the accident but could form no new long-term
memories.

Factual question: Why did Wozniak have amnesia?

                      (he hit his head)

Inference question: Why had Wozniak been practicing?

                      (he needed the experience)

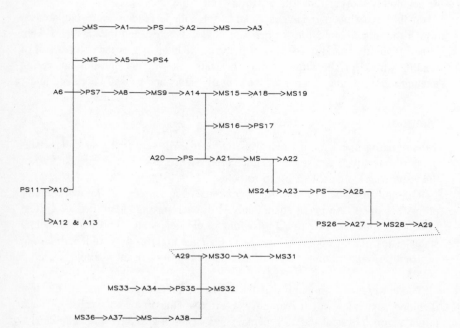

FIGURE 6.1. Event chain to accompany text in Table 6.1. Inferred
actions and states are indicated by unlabeled nodes.

Overall, the intact and abridged versions of each passage differed by approximately two grade levels according to the inference load formula. The abridged versions had an average inference load of 15.4 while the inference load of the intact versions averaged 13.1.

Ten questions accompanied each passage. Five were factual such that the correct answers were stated in the passage and five were inference. The correct answers to the inference questions could be inferred from the passages. Prior testing determined that these questions could not be correctly answered simply on the basis of background knowledge without reading the texts. These factual and inference questions had the same number of words. In isolation, they were read with equal speed (mean = 4.77 sec), $p > .05$.

The subjects read the passages one sentence at a time via a computer terminal. The subject controlled the presentation rate by pressing a control key to display each successive sentence. Reading times for the target sentences were automatically recorded as the interval between key presses. A randomly ordered sequence of factual and inference questions immediately followed each passage. The subject was instructed to read each question and to formulate an answer before pressing the control key. Pressing the control key removed the question and presented an answer prompt. The subject typed in an answer in response to the prompt. The interval from the onset of the question to the subject's key press was recorded as the latency to read a question and formulate an answer. The computer automatically recorded and scored the subject's answer as correct or incorrect. The latency to type in the answer was not recorded. Each subject read one intact and a different abridged passage in a random order.

Results

Separate analyses were done on the sentence reading times, the question-answering latencies, and the answer accuracy scores. Sentence reading times were the average time to read the four target clauses referring to actions, physical states, or mental states. The question-answering latencies for the five factual and five inference questions about each passage were averaged; only latencies for the questions the subjects correctly answered were included in the analysis since incorrect answers reflect a failure to correctly determine the underlying event chain. The accuracy scores were the average number of factual and inference questions answered correctly.

Reading Times. The mean reading times for the target sentences were analyzed with a 2 × 3 ANOVA. Version of the passage (intact vs. abridged) and type of sentence (actions vs. physical states vs. mental states) were within-subjects factors. All three types of target sentences were read more rapidly in the intact versions (mean = 2.89 sec) than in the abridged versions (mean = 4.29 sec), $p < .05$. There was also a significant interaction of passage version and

TABLE 6.3

Results of the first experiment comparing sentence reading times,
question-answering latencies, and accuracy scores for passages with
intact and abridged causal chains.

	Passage Version	
	Intact	Abridged
Reading time		
Actions	2.35 sec	4.32
Physical states	2.95	4.41
Mental states	3.65	4.44
Factual questions		
Latency	5.28 sec	6.03
Accuracy	86 %	78
Inference questions		
Latency	6.49 sec	6.61
Accuracy	60 %	62

sentence types, $p < .05$ (see Table 6.3). Relative to the abridged passages, the causal information in the intact passages had a greater facilitative effect on reading times for sentences referring to actions (mean difference = 1.97 sec) than for those referring to physical states (mean difference = 1.45 sec) or to mental states (mean difference = .79 sec).

There was also a significant main effect for sentence type, $p < .05$. Sentences referring to actions were read more rapidly than those describing physical states and sentences about mental states were read even more slowly than those about physical states. This reading time main effect is easy to interpret as the sets of action, physical state, and mental state sentences were matched in terms of average word length and were read equally rapidly in isolation. These results suggest that the sentence type main effect is not simply due to reading time differences for the target sentences but is itself a context effect. Given antecedent causal information, actions are more rapidly integrated into event chains than are physical states. Causal information has little effect on how rapidly mental states are comprehended and integrated into event chains.

Question-answering Latencies. A 2 × 2 ANOVA was used to analyze the mean latencies for correct answers to the questions. Passage version and question type (factual vs. inference) were within-subject factors. Factual questions were answered more rapidly than inference ones, $p < .04$. In isolation, factual and inference questions were read with equal speed; consequently, the question type main effects demonstrate that retrieving a fact that has been directly stated in a passage is more rapid than inferring a missing one.

156

The interaction of passage version and question type was also significant, p < .05 (see Table 6.3). Factual questions about abridged passages were answered more slowly than those about the intact passages. In contrast, passage version had no effect on the latency to answer inference questions. This interaction indicates that the abridgements disrupted overall comprehension of the event chains underlying the passages. For intact texts, the answers to the factual questions were directly represented in the event chains. But for the abridged texts, some of these facts were not included in the event chains but could be inferred during question-answering. For both intact and abridged texts, the answers to the inference questions were not directly represented in the event chains; only some of these answers could be inferred to answer the questions.

Correct Answers.   The mean number of questions answered correctly was analyzed with a 2×2 ANOVA with passage version and question type as within-subjects factors. Only the main effect of question type was significant, p < .05. The subjects correctly answered more factual questions (mean = 4.2 of 5) than inference questions (mean = 3.1 of 5).

Discussion

These results confirm both implications of the event-chain approach (cf. p. 153) to analyzing the difficulty of texts: (1) The time required to read a sentence is determined, in part, by whether it refers to an action, physical state, or mental state and, in part, by how easily the reader can causally link the action, physical state, or mental state to preceding ones. Deleting the immediate causes of actions and states has decremental effects on comprehension of sentences referring to those actions and states. To understand the text, readers must infer the missing causes in order to connect the actions and states to the underlying event chain. (2) Abridging a passage also affects the speed, but not the accuracy, with which factual questions about a text can be answered. Although inference questions are answered more slowly and less accurately than factual questions, text abridgements do not lower readers' accuracy in answering inference questions. Speed and accuracy in answering inference questions are separable aspects of question-answering.

The event-chain approach assumes that readers must segment texts into clauses, identify each clause as referring to either an action, physical state, or mental state, and then construct the causally connected event chain underlying the text. This model of text comprehension processes accurately predicts that readers will have difficulty inferring missing actions or states, slowing sentence comprehension and question answering. Of interest is whether or not the event-chain analysis of texts is useful in revising texts so as to render them more comprehensible. The following study examines this question.

IMPROVING COMPREHENSIBILITY

Readability formulas do not appear to be adequate as guides for revising texts to make them easier to read and understand (Duffy & Kabance, 1982; Klare, 1974/75). Reducing sentence length and substituting shorter or more familiar words do not guarantee that younger or less-skilled readers will be able to understand a difficult text. The inference load analysis of text difficulty identifies three components of text difficulty: the densities of stated and inferred mental states, and the density of stated physical states. The inference load of a text may be raised or lowered by subtracting or adding clauses referring to these states. The following study compares college students' comprehension of texts varying in both Flesch readability (1974) and inference load.

Method

The subjects were 32 undergraduates who participated as a course requirement for their introductory psychology class. All were native speakers of English.

The materials were four passages selected from the Pauk (1982) reading series. The average grade-level of each passage using Flesch's (1974) formula was 11.5. The passages were then rewritten lowering their difficulty by reducing sentence and word length.

Two coders analyzed the causal structure of each passage and determined the corresponding event chain of actions and states. The two versions differing in Flesch readability shared a common event chain. The coders then calculated the inference load of each passage using the formula described above and in Kemper (1983). The coders then rewrote each passage, to increase or lower their inference load.

These revisions resulted in four versions of each passage: The versions orthogonally contrasted two levels of Flesch readability and two levels of inference load. The four versions of each set differed in whether their Flesch readability was high (average = 11.5 grade) or low (average = 7.3 grade) and whether their inference load was high (average = 11.8) or low (average = 7.5 grade). Extracts from four versions of one set are given in Table 6.4.

Eight questions accompanied each passage. There were two types of questions: factual questions and inference questions. The answers to factual questions were explicitly stated in all four versions of the passage. The answers to the inference questions were not but could be inferred from information stated in the passage. The length of the questions varied across the sets of factual and inferential questions. Examples are given in Table 6.4. Inference questions averaged 8.1 words while factual questions averaged 9.2 words. Thus, differences in question-answering latency confound question type with length.

The subjects were tested individually. Each read four passages and answered eight questions about each passage. Each subject read one version from each set

TABLE 6.4

Extracts from four versions of one passage that vary orthogonally in inference load and Flesch readability. One factual and one inference question follow the extracts. The original passage is adapted from Pauk (1982).

Low Inference Load and Low Flesch Version

Low Inference Load and High Flesch Version

High Inference Load and Low Flesch Version

High Inference Load and High Flesch Version

A person moving on quiet feet can sneak right up to one of these unsuspecting critters. An armadillo doesn't seem to actually hear sounds in the air; instead it depends primarily on "feeling" ground vibrations. It must initially detect an unaccustomed vibration. It will push up on its haunches because it is trying to pinpoint by smell what has invaded its privacy.

High Inference Load and Low Flesch Version

A person moving on quiet feet can sneak right up. One of these critters will not suspect a thing. An armadillo doesn't seem to actually hear sounds in the air. It depends primarily on "feeling" ground vibrations. It must initially detect a new vibration. It will push up on its haunches. It is trying to pinpoint a smell. It will smell what has invaded its privacy.

Low Inference Load and High Flesch Version

A person moving on quiet feet can sneak right up to one of these unsuspecting critters. The person will not cause the ground to shake and will surprise the armadillo. An armadillo doesn't seem to actually hear sounds in the air. It depends primarily on "feeling" ground vibrations. It must initially detect an unaccustomed vibration. Then the armadillo will become curious and push up on its haunches to sniff the air. The armadillo will try to pinpoint by smell what has caused the ground to vibrate by invading its privacy.

Low Inference Load and Low Flesch Version

A person moving on quiet feet can sneak right up. One of these critters will not suspect a thing. The person will not cause the ground to shake. He will surprise the armadillo. An armadillo doesn't seem to actually hear sounds in the air. It depends primarily on "feeling" ground vibrations. It must initially detect a new vibration. Then the armadillo will become curious. It will push up on its haunches. It will sniff the air. The armadillo is trying to pinpoint a smell. It will smell what has caused the ground to vibrate. Then it will know what invaded its privacy.

Factual question: How can you sneak up to an armadillo?

(by moving on quiet feet)

Inference question: How well can an armadillo see?

(poorly)

159

and one passage with each combination of Flesch readability and inference load. For half the subjects, the four inferential questions preceded the four factual questions about each passage; for the other subjects, factual questions preceded inference questions. Sentence reading times could not be analyzed since the passage versions differed in sentence structure. Question-answering latencies and answer accuracy scores were collected as in the first study.

Results

Separate analyses of variance were used to analyze the mean number of questions answered correctly and the mean question-answering latencies. The question-answering latencies included the time to read a question and formulate an answer; the time to type in the answers was not recorded. Only the latencies for correct answers were analyzed since incorrect answers result from the subject's failure to understand the passage and remember the correct underlying event chain.

Accuracy.   A $2 \times 2 \times 2$ ANOVA was performed with Flesch readability (11th grade vs. 7th grade), inference load (high vs. low), and question type (factual vs. inference) was within-subject factors. In this analysis, only the main effect for inference load, $p < .01$, and the Flesch readability $\times$ inference load $\times$ question type interaction, $p < .01$, were significant (see Table 6.5).

Overall, lowering the inference load of the passages increased the accuracy of

TABLE 6.5

Results of the second study comparing question-answering latencies and accuracy scores when Flesch readability and inference load are orthogonally varied.

	Inference Load	
	High	Low
11th grade		
High Flesch readability		
Factual questions		
Latency	10.28 sec	10.31
Accuracy	78 %	90
Inference questions		
Latency	9.38 sec	7.48
Accuracy	58%	90
7th Flesch readability		
Factual questions		
Latency	10.17 sec	10.26
Accuracy	83 %	85
Inference questions		
Latency	9.26 sec	7.53
Accuracy	75 %	90

subjects' answers. The subjects' answers to factual questions were no more accurate than their answers to inference questions. Inspection of the significant three-way interaction reveals that inference questions were answered as accurately as factual questions for passages low in inference load regardless of their Flesch readability. However, for passages high in inference load and high in Flesch readability, factual questions were answered more accurately than inference questions. Yet for passages high in inference load and low in Flesch readability, factual questions were answered as accurately as inference questions. Apparently, when the overall difficulty of texts, as measured jointly by Flesch readability and inference load, is high, the subjects are unable to infer answers to the inference questions.

Latencies. A 2 × 2 ANOVA was performed on the mean question-answering latencies for each passage. Flesch readability, inference load, and question-type were within-subject factors. The results are given in Table 6.5.

The main effect for question type was significant, $p < .05$, as was the inference × question type interaction, $p < .05$.

As to be expected, the shorter inference questions (mean = 8.1 words) were answered more rapidly than the longer factual questions (mean = 9.2 words). Lowering the inference load of the passages facilitated answering the inference questions but had no effect on answering the factual questions.

The subjects answered inference questions about passages with low-inference loads more rapidly than ones about passages with high-inference loads.

Flesch readability had no effect on the question-answering latencies nor did it interact with inference load or question type.

Discussion

The inference load of a text did affect the speed and accuracy of subjects' answers. When the inference load of a text is increased from 7th- to 12th-grade reading levels, readers' accuracy in answering inference questions decreases 11% and their accuracy in answering factual questions decreases 24%. Further, the inference process that derives missing causal information to answer inference questions is slowed by the increase in inference load.

These results suggest that the event chain recovered from the text explicitly includes the answers to the factual questions. As the inference load of the texts increases, the event chain becomes less detailed; hence, subjects' accuracy in answering factual questions decreases. Although the event chains do not explicitly include the answers to the inference questions, an inference process similar to that used to construct the event chains can derive the answers. When the inference load of the texts is low, readers can accurately infer the answers but when inference is high, especially when the Flesch readability of the text is high, readers are unable to accurately infer the answers.

Simplifying the words and sentences of a text has little effect on the speed or accuracy of subjects' answers to questions about the text. Whether readers answer questions about explicitly stated facts or about plausible inferences from a text, their performance is similar for texts written at an 11th grade reading level and ones revised to a 7th grade reading level as measured by the Flesch readability formula.

Flesch readability affects text comprehension only when texts are already difficult to understand because they are high in inference load. The interaction of Flesch readability, inference load, and question type suggests Flesch readability measures a factor, sentence length, that affects how easily subjects can segment texts into clauses. When many causal inferences are required to construct the event chain underlying a text, subjects are less able to accurately segment long sentences into clauses. One interpretation of this effect is that subjects are less able to segment long sentences into clauses when they must also make many inferences; hence, some causal information is lost and the accuracy of answers to inference questions declines. Such an overload effect of Flesch readability is limited to texts high in inference loads and to inference questions.

CONCLUSION

There is an apparent discrepancy between the results of the first study and those of the second (see Table 6.6). In the first study, there was a loss of speed but no loss of accuracy for answers to factual questions with increases in the inference load of the passages; neither the speed nor accuracy of answers to inference questions were affected by inference load. In this study, the latencies for inferential questions as well as those for factual questions increased with the inference load of the passages. Increasing the inference load of the passages lowered the

TABLE 6.6

Effects of passage difficulty on college student's answers to factual and inference questions when grade level, as measured by the inference load formula, is systematically increased across a given range.

Increase in Inference Load grade level	Effect on question answering
13 > grade level > 15: (first study)	Speed traded for accuracy in answering factual questions No effect on inferential questions
10 > grade level > 13:	Loss of speed and accuracy in answering both factual and inference questions
7 > grade level > 11: (second study)	Loss of accuracy in answering both factual and inference questions Loss of speed in answering inference questions

accuracy of answers to inference questions but did not affect the accuracy of answers to factual questions. In other research, there was a loss of both speed and accuracy for answers to factual and inferential questions the inferential complexity of the passages increased (Kemper et al., 1985). The relative difficulty of the materials must be considered to explain these discrepancies.

As passage difficulty increases from 7th- to 11th-grade reading levels, the amount of information explicitly represented in the event chains declines, reducing the accuracy of answers to factual questions and increasing the difficulty, hence latency, of inferring answers to inference questions. As passage difficulty increases to 13th grade reading levels, the content of the event chains continues to decrease. As a result, there is a loss of both speed and accuracy for answers to inference questions; further, some answers to factual questions must be inferred and, hence, there is a loss of both speed and accuracy for answers to factual questions. As passage difficulty exceeds the reading level of the subjects, there is a further erosion of the content of the event chains. The answers to many factual questions must be inferred; however, speed can be traded for accuracy so there is no loss of accuracy. Once inference load exceeds the subjects' own reading level, they cannot construct a causally coherent event chain from the fragmentary information in the text. Further increases in inference load do not affect either the speed or accuracy of answers to inference questions as the subjects are unable to infer answers to the question regardless of how much time they allocate to the inference process.

This research on the effects of inference load on the event-chain analysis of texts has tested first year college students' understanding of texts ranging in difficulty from 7th to 15th (college junior) reading levels. Research in progress (Kemper, 1985) is investigating whether varying the inference load of a text can facilitate comprehension of readers from a wider range of grade levels. Results to date suggest that reducing the inference load of texts, relative to the reader's own grade level, does improve comprehension by 6th, 9th, and 12th grade students. The cumulative results support the proposed model of text comprehension: segmentation into syntactically defined clauses, identification of the clauses as referring to actions, physical states, and mental states, and the construction of a coherent event chain using these actions and states as well as ones inferred on the basis of a causal taxonomy.

ACKNOWLEDGMENTS

This research was supported by National Science Foundation grant IST-8110439. Portions of this chapter were presented at the annual meeting of the Midwestern Psychological Association, Chicago, May 6, 1983. Thanks to Nancy W. Denney, Meg Gerrard, Mabel Rice, and Maggie Schadler for their support and encouragement. Robert Estill, David Gleue, and Nelson Otalvaro helped to develop and test the inference load formula; I thank them for their assistance.

REFERENCES

Black, J. B., & Bower, G. H. (1979). Episodes as chunks in story memory. *Journal of Verbal Learning and Verbal Behavior, 18*, 309–318.

Black, J. B., & Bower, G. H. (1980). Story understanding as problem-solving. *Poetics, 9*, 223–250.

Bower, G. H., Black, J. B., & Turner, T. T. (1979). Scripts in text comprehension and memory. *Cognitive Psychology, 11*, 177–220.

Chafe, W. L. (1970). *Meaning and the structure of language*. Chicago: University of Chicago Press.

Dale, E., & Chall, J. S. (1948). A formula for predicting readability. *Educational Research Bulletin, 28*, 11–20.

Dale, E., & Chall, J. S. (1949). The concept of readability. *Elementary English, 26*, 19–26.

Daniel, C., & Wood, F. S. (1971). *Fitting equations to data: Computer analysis of multifactor data for scientists*. New York: Wiley-Interscience.

Duffy, T., & Kabance, P. (1982). Testing a readable writing approach to text revision. *Journal of Educational Psychology, 74*, 733–748.

Fillmore, C. S. A. (1968). The case for case. In E. Bach & R. H. Harms (Eds.), *Universals in linguistic theory*. New York: Holt, Rinehart & Winston.

Flesch, R. (1974). *The art of readable writing* (2nd Ed.). New York: Harper & Row.

Frederiksen, C. H. (1975). Representing the logical and semantic structure of knowledge acquired from discourse. *Cognitive Psychology, 7*, 374–458.

Graesser, A. C. (1981). *Prose comprehension beyond the word*. New York: Springer-Verlag.

Hirsch, E. (1977). *The philosophy of composition*. Chicago: University of Chicago Press.

Jarvella, R. J. (1971). Syntactic processing of connected speech. *Journal of Verbal Learning and Verbal Behavior, 10*, 409–416.

Kemper, S. (1982). Filling in the missing links. *Journal of Verbal Learning and Verbal Behavior, 21*, 99–107.

Kemper, S. (1983). Measuring the inference load of a text. *Journal of Educational Psychology, 75*, 391–401.

Kemper, S. (1984). The development of narrative skills. In S. A. Kuezaj (Ed.), *Discourse development*. Hillsdale, NJ: Lawrence Erlbaum Associates.

Kemper, S. (1985). *Facilitating comprehension by lowering inference load*. Unpublished manuscript. University of Kansas, Lawrence, KS.

Kemper, S., Otalvaro, N., Estill, R. B., & Schadler, M. (1985). Answering factual and inferential questions. In A. C. Graesser & J. B. Black (Eds.), *The psychology of questions*. Hillsdale, NJ: Lawrence Erlbaum Associates.

Kintsch, W., & van Dijk, T. A. (1978). Toward a model of text comprehension and production. *Psychological Review, 85*, 363–394.

Kintsch, W., & Vipond, D. (1975). Reading comprehension and readability in educational practice and psychological theory. In L. G. Nilsson (Ed.), *Memory: Processes and problems*. Hillsdale, NJ: Lawrence Erlbaum Associates.

Klare, G. (1974/75). Assessing readability. *Reading Research Quarterly, 10*, 62–102.

Lorge, I. (1939). Predicting the reading difficulty of selections for children. *Elementary English Review, 1*, 14–35.

McCall, W. A., & Crabbs, L. S. (1979). *Standard test lessons in reading*. New York: Teachers College Press, Columbia University.

Miller, G. A., & Johnson-Laird, P. N. (1976). *Language and perception.* Cambridge, MA: Harvard University Press.

Nicholas, D. W., & Trabasso, T. (1980). Toward a taxonomy of inference. In F. Wilkening, J. Becker, & T. Trabasso (Eds.), *Information processing by children.* Hillsdale, NJ: Lawrence Erlbaum Associates.

Norman, D. A., & Rumelhart, D. E. (1975). *Explorations in cognition.* San Francisco: Freeman.

Omanson, R. C., Warren, W. H., & Trabasso, T. (1978). Goals, inferential comprehension, and recall of stories by children. *Discourse Processes, 1,* 335–372.

Pauk, W. (1982). *Essential Skills Series.* Providence, RI: Jamestown.

Postal, P. (1974). *On raising.* Cambridge, MA: MIT Press.

Rosenbaum, P. R. (1967). *The grammar of English predicate complement constructions.* Cambridge, MA: MIT Press.

Sanford, A. J., & Garrod, S. C. (1981). *Understanding written language: Explorations in comprehension beyond the sentence.* Chichester, Great Britain: Wiley.

Schank, R. (1975). The structure of episodes in memory. In D. G. Bobrow & A. Collins (Eds.), *Representation and understanding.* New York: Academic Press.

Schank, R., & Abelson, R. (1977). *Scripts, plans, goals, and understanding: An inquiry into human knowledge structures.* Hillsdale, NJ: Lawrence Erlbaum Associates.

Turner, A., & Greene, E. (1977). *The construction of a propositional text base* (Technical Report). University of Colorado.

Warren, W. H., Nicholas, D. W., & Trabasso, T. (1979). Event chains and inferences in understanding narratives. In R. O. Freedle (Ed.), *New directions in discourse processing,* Vol. I. Hillsdale, NJ: Lawrence Erlbaum Associates.

7 Syntactic Complexity and
Reading Acquisition

Stephen Crain
Donald Shankweiler
University of Connecticut and Haskins Laboratories

INTRODUCTION

Learning to read is difficult for most people and complete mastery usually requires years of practice. In this paper we explore how the difficulties are related to linguistic structure. We focus primarily on one component of the language apparatus, the syntactic component, and consider the role of syntactic complexity in the problems of reading. These problems are most transparent at the early stages of learning, and therefore, it should prove most revealing to compare beginning readers who are progressing at the expected rate with those who are failing to make normal progress.

The approach we take assumes that the language faculty is composed of several autonomous subsystems, or modules. The modules are autonomous in the sense that they develop and function according to operating principles that are specific to them, i.e., not shared by other subsystems of language or other cognitive systems. Although these subsystems are intertwined in normal language use, experiments can be devised to disentangle them. The importance of this step has not always been recognized, however. We argue that failure to take account of the modular organization of language has led to many apparently conflicting findings concerning the syntactic competence of young children. We will show, moreover, that the concept of language as a modular system has important implications for understanding how reading is acquired and for interpreting the difficulties that so often arise.

A modular view of the language apparatus raises the possibility that a single component may be the source of reading difficulty. We assume that levels of language processing are organized in a hierarchical fashion and that the flow of

167

information is unidirectional and vertical ("bottom up") such that lower levels serve as input to higher levels and not the reverse. This means that if a lower-level component is implicated in reading difficulty, manifestations may appear at higher levels. A lower-level deficit may, therefore, masquerade as a complex of lower-level and higher-level deficits. We argue that this is what often happens in cases of childhood reading disability: the verbal short-term memory system, hereafter called working memory, which briefly retains a phonological record of the input, is largely responsible for difficulties in processing complex syntactic structures. In developing a modular approach to reading difficulties, we were influenced by the work of M. L. Kean (1977) on the analysis of language deficits in aphasia. By seeking a unified account of language problems associated with reading difficulties we may be able to move toward an explanation of what would otherwise look like an aggregate of individual differences between good and poor readers.

There are many unanswered questions about how reading exploits the language apparatus. In order to identify the questions and examine them it is important to say what we mean by the term "language apparatus." We use it to cover both linguistic structures and the processing systems that access and manipulate these structures. The structures include the language user's stored knowledge of rules of phonology, morphology, syntax, semantics, and pragmatics. The processing systems that invoke these structures include the verbal working memory system, the syntactic parsing mechanism, and the semantic and pragmatic processors.

Since our concern is not exclusively with the reading process but more generally with the question of what makes a sentence complex, we have found it appropriate, indeed necessary, to consider the problems associated with reading from the standpoint of language acquisition. For the most part these two aspects of cognitive development have been studied independently, but we have found compelling reasons to bring them together.

Broadly speaking, there are two ways to view the relationship between children's acquisition of language and the subsequent development of reading abilities. Each view of the relationship offers an explanation of the important facts about reading; namely, why it is hard to learn to read, and why reading, unlike speech, is not universal. The differences between the views are fundamental. Each conceives of syntactic complexity in a different way and each has a different conception of language acquisition. One view is that reading demands more syntactic competence than beginning readers have at their disposal. This view assumes that some aspects of syntax that are necessary for reading are not yet in place in the beginning reader. Since reading problems are seen as a result of missing structures, we call this position the Structural Deficit Hypothesis (SDH).

The second view locates the problem elsewhere. It supposes that most syntactic structures are mastered well before the child begins to learn to read, and therefore that the source of reading difficulty lies in the subsidiary mechanisms that are used in language processing, mechanisms that may require modification in order to accommodate print. This position is called the Processing Deficit Hypothesis (PDH).

These hypotheses are somewhat idealized, but they provide a framework from which to direct the search for causes of the difficulties encountered in mastery of reading, and each offers a distinctive perspective on the nature of syntactic complexity. In the later sections we consider how each hypothesis squares with research on language acquisition (section 3.A), with emphasis on one syntactic construction, the restrictive relative clause (3.B). We then focus on the plight of the poor reader; Section 3.C gives an account of an experiment designed to determine which hypothesis can best explain failures to comprehend sentences containing relative clauses. Section 3.D explores the implications of empirical findings showing that poor readers have problems with lower-level language operations. We raise there the possibility that these difficulties may, in turn, have ramifications for processing language structures at higher levels. We argue, moreover, that written language places special demands on the subsidiary language processors such that reading comprehension is often more limited than comprehension of spoken sentences.

On the empirical side, our conclusions are tentative; much research remains to be done. On the theoretical side, we offer a new perspective on reading and its problems—one that ties reading research more securely to current linguistic and psycholinguistic research.

2.   TWO HYPOTHESES ABOUT READING ACQUISITION

In this section we fully sketch the two hypotheses that were briefly introduced earlier. First we examine their different conceptions of the sources of syntactic complexity. From these conceptions are derived different explanations about what makes reading hard to learn. Ultimately our concern is with the different empirical predictions of the two hypotheses, since, in our view, one of the principal tasks of the psycholinguistics of reading is to discover which hypothesis comes closer to the truth.

A.   The Structural Deficit Hypothesis

The first proposal is based on the premise that some syntactic structures are inherently more complex than others. The supposition that linguistic materials are ordered in complexity invites an inference about the course of language acquisition; namely, that language acquisition proceeds in a stepwise fashion, beginning with the simplest structures and culminating only when the most complex structures have been mastered. This view of the course of language acquisition provides a foundation for hypotheses about learning to read and about the factors that distinguish good and poor readers. In this way, the SDH is intimately linked with a particular viewpoint on language development.

The SDH maintains that, at the time reading instruction begins, children are only partway through the course of language acquisition. If true, this hypothesis of gradually unfolding competence could explain why reading is delayed in most children until they are 5- to 7-years-of-age. Moreover, the difference between successful and unsuccessful readers could be attributed to further lags in primary language abilities in some children or to deficient instruction and/or experience with written language. This view may also contain implications for the role of experience. Although the early development of language requires only immersion in a speaking environment, the later development of language, as well as the early stages of reading, may require both graded inputs and extensive experience.

To develop this hypothesis further, we consider first the claim that syntactic structures differ in inherent complexity. As a case in point, it has been claimed that a sentence containing both a main clause and a subordinate clause, such as (2), is more complex than a coordinate structure, as in (1) (see section 3.B).

(1)   The dog hit a cat *and* bit a rat.
(2)   The dog hit a cat *that* bit a rat.

Syntactic differences between (1) and (2) can be gleaned from a cursory examination of the following, hypothetical tree-diagrams:

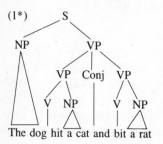

One difference is in the number of syntactic constituents in (1*) and (2*). Notice that there is a higher ratio of phrasal categories to words in (2*). Another difference is that (2*) but not (1*) contains a "missing" noun phrase, indicating that a constituent has been "moved" by transformational rule.

It is an empirical question whether or not these structural differences contribute to difficulties in processing either in speech or in reading (see Fodor & Garrett, 1967; Kimball, 1973). This possibility could be tested by measuring reaction-time latencies to sentences like (1) and (2) on some reading task that is sensitive to ease of processing. But in the research discussed here the indicator of the relative complexity of syntactic structures is the following: one structure is simpler than another if children can speak and comprehend it first. Returning to our examples, if sentences like (2) take longer to master than sentences like (1), this would be attributable to the relative complexity of (2*) as compared to (1*).

As we noted, the SDH makes an explicit prediction about reading acquisition: The structures that beginning readers and poor older readers find most difficult are just those that appear last in the course of language acquisition. Advocates of the SDH, then, would point to data on the late acquisition of specific structures in poor readers, particularly those structures underlying complex sentences (e.g., Byrne, 1981; Fletcher, Satz, & Scholes, 1981; Vogel, 1975). The SDH regards learning to speak and learning to read as continuous processes that tap the same cognitive abilities, but it is argued that reading is difficult largely because many of the primary linguistic abilities that support it are acquired late.

B. The Processing Deficit Hypothesis

We now introduce an alternative account of the fundamental facts of reading acquisition. Based on a different conception of linguistic complexity, this hypothesis supposes children have already acquired a great deal if not all of the primary linguistic apparatus by the time they begin to learn to read. But in addition to this, reading demands a number of secondary processing mechanisms to interface spoken language and an orthographic system of representation. These subsidiary mechanisms include verbal working memory, routines for identification of printed words, and the syntactic, semantic, and pragmatic processors.

Because many of the same structures are used in reading and speech, it is easy to overlook the possibility that reading may make special demands on the language processing systems beyond those required for speech. In speech processing, word identification, syntactic parsing, and semantic composition of word meanings are all highly automatic from the earliest stages of language acquisition. In reading, these processes must be reshaped to interface with a new input source. At the lowest level, a system for gaining access to the mental lexicon from print must be mastered to the point that it is both rapid and accurate. Until this is accomplished, higher-level processes such as syntactic parsing and semantic composition may be inhibited, reduced to a level far below the level at which they function in speech.

To make this discussion more concrete, suppose that working memory resources are exhausted by the task of identifying words from their orthographic representations. In that case, higher-level syntactic and semantic processing may be preempted. Much evidence exists that word recognition difficulties persist for a long time in early readers and that good and poor readers are sharply distinguished in orthographic ("decoding") skills (Gough & Hillinger, 1980; Perfetti & Hogaboam, 1975; Shankweiler & Liberman, 1972). If it could be shown further that when the pressures on working memory were reduced, beginning readers could comprehend structures that were otherwise problematic, this would provide confirmation for the PDH.

To develop this account, and to explain that the PDH offers a different view of syntactic complexity, we must consider further the implications of the early acquisition of syntax, a tenet we take to be central to this hypothesis. To this end, we draw upon the modularity hypothesis introduced earlier, which can be contrasted with the view that knowledge of language is a composite of more general cognitive faculties (for a recent statement, see J. A. Fodor, 1983). One tenet of the modularity thesis is the innate specification of language structures. Neurological evidence for the innateness of the language faculty is extensive. Among the facts that should be mentioned are the existence of special brain mechanisms present from birth, and evidence of dissociation between patterns of sparing and loss in language and other cognitive abilities in cases of brain damage (Dennis, 1980; Milner, 1974; Whitaker, 1976).

It is difficult to find psycholinguistic evidence that a *particular* linguistic structure, such as syntax, constitutes a submodule of the language component. Even the apparent innateness of some ability does not guarantee modular organization. An ability might, in principle, be innate and also multifactorial in composition. There are, however, some general guidelines for detecting modular organization, and tests for innateness are certainly among them. In the best case, an innate system could be expected to unfold rapidly, with much latitude regarding input from the environment, and with minimal interaction with concurrently developing systems (in Fodor's terms, "informationally encapsulated").

The acquisition of syntax adheres closely to these guidelines for innateness and, by extension, seems to conform to the modularity hypothesis. If the recent findings of early mastery of complex structures can be generalized (see section 3A), this would constitute strong empirical support for one tenet of linguistic theory, namely the hypothesis that there is an innately specified "Universal Grammar." The theory of Universal Grammar maintains that the language module develops into a rich and intricate system of rules much more rapidly than many other cognitive structures because of its innately specified content. Children seem to know too much too soon and they take too few wrong turns for the acquisition of language to be explained without supposing that it is both guided and constrained by innate principles (for further discussion, see Chomsky, 1971, 1975, 1981; Hamburger & Crain, 1984; and Lasnik & Crain, 1985).

Our specific concern here is with syntactic structure. If syntactic structure is largely built into the blueprint for development, then it makes little sense to ask if some syntactic constructions are harder to learn. Each construction simply develops in its own time, according to a predetermined schedule, regardless of its specific properties. In this way, the PDH calls into question the notion of linguistic complexity advanced by the SDH.

One possible advantage of modular organization, then, is that extreme structural complexity (by pretheoretic standards) can come "prewired." And what is not prewired may nonetheless be rapidly acquired, since the modular character of the linguistic system may endow it with heavy internal constraints on the types of hypotheses that a child can entertain. One way that children's grammar formation is believed to be constrained is in the structure-dependent nature of rules. A structure-dependent rule is one that is based on an abstract schema that partitions sequences of words into constituent structure. By contrast, a structure-independent rule, such as a simple counting rule, is applied directly to sequences of words themselves, without partitioning them into abstract functional units.

The theory of Universal Grammar maintains that children invariantly adopt structure-dependent rules in the course of grammar formation, eschewing structure-independent rules even when much of the available data is consistent with hypotheses of either type (Chomsky, 1971, 1975). Moreover, children are predicted to opt for structure-dependent rules even if structure-independent rules are computationally *less complex*. In the next section we present evidence of children's acquisition of an apparently complex rule at a time when a simpler rule would suffice.

To summarize, the two views we have presented make different predictions because they locate the source of reading difficulties in different components of the language apparatus. In essence, the views turn on the distinction between structure and process. On the first view there is a structural deficit, i.e., a deficit in stored knowledge. On the second view the problem is one of process, i.e., access and use of this stored knowledge. What is common to these hypotheses is that each attempts to locate the *causes* of reading difficulties. In this way they go beyond description and move towards explanation.

Each hypothesis attempts to account for the same basic facts about reading, but ultimately they diverge. Both predict that beginning readers will have difficulty reading some linguistic material, but on the SDH they should have trouble understanding complex linguistic structures even when these are presented in the speech mode. This hypothesis maintains that the late emergence of some structures places an upper bound on both the reading skills and the spoken language skills of the young reader. On the PDH, beginning readers will have achieved a high level of mastery of the grammatical operations that are required for speaking and understanding spoken sentences. The strongest version of the PDH would hold that all of the primary language apparatus is in place before formal instruction in reading begins. But even in this strong version, reading and writing will be acquired gradually, with some difficulty and with uncertain results, precisely because they tap abilities that may appear to be peripheral to the language module, though closely associated with it (Liberman, Shankweiler, Fischer, & Carter, 1974; Mattingly, 1972; 1984; Rozin & Gleitman, 1977; Shankweiler & Liberman, 1976). The PDH predicts that most beginning readers may be competent to deal with complex linguistic constructions in spoken language, whatever the attained level of reading skill, within the constraints imposed by their limitations in processing capacity.

It is important to point out, in this connection, that we are discussing performance here, and not competence. Poor readers' performance on complex sentences may often be faulty. But, according to the PDH, the failures in comprehension should be ascribed to secondary processing limitations, such as limitations on working memory, and not to lack of syntactic competence per se. Beginning readers and those with persisting difficulties may not be able to make use of their underlying grammatical competence because lower-level processing may preempt higher-level processing. Only by experimental means can we assess underlying competence when performance is faulty: the prediction of the PDH is that syntactic competence should be revealed in contexts that reduce the processing demands on the secondary language apparatus. In the next section we discuss how primary and secondary linguistic abilities may be successfully teased apart in studies of language acquisition.

3. IMPLICATIONS OF LANGUAGE ACQUISITION FOR READING

This section reviews aspects of language acquisition that are relevant to the two hypotheses about the sources of reading difficulty. The SDH distinctively predicts, as we noted, that relatively more complex linguistic structures emerge only at the later stages of language development. By contrast, the PDH predicts rapid acquisition of complex syntactic structures. As a test of this difference, the following experiment addresses the claim of Universal Grammar that children adopt only structure-dependent rules even if there exist viable alternative rules that appear to be considerably simpler. Following this, we shift our attention to the acquisition of another syntactic construction, the restrictive relative clause. We consider first its course of acquisition in normal development; then we present a study of the comprehension of this construction by good and poor readers.

A. Structure-Dependence in Language Acquisition

It is Chomsky's hypothesis that children unerringly adopt structure-dependent rules. To test this hypothesis Crain and Nakayama (in press) developed an experimental task, in the form of a game, to elicit yes/no questions that are amenable in principle either to structure-independent or structure-dependent analyses. For yes/no questions, the structure-independent strategy might be as follows:

Move the *first* "is" (or "can," "will" etc.) to the front of the sentence.

Notice that this principle gives the correct question forms for many simple sentences, as in (3).

(3) John is tall.   Is John tall?
     Mary can sing very well.   Can Mary sing very well?

Since the structure-independent strategy produces the correct forms in simple cases, and since it appears to be computationally simpler than the structure-dependent operation, we might expect some children to adopt it were it not precluded by Universal Grammar. However, the structure-independent rule produces incorrect question forms for more complex cases, as examples (4) and (5) illustrate.

(4) The man who is running is bald.
(5) *Is the man who __ running is bald?
(6) Is the man who is running __ bald?

Applying the structure-independent strategy to sentence (4) results in the ungrammatical question (5). The correct form (6) comes from the application of a rule that treats "the man who is running" as a constituent. It is the auxiliary verb following this constituent, the entire subject noun phrase, that must be fronted.

To discover whether children could be induced to give structure-independent responses such as (5), sentences like (7) were used.

(7) Ask Jabba if the man who is running is bald.

Sentences like (7) evoked corresponding yes/no questions from thirty 3- to 5-year-old children. These children were enjoined by one experimenter to pose questions about a set of pictures to Jabba the Hutt, a figure from "Star Wars," that was concurrently manipulated by a second experimenter. Following each question, Jabba would be made to look at the picture and give an appropriate response. This game was used to determine whether structure-independent questions such as (5) would be produced, as opposed to correct question forms like (6).

Crain and Nakayama found that the children *never* produced structure-independent utterances. Thus, the structure-independent strategy was not adopted in spite of its simplicity and in spite of the fact that it produces the correct question forms in many instances. Crain and Nakayama also provide evidence that even children as young as three base their rule for forming yes/no questions on the syntactic properties of sentences; they do not restrict its application to referential NPs, as claimed by Stemmer (1982), who advocates a *semantic* account of the acquisition of this construction. In this connection, Crain and Nakayama's subjects proved to be totally insensitive to the semantic properties of the noun phrases they encountered, which included abstract NPs (e.g., running, love) and expletives (e.g., it, there) in addition to referential NPs (e.g., the boy). Thus, yes/no question formation proved to be an instance of the developmental autonomy of syntax.

This experiment on structure-dependence serves to sustain the modularity hypothesis. Notice that each of the criteria of a modular system is met in this aspect of language development: early acquisition of complex structures, system-internal constraints on hypothesis testing, as illustrated by the formation of yes/no questions, and informational encapsulation, in the form of the developmental autonomy of syntax and semantics. It is worth emphasizing the importance of universal constraints on grammar formation, such as structure-dependence, for language learnability. By forestalling wrong turns that might otherwise be taken, these constraints obviate the need for ''negative data,'' which are presumably unavailable. The findings of Crain and Nakayama, then, provide striking support for the biological efficacy of Universal Grammar.

The concept of language as a modular system has implications both for the acquisition of syntax and for reading. If the language faculty is truly modular, then the primary language abilities of both good and poor readers should be in place before reading instruction begins. It is surprising that research addressing the comprehension of syntax by good and poor readers is so sparse. In the following section, we present the results of recent studies conducted by one of us on the acquisition of relative clauses by young children, and in section 3C we present a study, by the other author, that suggests that poor readers have these structures, though their processing of them is to some extent impaired.

B. The Acquisition of Relative Clauses

Full syntactic competence is revealed by performance with complex linguistic constructions such as the restrictive relative clause. This construction is complex in its syntactic, semantic, and pragmatic properties. For instance, because it is the product of a movement transformation, it contains a superficially empty noun phrase as one of its constituents. This empty constituent must be assigned an interpretation based on some overt noun phrase elsewhere in the sentence. Difficulties of interpretation may be encountered at sites like these where movement leaves a gap (indicated by "__" in (8)). At these positions principles of semantic interpretation must be applied. For instance, in sentence (8) the relative clause, "who we visited __ in Amherst," depends on the preceding noun phrase "the man" for its interpretation.

(8) The man who we visited __ in Amherst listens to WFCR.

Often, the head noun phrase of a restrictive relative clause refers to a set of entities in the surrounding context. Thus, a sentence like (8) would normally be used when more than one man has been introduced into the discourse. The set referred to by the general term "man" is then restricted in scope by the content of the clause; in the present example, reference is restricted to just the man who was visited in Amherst. Both of these properties of sentences containing relative clauses may contribute to processing complexity, and indeed, such sentences are frequently misinterpreted, especially by people with language impairment, like mentally retarded people (Crain & Crain, in preparation) and aphasics (Caramazza & Zurif, 1976).

The examples in (9) display four types of relative clauses, the characteristics of which are indicated by the preceding code letters. The first letter refers to the grammatical role of the noun phrase that bears the relative clause. In the first two examples the subject of the main clause is modified by a relative clause, whereas, in the last two examples, the relative clause is attached to the direct object. The second code letter refers to the grammatical role of the missing noun phrase in the relative clause. In the first and third examples, the relative clause has a missing subject. The direct object is superficially empty in the second and fourth. These varieties of relative clauses have received the greatest amount of attention in the literature (but also see deVilliers, Tager-Flusberg, Hakuta, & Cohen, 1979).

(9) SS The dog that — chased the sheep stood on the turtle.
     SO The dog that the sheep chased — stood on the turtle.
     OS The dog stood on the turtle that —chased the sheep.
     OO The dog stood on the turtle that the sheep chased —.

It is commonly believed that children even beyond the 5th year frequently misinterpret sentences with relative clauses, especially OS and SO relatives. Both Sheldon (1974) and Tavakolian (1981) found that many children would act out an OS relative, like the example above, by having the (toy) dog stand on the turtle and then chase the sheep. Tavakolian observed that this action sequence is a correct response to a sentence in which the two clauses are conjoined, as in (10).

(10) The dog stood on the turtle and chased the sheep.

This kind of misinterpretation led Tavakolian to suggest that children younger than six have not yet developed the grammatical competence needed to comprehend syntactic structures as complex as relative clauses. She argued that the "conjoined-clause" response reflects a stage of acquisition at which children have not yet attained full competence with the hierarchical constituent structure of relative clauses. She points out further that children are already productively using conjoined clauses at the age at which they misinterpret relative clauses (cf. Brown, 1973; Limber, 1973). It was concluded, therefore, that they tend to adopt a less differentiated conjoined-clause analysis when confronted with sentences with relative clauses, until some later stage of acquisition.

Although Tavakolian's conjoined-clause hypothesis is still widely accepted, several researchers have found that children can be diverted from the conjoined-clause response to relatives by careful selection of test sentences. Solan and Roeper (1978) found that sentences containing relative clauses evoke very different error rates depending on their semantic content. Their subjects produced more errors with sentences like (11) than with sentences like (12), which contain a relative clause that can be interpreted more naturally as modifying the object of the matrix sentence rather than its subject. In addition, Goodluck (1978) found that children made fewer incorrect responses when the number of *animate* noun phrases was reduced, as in (13).

(11)   The dog kicked the sheep that jumped over the pig.
(12)   The girl petted the sheep that licked the cow.
(13)   The dog kicked the sheep that jumped over the fence.

In accord with the PDH, these findings favor a performance account, rather than a competence account, of children's errors. Given that children misinterpret only a subset of sentences bearing the same structure, a nonstructural explanation of their errors seems to be required.

A direct test of the conjoined-clause hypothesis was conducted using a picture verification paradigm (Crain, Epstein, & Long, in preparation). In this study, 3- to 5-year-old children heard sentences containing relative clauses like (14). Then they were asked to select one of two pictures, which depicted the events expressed in sentences (14) and (15). According to the conjoined-clause hypothesis, children should have preferred the picture corresponding to (15).

(14)   A cat is holding hands with a man that is holding hands with a woman.
(15)   A cat is holding hands with a man and is holding hands with a woman.

Conjoined-clause responses were evoked only 10% of the time in this task. That is, children matched sentences containing relative clauses with the appropriate pictures and not with pictures representing a conjoined clause interpretation of the sentence. This finding suggests that children's misinterpretations of OS relatives in earlier studies should not be viewed as a reflection of incomplete syntactic development. Instead, misinterpretations in these studies were probably attributable to task complexity. By contrast, the picture verification technique appears to be a simple and direct test of comprehension. Sentences like (14), tested in this way, proved to be well within the capacity of three-year-old children.

Additional evidence that children have mastered the relative clause comes from an elicited production study by Hamburger and Crain (1982) who found that 4-year-old children consistently produced and understood restrictive relative clauses in contexts that were appropriate for them but inappropriate for conjoined clauses. These authors argue that previous research ignored what they called the "felicity conditions" on the use of relative clauses. One felicity condition is that the events depicted by the relative clause are presupposed to be true. For example, an utterance of sentence (16) is normally felicitous only if it is already known to both speaker and hearer that a particular cow has previously jumped over some contextually salient fence.

(16)   The sheep pushed the cow that jumped over the fence.

A second pragmatic constraint, noted above, requires that there be a set of objects corresponding to the head noun of the relative clause. In the present example, there should be at least one other cow from whom the fence-jumper needs to be distinguished. The relative clause serves to restrict the set, in this case to the cow that jumped the fence. If this constraint is not met, i.e., if only a single cow is present, the sentence without the relative clause (i.e., "The sheep pushed the cow") would convey as much information. In the experiments cited above (that evoked high error rates), sentences like (16) were used with only one cow present in the experimental workspace. This fact alone may have resulted in poor performance by children except, perhaps, when other processing demands were sufficiently reduced. As noted, poor performance has sometimes been attributed to children's ignorance of the syntactic rules for relative clause construction. Suppose, however, that a child had mastered not only the syntax of relative clauses, but also the presuppositions associated with their use. Such a child might still be unable to relate sentences with relative clauses to the (inappropriate) circumstances provided by the experiment. Hamburger and Crain propose that the failure to satisfy presuppositions renders sentences quite unnatural in the experimental context, encouraging subjects to think of the task as unrelated to normal contextually sensitive language use. If so, their responses would not be indicative of their grammatical knowledge.

This brief review shows that different tasks and procedures lead to different conclusions about the acquisition of complex syntax. Resolution of these conflicting results is important for reaching a decision on whether the SDH or the PDH gives a better account of the source of reading difficulty. We would appeal to the competence-performance distinction as an aid to resolve the conflict. Since performance and not competence is what is directly observed, negative findings are not necessarily indicative of children's incompetence. Though elusive, syntactic competence can be revealed in contexts that minimize semantic and pragmatic processing complexities. By eliciting successful performance in these controlled contexts, we can be confident that competence exists.

These observations underscore the need to disentangle aspects of structure and process. We have just seen that if a test sentence contains presuppositions that go unheeded in an experimental task, it cannot validly assess a subject's knowledge of syntax. The fact that syntax, semantics, inference, and so forth, are normally interwoven in discourse makes it difficult to isolate any one of these, even by experimental design. Although these methodological problems may seem obvious when pointed out, a large proportion of the existing research both on normal and language-impaired populations has paid them little heed. As a result, the research literature may give a misleading picture of the linguistic competence of young children, portraying them as ignorant of complex structures until well after the age at which reading instruction begins. Thus, much of the research appears to support the SDH. However, a reinterpretation of the empirical findings on the acquisition of syntax leads to a different conclusion. Several recent studies, which have respected the methodological problems we have been discussing, seem to show that even 3-year-old children have acquired the complex syntax denied by earlier investigators. These findings, then, support the PDH.

C. Comprehension of complex syntax by good and poor readers

Until now we have not discussed the problems of the poor reader directly. We have presented several issues in the assessment of syntactic competence in young children, and attempted to show how these issues bear on the two hypotheses about the nature of the obstacles that lie in the way of becoming a good reader. We are now ready to apply the findings on language acquisition to the problems of learning to read with comprehension.

The literature we have reviewed on the acquisition of the restrictive relative clause has shown that very young children sometimes produce and comprehend complex syntactic structures of this sort. We know, however, from other work, including the findings presented in this section, that even much older (school-age) children who are poor readers have difficulties understanding complex spoken sentences, including those containing restrictive relative clauses. Our task in this section is to explain how the difficulties in understanding these structures might have arisen. To that end, we present the results of a recent study designed to locate the source of comprehension failures in poor readers, using a variety of sentences containing the restrictive relative clause. These studies underscore many of the theoretical and methodological problems that concerned us in the preceding discussion.

In the light of the foregoing findings on young children, it is to be expected that relative clause structures should already be well established in the internalized grammars of 8- or 9-year-old children. It is conceivable, however, that even by this age some children (i.e., poor readers) may have attained only partial mastery of these structures. It is important to find out whether certain forms of relative clause structure are missing from their grammars, because, as we have argued, if poor readers were absolutely unable to comprehend some types of restrictive relative clauses, this would be strong support for the SDH.

According to the PDH the difference between good and poor readers should be one of degree. The PDH, too, would predict that poor readers would have difficulties understanding complex structures such as relative clauses, but crucially, they should not fail to comprehend them altogether. If they give the same pattern of responses as good readers, but do not achieve as high a rate of success, this would support the PDH. In this event, we would have to go on to ask what secondary processing mechanisms must be invoked to explain their difficulties.

We now discuss in some detail the results of an experiment that attempts to test directly the possibility that a certain processing deficit is responsible for poor readers' difficulties in understanding complex sentences not only in reading but also in spoken language. As we will see, the answer turns on the role of working memory in processing connected discourse. In spoken language comprehension, only structures that severely stress working memory will be expected to cause notable difficulties. We maintain that comprehension difficulties that are manifested in spoken language will be magnified in reading because reading places greater demands than speech processing on limited working memory resources. Until orthographic decoding skills are mastered and highly practiced, a reader cannot be expected to perform with print up to the ceiling set by performance in spoken language. The comparison between speech and reading is treated in the next section (3D), and at greater depth in Shankweiler and Crain (1986). See also Perfetti (1985) and Perfetti and Lesgold (1977).

Comprehension and recall of complex sentences containing four relative clause structures (as in sample sentences (9) above) were studied by Mann, Shankweiler, & Smith (1984). The children's comprehension was tested first, using a toy manipulation paradigm; on a later day, the taped sentences were presented again and rote recall was tested. Both tests were administered to the same groups of good and poor readers in the 3rd grade.

The experiment was designed to hold certain processing demands constant while varying the type of relative clause structure. Each of the test sentences mentioned three (animate) objects. As the examples in (9) illustrate, each set of test sentences mentioned the same objects, and each set contained the same ten words. Therefore, any differences in their meanings were carried by syntactic structure. The importance of controlling sentence length in a test of this kind is well recognized. Indeed, readability formulas assume that this is the most important variable in determining ease of understanding (Dawkins, 1975). But, as we will see, structure has large effects on comprehensibility that are independent of length.

The good and poor readers in this study were compared both with respect to the kinds of errors that occurred and the way these errors were distributed between the groups. As to the kinds of errors, it was expected that a conjoined-clause response might more often be made by poor readers than by good readers. This could mean that poor readers are heavily influenced by nonsyntactic processing factors, just as younger normal children are. Alternatively, these responses could imply, as the SDH would predict, that the grammars of poor readers are less differentiated than those of normal adults and more mature children of the same age.

The way the errors are distributed is also relevant to the two hypotheses. If there exists a specific syntactic deficiency over and above the difficulties of processing, we would expect, other things being equal, to find a different pattern of accuracy between groups on the four sentence types. Figure 7.1 displays the mean errors for each of the four sentence types, separately for good and poor readers. As expected, the types were not equal in difficulty. The poor readers

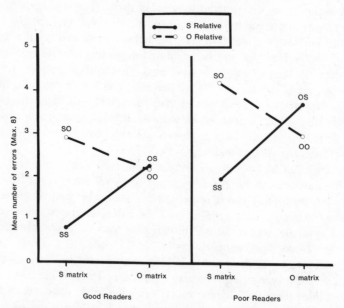

FIGURE 7.1.   Mean errors of good and poor readers in the third grade on four types of relative clause constructions (from Mann, Shankweiler, & Smith, 1984).

made more errors than the good readers on each. But when the four types were ranked in order of difficulty for good and poor readers separately, the ordering was the same for both groups. The lack of statistical interaction means that the poor readers were generally worse than the good readers in comprehension of relative clause sentences, but within this broad class, they were affected by syntactic variations in the same way as the good readers. The results give no evidence, then, that the poor readers in this study were deficient on any facet of the grammar pertaining to the interpretation of these relative clause sentences. The competence they displayed was essentially like that of the good readers.

We must nevertheless account for the fact that the poor readers made somewhat more errors than the good readers on the comprehension of each type of relative clause sentence. A likely explanation is found by comparing the groups on the test of rote recall of the sentences. As we noted earlier, the taped sentences were presented to the children a second time on another day and immediate recall was tested. In working memory for the sentences, as in the previous test of comprehension, the poor readers made significantly more errors than the good readers, and, again, the differences between the groups did not favor one type of sentence more than another. These results fit well with much earlier work that indicates that poor readers do consistently less well than good readers on a variety of tests of verbal working memory (see Jorm, 1979; Mann, Liberman, & Shankweiler, 1980; Shankweiler, Liberman, Mark, Fowler, & Fischer, 1979).

In keeping with the modularity hypothesis, it is important to appreciate that the memory deficits of poor readers are largely limited to verbal material. Tests of working memory for nonverbal material, such as unfamiliar faces and nonsense designs, do not distinguish good and poor readers (Katz, Shankweiler, & Liberman, 1981; Liberman, Mann, Shankweiler, & Werfelman, 1982). Thus the failure of the poor readers to do as well as the good readers on the test of sentence comprehension is probably largely a reflection of specifically linguistic working memory limitations on the part of the poor readers. But it is a limitation on efficiency of linguistic processing and not a limitation of structural competence. To make a further test of this possibility, it will be important to find out if poor readers have a higher success rate when the same structures are placed in contexts that minimize, not just control for, processing demands (such as presuppositions and parsing) that are otherwise confounded with syntactic complexity.

Having discussed the basis of poor readers' difficulties in sentence understanding in speech, we now turn to the consequences of these problems for reading. We have cited the evidence that poor readers have special limitations in use of the verbal working memory system that supports on-line language processing. We can now guess how handicapping such a limitation must be for reading, since the poor reader is also generally slow in decoding the individual words of the text. If the individual words are read too slowly, comprehension suffers, even if all the words are read correctly, because the integrative processes are disturbed by the slow rate of input. Perfetti and his colleagues have suggested that working memory limitations create a "bottleneck" that restricts the utilization of the higher level language processing systems, preventing proper comprehension of what is read (see, e.g., Perfetti & Lesgold, 1977).

The bottleneck hypothesis takes us some distance toward an explanation of the high correlation that has repeatedly been noted between (1) the speed and accuracy of identifying words and pseudowords in isolation, and (2) various measures of reading comprehension (Calfee, Venezky, & Chapman, 1969; Perfetti & Hogaboam, 1975; Shankweiler & Liberman, 1972). We view this correlation as a particularly strong indication that a low-level deficit can give rise to apparent deficits at higher levels. Because syntactic structure and propositional content are conveyed by sequences of words, it is generally supposed that working memory is needed for sentence comprehension, whether by speech or by reading. Since the verbatim record of incoming speech or printed text is extremely fleeting, the input to the working memory system is lost unless it is rapidly converted into a more durable form (Sachs, 1967). Because the working memory representation is so brief in duration and so limited in span, it has been proposed that the sentence parsing mechanism works rapidly on small chunks of text to decode linguistic information into more durable memory representations (Frazier & Fodor, 1978; Liberman, Mattingly, & Turvey, 1972).

We conclude this section with some remarks on the role of context in determining whether or not a sentence will be understood. Consider first the role context plays in spoken language comprehension. It was seen that children who are poor readers sometimes fail to comprehend spoken sentences that impose heavy processing demands on working memory. It was not easy, however, to demonstrate that poor readers are not as adept as good readers in sentence processing. The problems of the poor reader are ordinarily well-masked; they are revealed only under rather stringent conditions of testing, without contextual supports, in the "null context" (see Crain & Steedman, 1985). The difficulty in bringing these problems to light should not surprise us. Under ordinary conditions, listeners do have contextual support. It is only when we artificially deprive poor readers of this support that they are apt to fail. When support is available, 10-year-old poor readers display clear ability to benefit from it (Perfetti, Goldman, & Hogaboam, 1979). This too is not surprising. We have shown that even 3- and 4-year-old children are able to understand complex sentences in appropriate contexts.

In reading, the situation is complicated by the demands of orthographic decoding. It is obvious that young poor readers have a problem in comprehending complex sentences that are set down in print. But why can't they use context here as effectively as they do in perception of spoken sentences? Our response is that a working memory limitation has a more profound effect on reading comprehension than on comprehension of speech. As noted earlier, the beginning reader is required to develop a whole new apparatus for word recognition, incorporating a set of rules for getting from the orthography to preexisting lexical entries. Until the rules and the strategies for invoking their use are automatized, the would-be reader cannot use syntactic and pragmatic context effectively, because nearly the whole of the processing capacity is consumed by lower-level functions. This, we assume, is the point of the bottleneck hypothesis of Perfetti and his associates. The remainder of this section is concerned with working out the detailed implications of poor readers' lower-level deficits for performance on sentence processing tasks.

D. Consequences of a Low-Level Deficit for Higher-Level Processing

The preceding section gives a rough sketch of the source of comprehension difficulties that plague the beginning reader and many others who, though no longer beginners, are still struggling to gain mastery. If our analysis is on the right track, we have now moved beyond the stage of identifying correlates of reading difficulties. To the extent that we now have the beginnings of a theory, we stand in a position to make fairly detailed predictions about what will be difficult for children to read and to offer tentative suggestions about how these difficulties might be circumvented.

Since our concern here is with sentence understanding, our predictions involve syntactic structures and the mechanism that invokes them. We have no reason to suppose that different mechanisms perform this function in reading than in speech. But the bottleneck hypothesis anticipates that the syntactic parsing mechanism will be less efficient in reading at the early stages, when the reader is preoccupied with the identification of words in print. The poor beginning reader, as we saw, labors under a double handicap, since he or she has less than normal working memory capacity to begin with. In this section we discuss two ways that a working memory deficit may affect syntactic parsing: limitations in the use of syntactic parsing strategies, and the consequent overreliance on nonsyntactic parsing strategies.

The syntactic parser is a processor that tends to favor certain structures where more than one grammatical possibility exists partway through a sentence. Demonstrated parsing preferences have been used as an indicator of the relative complexity of syntactic structures. The subject's resolution of structural ambiguities is accomplished by decision-making strategies. Parsing strategies are used on line for ambiguity resolution, but they do not always result in the adoption of the correct structural analysis. When a listener or a reader is led to expect one particular syntactic organization by the first part of the sentence but is later required to reinterpret the structure, one might say that the perceiver has been led down a "garden path." As a consequence of limited working memory storage we would expect poor readers to show greater susceptibility to garden path effects.

Eye movements in reading can reveal these garden path effects, in the view of

Frazier and Rayner (1982). These investigators measured eye fixation times during sentences that would demand restructuring if the syntactic parsing strategy "Minimal Attachment" was being used (Frazier & Fodor, 1978). This is a parsing strategy that induces the reader to resolve local ambiguities most economically, by using the fewest possible nonterminal nodes in the constituent structure being assigned to the fragment of the sentence currently under analysis. Minimal Attachment predicts that a garden path will be pursued in example (17).

(17)   John believed the big burly policeman was lying.

The minimal analysis of the noun phrase beginning "the big. . ." would assign it the grammatical role of Direct Object of "believe." But "believe" also permits a Sentential Complement, and, in this example, the phrase "the big burly policeman was lying" serves this grammatical role. Since sentence parsing strategies are applied on-line, according to Frazier and Fodor, the Direct Object analysis should be pursued first, producing a garden path effect when the word "was" is encountered, since it is this word that indicates the necessity for reanalysis.

Investigation of eye movements in reading sentences like (17) revealed that eye fixations are prolonged on the word that was predicted to initiate reorganization, indicating that the Minimal Attachment analysis had been adopted (Frazier & Rayner, 1982). Measurement of eye movements is useful not only in evaluating models of the sentence processing mechanism by which structural ambiguities are resolved, but it can also potentially inform us about differences in the use of this mechanism by good and poor readers. One testable hypothesis, using the eye-fixation tracking technique, is that poor readers are less likely than good readers to recover from garden paths because of their working memory limitations (see Shankweiler & Crain, 1986, for further discussion of this hypothesis).

The need for working memory in sentence processing might seem to be vitiated by parsing strategies, such as Minimal Attachment, that have the parser operate on small segments of speech or text. In our view, however, the existence of on-line strategies strengthens, not weakens, the argument that working memory plays an essential role in language processing. As Frazier and Fodor (1978) point out, the fact that verbal working memory decays rapidly and has limited capacity requires parsing decisions to be made quickly. Since for many poor readers, working memory limitations are even greater than normal, we would expect them to be more dependent on these on-line strategies for ambiguity resolution.

Overreliance on nonsyntactic processing strategies is another expected manifestation of a working memory limitation. For example, upon encountering a pronoun in extended text, the reader must initiate a search for a referent. Although there are syntactic constraints on which noun phrases can serve as legitimate antecedents (Lasnik, 1976), we expect working memory limitations to lead poor readers to adopt nonsyntactic strategies based on proximity rather than hierarchical structure. In a recent study of this problem, it was found that poor readers tend to rely on a minimal distance strategy more often than good readers in determining the reference of reflexive pronouns, although the difference did not reach significance statistically (Shankweiler, Smith, & Mann, 1984).

It is worth emphasizing again that even rigid adherence to a structure-independent strategy by poor readers would not necessarily be indicative of syntactic incompetence, since there are so many other factors besides syntax involved in sentence understanding. Parsing preferences must be neutralized or factored out when the objective is assessment of active mastery of a particular syntactic structure. It is crucial that a subject's proclivity to use one structure at the expense of another must not be taken uncritically to indicate an incapacity to use the latter (Crain & McKee, 1986; Hamburger & Crain, 1984; Lasnik & Crain, 1985).

4. SUMMARY AND CONCLUSIONS

Previous research extending across languages and cultures indicates that the abilities that distinguish successful and unsuccessful readers are primarily in the language domain and not in the general cognitive domain, or in visual processing (Katz, Shankweiler, & Liberman, 1981; Liberman et al., 1982; Liberman & Shankweiler, 1985). Our focus, within this domain, has been on the relevance of syntactic complexity to reading acquisition and difficulties in comprehending text. We argued that in order to understand the special problems of comprehension in reading, we must address the problems of sentence understanding more broadly, by considering comprehension of speech as well. In pursuing these questions about the nature of syntactic complexity, we appealed to the distinction between structure and process, a distinction that enabled us to identify two possible sources of linguistic complexity in understanding spoken and written sentences. On one view, linguistic structures are taken to be ordered in complexity; on the other, it is not the structures themselves that make comprehension difficult, but the demands these structures make on the subsidiary processing mechanisms, especially verbal working memory.

Distinct predictions about the course of language acquisition arose from the different views of linguistic complexity. On the one hand, by adopting the thesis that language is a self-enclosed system, a module, the PDH predicts rapid acquisition of complex structures. On the other hand, a premise of the SDH is that some structures are inherently more complex than others. This would lead one to predict gradual, staged acquisition. These different conceptions of the course of language acquisition, in turn, yield different ways of viewing the problems of the beginning reader and the older unsuccessful reader. The SDH holds that these groups may not have acquired some of the language structures needed for learning to read successfully. The alternative is that the beginning reader has the language structures but has not yet managed to construct an efficient interface between these preexisting structures and the orthography, nor is he able to integrate the words of the text into higher order structures because of limitations on working memory. Each hypothesis can account for most of the basic facts about reading, and indeed, each often makes the same predictions. However, they identify different causes for failure to comprehend complex sentences, and these difference are amenable to empirical test.

Having developed the predictions, the next step was to examine the relevant empirical findings. First, it was shown that complex structures such as restrictive relative clauses and yes/no questions could be elicited successfully from children as young as three. These studies supported the rapid-acquisition scenario that the modularity hypothesis predicts and offered no support for the alternative staged-acquisition view. This led us to the second step in our argument. We asked whether subsidiary language mechanisms and not the language structures themselves might be the source of observed difficulties in the comprehension of complex syntax in reading. We expected the early stages of learning to read to be the most revealing. Accordingly, we sought an answer to this question by examining good and poor readers in the early grades. Studies of good and poor readers were presented that confirmed earlier claims that poor readers have difficulties in understanding complex sentences even when presented in spoken form. But these studies went on to suggest that the source of these difficulties was not a syntactic deficit as such. Instead, we found that good and poor readers were distinguished in efficiency of working memory, a subsidiary processing mechanism, rather than in syntactic competence. It is not clear whether the limitation is in the capacity of working memory per se, or whether it is in the "executive" or control component (Baddeley & Hitch, 1974). In Shankweiler and Crain (1986) we speculate that the control component of verbal memory is the site of the primary problem. In all events, the memory constraint would be expected to show up beyond sentence boundaries, for example, in relating pronouns to their antecedents.

In the preceeding section, we examined the implications of working memory limitations of the poor reader for the reading process itself. Building on the bottleneck hypothesis of Perfetti and his associates, we explained how a working memory limitation could be expected to inhibit higher-level processing of text, by slowing word decoding and making it less accurate. This perspective tells us why poor readers are far less able to understand complex sentences in print than in speech, and it also explains their difficulties with spoken language. Finally, this hypothesis yields fairly specific predictions about the strategies for syntactic parsing on which beginning readers and poor readers should be expected to rely (although the research to test these predictions has not yet been done).

It follows from the bottleneck hypothesis that if our goal is to increase reading comprehension in beginning readers and unsuccessful readers, the first priority is to improve skills in recognizing printed words. It was argued that deficits implicating lower-level components in the structural hierarchy may have important repercussions at higher levels. In this connection, we would add that there is evidence that the abilities that underlie word decoding can be successfully taught at any age (see Liberman & Shankweiler, 1985; Liberman, Shankweiler, Blachman, Camp, & Werfelman, 1980). If we are correct in our other conclusion that the syntactic structures needed for sentence interpretation are already in place long before children actually encounter these structures in print, then the main thrust of efforts to improve reading should be directed to the inculcation of those lower-level skills that pertain to use of the orthography. Only then can the working memory system be used effectively to gain access to the higher level syntactic, semantic, and pragmatic structures.

The position we have developed has definite implications, we believe, for the design and evaluation of appropriate text materials for beginning readers. It has long been appreciated that the beginning reader has special needs, but what these needs are has often been misunderstood. If the acquisition of the relative clause is indicative of the syntactic capacities of beginning readers, we should suppose that text designed for beginners need not simplify sentence structure. Since, in fact, the child of five or six is producing complex sentences in appropriate contexts, the avoidance of these complex structures in the text would likely be perceived as unnatural.

The findings we presented on early acquisition of complex structures suggest a caution, however. Complex syntactic structures, when used in reading materials, should appear in contexts that satisfy the presuppositions on their use, if good comprehension is to be achieved. We have seen that children as old as ten may have difficulties comprehending some sentences containing relative clauses, when these presuppositions are not met. One can expect, then, that without contextual supports, young children will often fail to display successful comprehension, but with these supports even texts containing complex syntactic structures may be read with understanding.

ACKNOWLEDGMENT

Portions of this research were supported by NSF Grant BNS 84-18537, and by a Program Project Grant to Haskins Laboratories from the National Institute of Child Health and Human Development (HD-01994). We would like to thank Alice Davison and Ignatius Mattingly for their comments on earlier drafts.

REFERENCES

Baddeley, A. D., & Hitch, G. B. (1974). Working memory. In G. H. Bower (Ed.), *The psychology of learning and activation* (Vol. 4). New York: Academic Press.

Brown, R. (1973). *A first language.* Cambridge, MA: Harvard University Press.

Byrne, B. (1981). Deficient syntactic control in poor readers: Is a weak phonetic memory code responsible? *Applied Psycholinguistics, 2,* 201–212.

Calfee, R. C., Venezky, R., & Chapman, R. (1969). *Pronunciation of synthetic words with predictable and unpredictable letter-sound correspondences.* (Tech. Rep. No. 71) Madison: Wisconsin Research and Development Center.

Caramazza, A., & Zurif, E. B. (1976). Dissociation of algorithmic and heuristic processes in language comprehension: evidence from aphasia. *Brain and Language, 3,* 572–582.

Chomsky, N. (1971). *Problems of knowledge and freedom.* New York: Pantheon Books.

Chomsky, N. (1975). *Reflections on language,* New York: Pantheon Books.

Chomsky, N. (1981). *Lectures on government and binding: The Pisa lectures.* Dordrecht, Holland: Foris Publications.

Crain, S., & Crain, W. M. (in preparation). *Restrictions on the comprehension & relative clauses by mentally retarded adults.* Unpublished manuscript, University of Connecticut. University of Massachusetts, Amherst, MA.

Crain, S., Epstein, S., & Long, Y. (in preparation). *Syntactic theory as a theory of language acquisition.* Unpublished manuscript, University of Connecticut.

Crain, S., & McKee, C. (1986). Acquisition of structural restrictions on anaphora. Proceedings of the *North Eastern Linguistics Society* (Vol. 16) University of Massachusetts, Amherst.

Crain, S., & Nakayama, M. (in press). Structure dependence in grammar formation. *Language, 63.*

Crain, S., & Steedman, M. (1985). On not being led up the garden path: The use of context by the syntactic processor. In D. R. Dowty, L. Karttunen, & A. Zwicky (Eds.), *Natural language parsing: Psychological, computational, and theoretical perspectives.* London: Cambridge University Press.

Dawkins, J. (1975). *Syntax and readability.* Newark, DE: International Reading Association.

Dennis, M. (1980). Capacity and strategy for syntactic comprehension after left or right hemidecortication. *Brain and Language, 10,* 287–317.

deVilliers, J. G., Tager-Flusberg, H. B. T., Hakuta, K., & Cohen, M. (1979). Children's comprehension of relative clauses. *Journal of Psycholinguistic Research, 8,* 499–518.

Fletcher, J. M., Satz, P., & Scholes, R. (1981). Developmental changes in the linguistic performance correlates of reading achievement. In *Brain and Language, 13,* 78–90.

Fodor, J. A. (1983). *The modularity of mind.* Cambridge, MA: MIT Press.

Fodor, J. A., & Garrett, M. (1967). Some syntactic determinants of sentential complexity. *Perception and Psychophysics, 2,* 289–296.

Frazier, L., & Fodor, J. D. (1978). The sausage machine: A new two-stage parsing model. *Cognition, 6,* 291–325.

Frazier, L., & Rayner, K. (1982). Making and correcting errors during sentence comprehension: Eye movements in the analysis of structurally ambiguous sentences. *Cognitive Psychology, 14,* 178–210.

Goodluck, H. (1978). *Linguistic principles in children's grammar of complement subject interpretation.* Unpublished doctoral dissertation, University of Massachusetts.

Gough, P. B., & Hillinger, M. L. (1980). Learning to read: An unnatural act. *Bulletin of the Orton Society, 30,* 179–196.

Hamburger, H., & Crain, S. (1984). Acquisition of cognitive compiling. *Cognition, 17,* 85–136.

Hamburger, H., & Crain, S. (1982). Relative acquisition. In S. Kuczaj, II (Ed.), *Language development: Syntax and semantics* (pp. 245–274). Hillsdale, NJ: Lawrence Erlbaum Associates.

Jorm, A. (1979). The cognitive and neurological basis of developmental dyslexia: A theoretical framework and review. *Cognition, 7,* 19–33.

Katz, R. B., Shankweiler, D., & Liberman, I. Y. (1981). Memory for item order and phonetic recoding in the beginning reader. *Journal of Experimental Child Psychology, 32,* 474–484.

Kean, M. L. (1977). The linguistic interpretation of aphasic syndromes: Agrammatism in Broca's aphasia, an example. *Cognition, 5,* 9–46.

Kimball, J. (1973). Seven principles of surface structure parsing in natural language. *Cognition, 2,* 15–47.

Lasnik, H. (1976). Remarks on coreference. *Linguistic Analysis, 2,* 1–22.

Lasnik, H., & Crain, S. (1985). On the acquisition of pronominal reference. *Lingua, 65,* 135–154.

Liberman, A. M., Mattingly, I. G., & Turvey, M. (1972). Language codes and memory codes. In A. W. Melton & E. Martin (Eds.), *Coding processes and human memory.* Washington, DC: Winston and Sons.

Liberman, I. Y., Mann, V. A., Shankweiler, D., & Werfelman, M. (1982). Children's memory for recurring linguistic and non-linguistic material in relation to reading ability. *Cortex, 18,* 367–375.

Liberman, I. Y., & Shankweiler, D. (1985). Phonology and the problems of learning to read and write. *Remedial and Special Education, 6,* 8–17.

Liberman, I. Y., Shankweiler, D., Blachman, B. A., Camp, L., & Werfelman, M. (1980). Steps toward literacy. In P. Levinson & C. C. Harris Sloan (Eds.), *Auditory processing and language: Clinical and research perspectives.* New York: Grune and Stratton.

Liberman, I. Y., Shankweiler, D., Fischer, F. W., & Carter, B. (1974). Explicit syllable and phoneme segmentation in the young child. *Journal of Experimental Child Psychology, 18,* 201–212.

Limber, J. (1973). The genesis of complex sentences. In T. E. Moore (Ed.), *Cognitive development and the acquisition of language.* New York: Academic Press.

Mann, V. A., Liberman, I. Y., & Shankweiler, D. (1980). Children's memory for sentences and word strings in relation to reading ability. *Memory & Cognition, 8,* 329–335.

Mann, V. A., Shankweiler, D., & Smith, S. T. (1984). The association between comprehension of spoken sentences and early reading ability: the role of phonetic representation. *Journal of Child Language, 11,* 627–643.

Mattingly, I. G. (1972). Reading, the linguistic process, and linguistic awareness. In J. F. Kavanagh & I. G. Mattingly (Eds.), *Language by ear and by eye: The relationships between speech and reading.* Cambridge, MA: MIT Press.

Mattingly, I. G. (1984). Reading, linguistic awareness, and language acquisition. In J. Downing & R. Valtin (Eds.), *Language awareness and learning to read.* New York: Springer-Verlag.

Milner, B. (1974). Hemispheric specialization: Scope and limits. In F. O. Schmitt & F. G. Worden (Eds.), *The neurosciences: Third study program,* Cambridge, MA: MIT Press.

Perfetti, C. A. (1985). *Reading ability.* New York: Oxford University Press.

Perfetti, C. A., Goldman, S., & Hogaboam, T. (1979). Reading skill and the identification of words in discourse context. *Memory and Cognition, 7,* 273–282.

Perfetti, C. A., & Hogaboam, T. (1975). The relationship between single word decoding and reading comprehension skill. *Journal of Educational Psychology, 67,* 461–469.

Perfetti, C. A., & Lesgold, A. M. (1977). Discourse comprehension and sources of individual differences. In M. A. Just & P. A. Carpenter (Eds.), *Cognitive processes in comprehension.* Hillsdale, NJ: Lawrence Erlbaum Associates.

Rozin, P., & Gleitman, L. R. (1977). The structure and acquisition of reading II: The reading process and the acquisition of the alphabetic principle. In A. S. Reber & D. L. Scarborough (Eds.), *Toward a psychology of reading: The proceedings of the CUNY Conference.* Hillsdale, NJ: Lawrence Erlbaum Associates.

Sachs, J. S. (1967). Recognition memory for syntactic and semantic aspects of connected discourse. *Perception and Psychophysics, 2,* 437–442.

Shankweiler, D., & Crain, S. (1986). Language mechanisms and reading disorder: A modular approach. *Cognition, 24,* 139–168.

Shankweiler, D., & Liberman, I. Y. (1972). Misreading: A search for causes. In J. F. Kavanagh & I. G. Mattingly (Eds.), *Language by ear and by eye: The relationships between speech and reading*. Cambridge, MA: MIT Press.

Shankweiler, D., & Liberman, I. Y. (1976). Exploring the relations between reading and speech. In R. M. Knights & D. J. Bakker (Eds.), *The neuropsychology of learning disorders: Theoretical approaches*. Baltimore, MD: University Park Press.

Shankweiler, D., Liberman, I. Y., Mark, L. S., Fowler, C. A., & Fischer, F. W. (1979). The speech code and learning to read. *Journal of Experimental Psychology: Human Learning and Memory, 5*, 531–545.

Shankweiler, D., Smith, S. T., & Mann, V. A. (1984). Repetition and comprehension of spoken sentences by reading-disabled children. *Brain and Language, 23*, 241–257.

Sheldon, A. (1974). The role of parallel function in the acquisition of relative clauses in English. *Journal of Verbal Learning and Verbal Behavior, 13*, 272–281.

Solan, L., & Roeper, T. W. (1978). Children's use of syntactic structure in interpreting relative clauses. In H. Goodluck & L. Solan (Eds.), *Papers in the Structure and Development of Child Language. University of Massachusetts Occasional Papers in Linguistics. Vol. 4*, 105–126.

Stemmer, N. (1982). A note on empiricism and structure dependence. *Journal of Child Language, 18*, 629–633.

Tavakolian, S. L. (1981). The conjoined-clause analysis of relative clauses. In S. Tavakolian (Ed.), *Language acquisition and linguistic theory*. Cambridge, MA: MIT Press.

Vogel, S. A. (1975). *Syntactic abilities in normal and dyslexic children*. Baltimore, MD: University Park Press.

Whitaker, H. (1976). A case of isolation of the language function. In H. Whitaker & H. A. Whitaker (Eds.), *Studies in neurolinguistics* (Vol. 2). New York: Academic Press.

8 The Study of Linguistic Complexity

Lyn Frazier
University of Massachusetts, Amherst

Psycholinguists have been trying to determine how grammatical information is acquired, mentally represented and used by humans to produce and understand natural language sentences. Here we are concerned only with mental representations and processing operations underlying adult comprehension of spoken and written language. The study of linguistic complexity is relevant to the endeavor to develop theories of human sentence processing for several reasons. Alternative theories of sentence processing typically make distinct predictions about the relative processing complexity of different constructions. Hence, complexity data is one of the primary sources of evidence used to evaluate psycholinguistic theories or hypotheses. Given the heavy reliance on complexity data, it is important to examine our assumptions about the relation between complexity data and specific grammatical representations or processing routines. If these assumptions are mistaken or overly simplistic, a seriously distorted picture of the language comprehension system may emerge from complexity investigations (see Forster, 1979, where this point is developed in detail). Finally, an understanding of the complexity of various linguistic structures is crucial if we are to evaluate the hypothesis that the grammars of natural languages are, at least in some respects, shaped by the exigencies of human processing mechanisms (see Frazier, 1985).

Section 1 briefly compares the approach to linguistic complexity motivated by the general sorts of concerns outlined above with more applied approaches, in an attempt to elucidate differences in the goals and underlying assumptions of each. Section 2 illustrates how and why our interpretation of complexity data is influenced by our assessment of the nature of the comprehension task and the architecture of the language processing system (i.e., by the nature of the component subsystems involved and the relations between them). Section 3 reviews some of the empirical findings on processing complexity and particular psycholinguistic proposals offered to capture or explain them. Section 3.1 focuses on syntactic processing complexity. It is argued that there are several quite distinct sources of difficulty that contribute to the complexity of assigning a syntactic analysis to an input sentence. Section 3.2 takes up lexical complexity. It is suggested that the question of how much a particular lexical item contributes to the complexity of processing an expression containing the item may be misguided; the very notion of "lexical entry" may need to be reexamined. Section 3.3 looks at semantic processing. It explores a rather tentative proposal concerning the reason why large and robust inherent complexity differences have not been observed for various types of words and (simple) phrases.

1. MOTIVATION FOR LINGUISTIC COMPLEXITY METRICS

Measures of linguistic complexity have been developed for several very different reasons. More applied approaches to the complexity problem have been motivated by the attempt to develop an accurate and reliable measure of linguistic complexity that could be used to select appropriate reading material for particular populations and to provide an objective measure for evaluating an individual's language skills. My impression is that most investigations of this sort are characterized by the fact that they look directly to the properties of a text to identify variables that correlate with processing complexity, e.g., factors such as legibility, length, and frequency of the words in a text, the number of prenominal modifiers, etc. Work in this area seems to implicitly assume that an explicit complexity metric will provide a useful tool and, in this sense, developing an accurate metric is an end in itself.

In sharp contrast, more theoretically oriented approaches are typically motivated by the attempt to evaluate and refine theories of the human language processor. Thus, the interest is not so much in the particular complexity metric that happens to be correct, but rather in what this metric reveals about the fundamental properties of the human language capacity. It seems unlikely that *direct* measures of complexity (tallying up the value of various variables taken directly from the text) will by themselves lead to very refined measures capable of predicting the precise complexity of each portion of a text or reveal the nature and source of differences in processing complexity. Thus, while direct measures may provide a gross estimate of the overall complexity of a text, I assume that ultimately it must be a theory of human language comprehension which will provide (embody) the complexity metric for processing, since it is this theory which will characterize the complex interplay of different factors that contribute to complexity and reveal the reasons why some materials are more difficult to understand than others.

Another difference between applied and theoretically oriented studies of complexity emerges from the focus or central concern of the investigators. Typically, investigators working in more applied areas are concerned with characterizing and accounting for individual variability in linguistic performance; whereas, investigators with more theoretical orientations are usually concerned with identifying and explaining the commonalities in the underlying mechanisms of different individuals. Indeed, theoretical studies usually assume that there is significant uniformity in the basic linguistic knowledge, comprehension routines, and memory and computational resources available to all intact humans. In the case of auditory comprehension, there seems to be widespread consensus about the correctness of this view. This consensus is based on two basic facts: All intact humans automatically acquire the ability to process whatever natural language they happen to be exposed to as children; and, across individual speakers of a given language, the relative processing complexity of particular words, sentence structures or passages is quite uniform.[1]

The fundamental differences in the focus of theoretical and applied investigators naturally lead to different questions being asked and thus, not too surprisingly, to a somewhat different view of language. Note, however, that the individual variability in language performance that will be of interest to those working on language-related disabilities is variability that lies outside the range of variability exhibited within and across individuals with no language difficulties. Hence it would seem unwise to permit the study of uniformity and the study of individual variability proceed in complete isolation.

We turn now to the relation between complexity data and a theory of language comprehension. The point of the discussion is to show how the interpretation of complexity data depends on the assumptions one makes about the structure of the language comprehension device.

2. STRUCTURE OF THE LANGUAGE COMPREHENSION TASK

The task of processing a sentence may be elucidated by drawing an analogy with a familiar situation. Consider the structure of the standard crossword puzzle game in which some compulsive individual completes the puzzle in a single

---

[1]The studies cited later are typically of the form: construction X takes longer to process than construction Y across subjects. This, of course, suggests that whatever processing principles or mechanisms underlie the complexity differences (e.g., predict them) are also shared by different individuals. It is logically possible for distinct principles or mechanisms to give rise to the same complexity ranking of various constructions. However, in actual practice, it is often difficult to imagine explanatory alternatives in the case of *general* principles responsible for predictions about the relativity complexity of a large range of different constructions types.

uninterrupted sitting. The time needed to complete the entire puzzle will simply be the sum of the time needed to complete each word of the puzzle. In principle, language comprehension might proceed in this fashion, with the time needed to comprehend a sentence being a direct reflection of the time needed to complete each step of the comprehension process.

Now consider an unorganized group of people working on the same puzzle without even an informal division of labor, so that a number of people might all happen to be working on the same word at the same time. In this case, the time needed to complete the puzzle will not provide an indication of the number or complexity of the steps performed to complete the puzzle. It will not even reflect the sum of the fastest solution to each word contained in the puzzle. Further, on different occasions, the time needed to complete the puzzle could differ substantially due to accidentally efficient or inefficient allocation of resources. If human language comprehension proceeded in a similar manner, then reliance on processing time data in developing theories of language comprehension would be quite unrevealing and potentially misleading. Fortunately, empirical evidence shows that language processing does not proceed in this manner; processing principles have been identified which are quite successful in predicting the processing time of various linguistic constructions. This fact alone argues that sentence comprehension is not haphazard or completely unstructured, with no principled division of labor.

Imagine now that there is some nonarbitrary division of labor in the group of crossword puzzle fanatics that draws on the special talents of the individual players, ensuring that the historians, geologists, and physicists are each assigned to appropriate clues which fall in their particular specialized domain. If each of the specialists may write down a solution as soon as it has been discovered, and each specialist is working on an equal number of problems, then the time to solve the puzzle will reflect the complexity of whatever operations (i.e., whichever specialist) happens to take the longest. The time taken by other specialists to accomplish their tasks would be reflected in the total solution time only in puzzles that increased the number or complexity of their operations in relation to the other experts. This division of labor begins to resemble what is known presently about language processing in that we may manipulate the complexity of one type of processing, holding other properties of the linguistic input constant, and see effects on response times requiring comprehension of the input. E.g., holding lexical frequency constant one may see the effect of the complexity of various syntactic structures, holding syntactic complexity constant one may observe the effects of minor lexical differences. We would expect these effects to be truly additive (with the difference between, say, a sentence containing a high- vs. low-frequency word in a syntactically complex structure being identical to the difference obtained when these words occurred in a syntactically simple structure) only in circumstances where the relevant processors are serially arranged, so that the later processor may begin operating only once the earlier processor has completed its operations. The experimental evidence pertaining to this issue has been mixed, with some investigators finding additive effects of syntactic and semantic complexity (e.g., Forster & Olbrei, 1973) and lexical and semantic effects (Inhoff, 1983), and others finding interactive effects (Marslen-Wilson & Tyler, 1980).

Returning to our crossword puzzle game, imagine now that there is an optimal ordering of the output of our specialists. Regardless of when any particular specialist has solved his particular problems, the physicist is required to write down his solution before the geologist, who in turn must report her results before the historian. Any delays imposed by the physicist's deliberations will now contribute to the total solution time just in case the geologist and historian have already completed their tasks successfully and are standing by twiddling their thumbs. By contrast, if the geologist is still puzzling over some difficult clue, slow solution times on the part of the physicist will not affect the overall solution time at all. In short, given this organization there is no particular premium to speedy solutions on the part of the earliest processors (i.e., those that must report first).

In various respects the crossword puzzle game, as idealized here, is not comparable to the language processing task. Above, it is implicitly assumed that each specialist is producing error-free solutions and is uninterested in the solutions of the other experts, requiring no information from them in the completion of their own specialized subtask. In sharp contrast, grammatical processing subsystems often must operate on the representations identified or constructed by other grammatical subsystems. Thus in language there is at least a partial inherent ordering of the information flow: Syntactic category assignments must presumably await the identification of lexical items under most circumstances; semantic interpretation of an item in a phrase must be delayed until a constituent structure analysis has identified the syntactic role of that item within the phrase, etc. Thus we would expect there to be an optimal ordering of solutions in at least some of the subtasks of language comprehension, and thus optimal and nonoptimal relations that could in principle obtain between language processing subsystems.

The grammatical subsystems of the comprehension device may be identified with the specialized experts in the crossword puzzle game in terms of a task and knowledge decomposition that can be specified in advance. The historian's domain of expertise may be identified in advance of any particular crossword puzzle, and it will define a natural and reasonably efficient procedure for parcelling out tasks. Clues (tasks) that do not fall under the domain of any of the experts would presumably be relegated to some generalist. If this generalist is to operate efficiently, one would expect its solutions to be constrained by the structure resulting from the solutions entered by all of the experts. This, I suspect, is similar to the language comprehension system and perhaps provides one of the crucial advantages of a modularized language processing device: The grammatical subsystems may each construct representations of an input on the basis of specialized knowledge known in advance to be relevant (e.g., the phonological constraints of the language limit the possible phonological and lexical structures postulated regardless of the particular input) and the ultimate grammatical representation resulting from the operation of the grammatical subsystems may be viewed as defining the task presented to the general cognitive processing system and placing limitations on its solutions. Without some such division of linguistic and nonlinguistic labor, language comprehension would surely amount to an anagram task in which communication of a message not confirming the perceivers expectations would be impossible. That is, grammatical information would merely provide another source of information for arriving at a good guess about the intended meaning of an input. It would be attributed no distinguished role in limiting the interpretation of the input to one consistent with the grammar.

There are two general morals that can be drawn from the above observations. First, in terms of the overall complexity of understanding a discourse or text, one would expect this to be predominantly a function of whether information is available when it is needed. It is of course only a theory of language comprehension, in particular, one specifying the architecture of the overall system (i.e., the relation between subsystems) and the operations available within each component of it, that will make explicit when particular types of information must be available in order to lead to correct decisions and decisions that are sufficiently rapid not to delay the output of the overall system. The reasoning behind this claim is straightforward. Presumably the individual operations involved in language processing (e.g., accessing grammatical information or using it to assign some syntactic role to an input word) are themselves very routine and well within the capacity of all normal humans. Thus it is not to the individual operations themselves that we should look for assessments of overall comprehension complexity.

The second moral is also straightforward. Unless experimental tasks tap into the operations of just a single module (cf. Fodor, 1983; Forster, 1979), it will not be evident from response time data alone whether differences in response time reflect the operation within a processing module or complexity due to nonoptimal functioning of modules with respect to the operation of other modules, in the absence of some account of the architecture of the overall system. This suggests, I think, that experimental investigations must place more emphasis on designing studies that can be interpreted within the framework of an explanatory theory of language comprehension if they are to substantially contribute to our understanding of even the descriptive facts about language processing. This, together with independent confirmation of hypotheses from other sources of data (preference data, error data, priming studies, etc.) will permit response time data to be informative rather than misleading.

3. SOURCES OF PROCESSING COMPLEXITY

We turn now to various sources of complexity that have been documented in the psycholinguistic literature. The emphasis will be on identifying the principles that capture the dimensions along which complexity might vary. We begin with an attempt to identify the distinct types of complexity in assigning a syntactic structure to an input sentence.

3.1 Syntactic processing

Given the existence of constraints on the immediate memory and computational capacity of the human language processor, syntactic ambiguity poses a difficult problem for the processor. There are indefinitely many sentences in a natural language and thus it is in principle impossible for each sentence to be prestored in memory. Hence, we will assume the processor uses the syntactic wellformedness constraints of the language to assign a syntactic structure to a sentence. It will also be assumed that the point of assigning a syntactic structure to an input is to determine what a sentence actually does mean, i.e., to distinguish the permissible meanings of a sentence from the larger set of meanings that result from randomly combining the meanings of the lexical items in the sentence.

If the processor must compute all possible analyses of an ambiguous input, this should impose memory and computational demands on the processor that are larger than the demands imposed by a corresponding unambiguous sentence. Delayed analysis of an ambiguous input would also impose a memory burden on the processor assuming that it is difficult to hold relatively unstructured materials in memory. Pursuing just a single analysis of an ambiguous input will also turn out to be costly if the chosen analysis subsequently proves to be incorrect, since the processor will need to revise the initial analysis. Thus, on any account, the analysis of an ambiguous input should at least at times be complex if the analysis of the input must be "computed" (i.e., constructed by rule, not merely looked up in memory).

It is important to emphasize that the complexity of processing ambiguous inputs will persist regardless of whether the input is fully ambiguous (ultimately open to more than one analysis) or only temporarily ambiguous, i.e., the initial portion of a sentence may be open to more than one analysis but subsequent items may be consistent with only one of these analyses. The processor typically cannot know in advance if or when information will arrive that will disambiguate an ambiguous portion of a sentence, nor is there usually a guarantee that such information will be superficially identifiable. Thus, apart from exceptional circumstances where the disambiguating information is guaranteed to arrive immediately after the ambiguous string, the pervasive temporary ambiguities in the analysis of natural language inputs will pose the same problems for the processor as full ambiguity. In short, from the perspective of the processing system, the distinction between temporary and full ambiguity is a post-hoc one.

Table 8.1 presents several types of temporarily ambiguous strings to illustrate the range of temporary syntactic ambiguities (falling under the Minimal Attachment and Late Closure strategies that are discussed below).

Consider the ambiguous string *the girl that Bill liked* in sentences (1)–(4).

TABLE 8.1

1. Since Jay always jogs <u>a mile</u>... (subject of main clause vs. object of subordinate clause)

   a. seems like a short distance to him.
   b. this seems like a short distance to him.

2. The newspaper only reported that the incident happened <u>yesterday morning</u>... (low vs. high attachment of adverb)

   a. today.
   b. in the late edition.

3. John knew <u>the answer</u>... (subject of complement clause vs. direct object of matrix clause)

   a. was correct.
   b. by heart.

4. Ernie kissed Sally <u>and her sister</u>... (sentential vs. noun phrase conjunction)

   a. laughed.
   b. too.

5. I mailed the package <u>for Susan</u>... (attachment of PP into NP vs. VP)

   a. to Frank.
   b. because she couldn't.

6. Fred gave <u>the child a dog</u>... (relative clause vs. direct object of dative verb)

   a. bit some candy.
   b. for his birthday.

7. The man <u>offered some coffee</u>... (reduced relative clause vs. main clause)

   a. said he'd given up all his old vices.
   b. to his friends.

8. We visited the <u>Smiths</u>... (possessive modifier vs. head)

   a. summer home.
   b. frequently.

9. <u>That sheep lived in Australia</u>... (sentential subject vs. main clause)

   a. upset Tommy.
   b. with my uncle.

10. Jimmy programmed the computer <u>to</u>... (low attachment as complement vs. high attachment as in-order to clause)

    a. do all his homework.
    b. escape doing his homework.

This string may be interpreted as a relative clause, as indicated in (1a), or as an indirect object followed by the beginning of a sentential complement as indicated in (1b). The fully ambiguous sentence (1) and the temporarily ambiguous sentence (2) are identical up until the final word of the sentence. Before the processor encounters this word, there is no way to determine if or when disambiguating information will occur, or what form the disambiguating information will assume.

(1)   John told the girl that Bill liked the story.
   a.   John told [the girl that Bill liked] the story.
        (Releative Clause)
   b.   John told the girl [that Bill liked the story].
        (Complement Clause)

(2)   John told the girl that Bill liked the eggplant.
      (Complement Clause Only).

(3)   John told anyone that Bill liked the story. (Relative Clause Bias)

(4a) Susan didn't believe that John told anyone that Bill liked the story.
      (Ambiguous)

(4b) John didn't tell anyone that Bill liked the story.
      (Ambiguous)

A comparison of sentences (3) and (4) may illustrate the complexity of the information that may serve to disambiguate or bias the interpretation of an ambiguous string. A sentence like *John told anyone the story* is slightly odd (though not entirely anomalous due to the interpretation appropriate for just anyone). Thus sentence (3) is strongly biased toward the relative clause analysis of the string *anyone that Bill liked*. However, sentence (3) would not be biased toward a relative clause analysis if the sentence were embedded in a context containing a negative, e.g., *Susan didn't believe* . . . Thus the sentences in (4) are not biased toward the relative clause interpretation. The biasing information that serves to disambiguate (3) is clearly nonlocal information that need not be contained in the same clauses as the ambiguous string.

It is reasonable to suppose that at least under certain circumstances the ambiguity in the syntactic analysis of a sentence persists despite the presence of *prior* disambiguating information (see, for example, Ferreira & Clifton, 1986, where it is shown that readers initially compute an incorrect syntactic analysis of certain sentences even when preceding context provides information which in principle could have been used to disambiguate the sentence). We may thus distinguish two types of temporary ambiguity: horizontal ambiguity which persists even when all information has been extracted from preceding sentence and discourse context; (as in (1) above) and, vertical ambiguity due to delayed use of information which in principle may be extracted from material preceding the ambiguous string but which is in fact not exploited by the processor until some time after the initial syntactic analysis of the string.

It is common practice to refer to a structure as ambiguous only if it contains no information which in principle could be used to dictate its correct analysis. This type of ambiguity is what I have called "horizontal" ambiguity. In other words, during the "left-to-right" process of a sentence, there is no conceivable language processing system that could reliably assign only one analysis to the structure and be guaranteed of assigning the ultimately correct analysis without consulting information from subsequent items that have not yet been received.

In addition to these horizontal ambiguities, there may, however, also be ambiguities that result because the processing system does not immediately use certain information that can be derived from items that have already been processed. For example, assume that the language processing system immediately uses subcategorization information specifying that *put* is the kind of verb that requires both a direct object noun phrase and a locative prepositional phrase, whereas *write* does not require a locative phrase and may occur with just a direct object noun phrase. In this case, the string in (5a) is unambiguous whereas in (5b) *the book in the tent* may be analyzed either as a complex noun phrase referring to a particular book or as a simple noun phrase followed by a locative phrase indicating where Ernie wrote the book.

(5)   a.   If Ernie put the book in the tent then . . .
      b.   If Ernie wrote the book in the tent then . . .

But imagine for a moment a language processing system that delays the use of subcategorization information about the possible complements of these verbs, consulting this information, say, only at the end of a sentence. In this case, (5a) like (5b) would be syntactically ambiguous since the processor will not yet have exploited the information about *put* which will ultimately disambiguate (5a). There would still be no horizontal ambiguity in (5a), since in principle information is available to disambiguate this string; however, given the above assumptions, there would be a vertical ambiguity in (5a) because the disambiguating information will not yet have consulted by our hypothetical processing system when the ambiguous phrase is encountered (see Frazier, Clifton, & Randall, 1983, Ferreira & Clifton, 1986, for actual examples of this type).

Immediately below we turn to evidence concerning the decision principles that characterize the decisions made in the initial syntactic processing of horizontal ambiguities. It is natural to suppose that an account of vertical ambiguities will require a theory of distinct modules or subcomponents involved in language comprehension and the relation between them, explaining why the use of certain information types is delayed.

In several papers, my colleagues and I (Frazier, 1979; Frazier & Fodor, 1978; Rayner, Carlson, & Frazier, 1983) have presented evidence that the processor deals with temporary ambiguity by initially pursuing the analysis which requires the fewest syntactic nodes. Consider (6), where the noun phrase *the answer* may be attached directly to the verb phrase node dominating *knew*, as in (6a), or it may be dominated by a sentence node if it is the subject of a sentential complement of *knew*, as in (6b). The former analysis requires the postulation of fewer syntactic nodes, since no new S-node is required when the ambiguous phrase is encountered. According to fewest nodes or "Minimal Attachment" strategy, (6b) but not (6a) will create difficulties for perceivers since their initial analysis of the ambiguous phrase will have to be revised (only) in (6b). In cases where two competing analyses of the input sting require the postulation of an equal number of nodes, an incoming item is incorporated into the phrase currently being processed. This "Late Closure" strategy predicts perceivers will initially analyze *tomorrow* as a constituent of the lower clause *Mary is arriving* in (7a) and (7b). In (7b), this decision will have to be revised due to the tense of the verb *arrive*.

(6)   Lydia knew the answer . . .

    a. Lydia knew the answer by heart.

    b. Lydia knew the answer was correct.

(7) a. Brenda will announce that Mary is arriving tomorrow.

    b. Brenda will announce that Mary arrived tomorrow.

Thus one source of processing complexity derives from the operations needed to revise an initial incorrect analysis of a sentence, e.g., in (6b), *the answer* must be taken to be the subject of a sentential complement to *know* not a simple direct object of *know;* (6b) thus requires the insertion of an extra S-node dominating the temporarily ambiguous noun phrase.

Differences in the complexity of processing unambiguous syntactic structures also exist. Assuming that the processor attempts to incorporate each word of an input into a constituent structure representation of the sentence as the word is encountered (cf. Frazier & Rayner, 1982), we would expect an increase in complexity to result when numerous operations are warranted by each of several adjacent words. For example, the sentence in (8) is difficult to process due to the need to postulate numerous nonterminal nodes all at once over, say, a three word window, as illustrated in (8a).

(8) That that John left bothered Mary upset me.

    a.

Sentences also differ in the memory requirements that they impose on the processing system. Wanner and Maratsos (1978) propose that "fillers" (e.g., phrases like *who* that control the interpretation of empty positions in the sentences as in "Who does John like _____?") must be stored in a special memory buffer until they may be assigned to a "gap" (e.g., the position after *like* in the constituent structure of *Who does John like?*). Frazier (1984) suggests that certain word orders (placement of heads of phrases consistently before, or consistently after, their complements) may facilitate sentence processing by permitting rapid semantic integration of sentences, thereby reducing the memory load imposed by a sentence. It is also suggested that constraints on filler-gap dependencies may reduce the memory burden associated with processing sentences, by defining "islands of certainty" where reliably correct decisions can be made, thereby alleviating the need for the processor to maintain nonsemantic representations of the input once a semantic interpretation has been assigned to it.

In short there are several types of complexity involved in syntactically processing sentences. Complexity may result from the need to revise an initial incorrect analysis of a sentence (e.g., as in sentences where Late Closure and Minimal Attachment analyses prove to be incorrect), from a concentration of normal processing operations that are warranted all at once rather than spread evenly throughout the sentence (e.g., postulating lots of nonterminals over a short stretch of input) or from the memory burden imposed by the need to maintain unstructured material or material that has not been semantically interpreted (see Frazier, 1985, for more detailed discussion).

Before turning to a discussion of the complexity associated with the lexical processing of sentences, it should be pointed out that at present there is no explicit complexity metric which permits us to compare complexity due to these different sources. Thus the principles concerned with the analysis of temporarily ambiguous strings predict that a sentence which violates a strategy like Minimal Attachment will be more difficult to process than one that does not, and a string with a high nonterminal-to-terminal ratio will be more difficult than a corresponding string (controlled for lexical complexity) with a low nonterminal-to-terminal ratio. As a matter of empirical fact it is known that, say, a Nonminimal Attachment sentence (one that violates the Minimal Attachment strategy) is more complex than a corresponding unambiguous sentence that requires postulation of just as many syntactic nodes (cf. Rayner, Carlson, & Frazier, 1983, discussion of Experiment 1). In this sense violation of a parsing strategy is more costly than expected simply on the basis of a high local nonterminal-to-terminal ratio. However, precisely how high a local nonterminal ratio would be necessary to render an unambiguous sentence as difficult to process as a temporarily ambiguous ("garden path") sentence is not known. That is, there is no general unit of complexity (defined either in terms of time or number of computational operations) which would permit us to predict in "absolute" terms the complexity of a sentence and compare the complexity contributed by distinct sources of complexity, i.e., at present we cannot predict that an isolated sentence will be complex to degree *n*.

3.2 Lexical Processing

The issues surrounding lexical contributions to processing complexity are in many respects different from those concerning syntactic processing complexity. If lexical items are defined as linguistic units stored in memory (morphemes, words and idioms), lexical analysis of an input will often entail identifying a representation already stored in memory (i.e., looking up information in the mental dictionary), rather than actively computing a representation by rule. As a result, the complexity of a lexical item might be viewed in terms of (a) the complexity of the lexical representation of that item (e.g., the number of symbols in its entry), (b) how difficult or time consuming the item is to recognize (e.g., how hard it is to identify the appropriate entry in the mental lexicon), and/or (c) the item's contribution to the processing complexity of the phrase or sentence it occurs in. We will take up each of these issues in turn.

3.2.1 The complexity of the lexical entries.   Here we examine the idea that the mental representation of certain lexical items may be more complex than that of others. After pointing out reasons why this hypothesis is difficult to evaluate empirically, it will be suggested that the very idea of a "lexical entry" (i.e., an entry in the mental dictionary containing phonological, orthographic, syntactic and semantic information about an item) may be misguided and rest on unwarranted assumptions.

To my knowledge, the only complexity metric that has been considered for lexical entries is a simple symbol-counting metric. Basically this predicts that the longer a lexical entry is (i.e., the more symbols it contains), the more complex it is for purposes of processing. (See Jackendoff, 1975, for arguments that this metric does not necessarily predict that longer entries are more complicated to acquire, because the entering of predictable information may be relatively cost-free due to the operation of redundancy rules.) The length and (given this metric) the predicted complexity of a lexical entry will crucially depend on the organization of mental representations into lexical entries. It will depend, for example, on whether noun-verb duals (e.g., *fire*$_{Noun}$–*fire*$_{Verb}$) share a lexical entry and on which morphologically related items (e.g., *serene–serenity*) share a common entry. A few studies have examined these questions (e.g., Bradley, 1979; Forster, 1976; Murrell & Morton, 1974; Stanners, et al., 1979; Taft, 1976), but the vast majority of work on word recognition has focused on the processing of monomorphemic words and thus no generally accepted view of the basic principles governing lexical organization has emerged to date. Hence, at present, the symbol-counting metric is at best only partially defined.

Nevertheless, various attempts have been made to evaluate the predictions of this metric, given independent hypotheses about the composition and organization of particular lexical representations. Cutler (1982) provides a detailed review of this research and concludes that the number of symbols contained in its lexical entry does not influence the complexity of processing a word (see also Rayner & Duffy, 1986).

One problem, however, is the relation between processing operations and measures of processing complexity. The information in a lexical entry may contribute to actual processing complexity whenever the lexical item occurs in a sentence (in accordance with the symbol-counting metric) but may contribute to measures of complexity only if the information is directly involved in the processing being accomplished at the point when complexity is measured (e.g., when subjects initiate a response). This possibility is extremely difficult to distinguish from the possibility that increasing the information in a lexical entry (i.e., the number of symbols in it) increases processing complexity only *if* the information is relevant to the sentence being processed. This latter possibility would violate the symbol-counting metric. For examples, Inhoff (1983) presents eye movement data showing that fixations on factive verbs—verbs such as *know* or *realize* which imply the truth of their complements—are no longer than fixations on a controlled set of nonfactive verbs; however, when a false complement is embedded under a factive verb (e.g., *John knows 2+2 = 5*) the complement takes longer to read than when the same complement is embedded under a nonfactive verb. Which of the above possibilities do these results support? They seem most compatible with the view that factive verbs take no longer to process than nonfactive verbs, since no difference was observed in the fixation durations associated with the verbs themselves. However, it is difficult to interpret the results as truly compelling evidence against the symbol counting mechanism since we cannot entirely exclude the possibility that the complements of factive verbs take slightly longer to process than the complements of nonfactive verbs, but the difference is observable only when magnified, e.g., when the complement disconfirms the lexical expectation. However, despite these difficulties of interpretation, what does seem clear is that large local increases in complexity do not depend simply on the length of lexical entries per se.

To my knowledge, every study investigating the complexity of long lexical entries has in fact looked only at one component of a lexical representation (e.g., its semantic representation), presumably on the assumption that the complexity of other aspects of the representation (e.g., phonological, or syntactic) would vary randomly and thus be essentially equivalent across sets of items that differed in some other respect. However, the situation may be that components of a lexical representation other than those explicitly manipulated (whether they in fact do vary randomly or are confounded with the property of interest) are simply irrelevant. In other words, the very notion of a "lexical entry" may be a convenient fiction, with no status in a theory of language other than as a short-hand label for a certain (albeit nonarbitrary) cluster of information.

Consider the various distinct kinds of information that must be stored for a lexical item. Information about its phonological form will presumably be couched in terms of distinctive features of individual segments and information about the relations between those segments (how they are arranged into constituents such as syllables, feet, etc.). Information about the syntactic category of an item (e.g., noun vs. verb) and about the category and obligatoriness of any complements (e.g., whether a verb may or must occur with a noun phrase object) must be represented. In addition, there must be a semantic representation of the item and a specification of the number and thematic role of any arguments it takes. Morphological features entering into the agreement rules of the language must also be stored, at least for certain items (e.g., the number and gender of *her*). In short, the information that must be stored for lexical items will need to make reference to several theoretically distinct vocabulary types, overlapping with the vocabulary of syntactic, semantic, morphological, and phonological rules or principles. Surely we would be absolutely startled to find that in any interesting sense the complexity of a "lexical entry" with 100 semantic symbols and only 10 phonological ones was the same as the complexity of an entry with 100 phonological symbols and only 10 semantic symbols.

The implausibility of this view of lexical entries immediately gives rise to the question of whether the symbol counting metric merits any consideration with respect to individual components of lexical representations, e.g., is a longer phonological representation more complex than a shorter one? On the face of it, it would appear that the length of a phonological representation (i.e., the number of symbols it contains, not the length of the word) could contribute at most to the complexity of holding the item in some immediate memory store; with respect to actual processing operations (e.g., those involved in recognizing a perceptual input) it would certainly seem more likely that the familiarity of the item (whether it has been encountered recently or frequently), the regularity of the item (whether it corresponds to the phonological regularities of the language), the length of the item (measured in numbers of segments or syllables) and the confusability of the item (whether it is easily distinguished from all other lexical items of the language) will be more important than the number of symbols in the phonological representation per se.

With respect to syntactic and semantic representations, it might intuitively seem correct that longer representations will be more complex than shorter ones for reasons other than memory burden, since longer representations will often result when a lexical item is syntactically or semantically ambiguous. Thus, the obligatorily intransitive verb *die* will only be associated with a single "subcategorization frame" (cf. Chomsky, 1965), as indicated in (9a), whereas an optionally transitive verb like *walk* may be associated with two distinct frames, as indicated in (9b).

(9) a. die
         verb
         [_____ (PP)] (e.g., John died at home.)

b. walk
      verb
    [_____ (PP] (e.g., John walked to the store.)
    [_____ NP (PP)] (e.g., John walked the dog to the
      store.)

However, if we were to claim that it is the length of the syntactic entry for *walk* per se that is responsible for any processing complexity associated with this item (relative to *die*) then we would (falsely) predict that the complexity associated with *walk* will persist regardless of whether it is used in its most frequent (intransitive) form or in its less frequent (transitive) form. Clifton, Frazier, and Connine (1984) show that intransitive sentences containing obligatorily intransitive verbs are processed no more quickly than corresponding sentences containing optionally intransitive verbs that occur most frequently in their intransitive form, disconfirming the above prediction. In sum, there is at present no reason to believe the symbol counting metric provides a measure of lexical processing complexity regardless of whether it is applied globally to all of the symbol-types of a lexical representation or just to symbols of a given type.

   Indeed, the above considerations might suggest that attempts to assess the complexity of a lexical entry are fundamentally misguided. Attention might be focused instead on how particular types of lexical representation (e.g., phonological representations, syntactic representations, etc.) are mentally represented, organized, and used in language processing. Before turning to these issues, note that the above observations may pose a challenge to the notion "lexical entry," i.e., Does the concept "lexical entry"—a mental construct containing representations couched in various distinct vocabulary types—warrant any status whatsoever in a theory of language? To address this question we must ask whether explaining any grammatical facts or psycholinguistic facts requires reference to this notion.

   We might ask, for example, whether reference to the distinct information types in a lexical entry is needed in an account of the grammatical constraints of the language. For example, the fact that the verb *convict* has second syllable stress, whereas the noun has initial stress, would seem to suggest that phonological rules must have access to information about the syntactic category of a form. However, whether this is so, depends on the precise assumptions that are made about phonological representations. Information about stress might be represented in a lexical representation in terms of the relative strength of syllables or the relation between them; the correlation between initial stress and nouns might only serve as a redundancy rule (see Jackendoff, 1975) making the grammar more highly valued, easier to learn, if nouns conform to the general pattern and carry initial stress.

   The strongest evidence in favor of lexical entries may derive from the influence of the orthographic shape of a word in experiments where subjects must determine whether two auditorily presented words rhyme. The fact that such effects can be demonstrated (cf. Donenwerth-Nolan Tanenhaus, & Seidenberg, 1981) even under the circumstances where orthographic information is not only irrelevant to the task but, further, may only interfere with subjects' performance makes it difficult to explain them without appeal to some notion like a lexical entry. (I do not consider automatic semantic priming effects to be comparable because such effects might more easily be claimed to lie outside the domain of a lexical entry.) But even this type of effect may be attributed to subjects' need to overcome frequently used strategies developed in more normal language situations, e.g., if phonological recoding is often a normal part of reading, a strategy of relating phonological and orthographic representations of an input may be sufficiently automatized that it must be suppressed under other circumstances.

The absence of compelling evidence for the existence of entries in the mental lexicon that look anything like the entries in an ordinary dictionary (i.e., entries containing information about the form, syntactic restrictions and meaning of an item) may indicate that more serious attention should be paid to alternative views of the mental lexicon. For example, it may be more appropriate to think in terms of a lexicon of phonological representations, containing only phonological information and organized according to phonological principles, a lexicon of syntactic representations organized according to syntactic principles, and so forth. (Of course, we must assume that a phonological representation may contain a pointer to one or more representations in the syntactic lexicon, etc.) Clearly this view is substantively different from the view where individual lexical entries contain representations of various types. For instance, the question of sharing a common entry may receive several (contradictory) answers on the view that there are several distinct lexicons, e.g., the noun *vent* and the verb *vent* might share a representation (or a location or address) in the phonological lexicon, but not in the syntactic lexicon.[2]

3.2.2. The complexity of recognizing lexical items.   What determines how long it takes to access a particular lexical item (i.e., to perceptually process an input and find its phonological or orthographic representation in the lexicon)? Current evidence suggests that the determinants of lexical access time may depend on what type of item is being accessed. Closed class items ("function words" such as determiners, quantifiers, prepositions, etc.) may be processed differently than open class items (see Bradley, 1978, but also Gordon & Car-

---

[2]Though I will not review the argument here, Fay and Cutler (1977) present evidence that a single lexicon is exploited for purposes of production and perception. At first blush, this might appear to contradict the suggestion in the text that there are several distinct lexicons, organized along distinct types of principles. However, in the present context, the (relevant) conclusion that follows from their argument is simply that language producers must be able to use semantic information to access phonological representations organized according to phonological principles and thus, in fact, their evidence is quite consistent with the suggestion in the text.

amazza, 1982). There is also an indication that some morphologically complex items are processed differently than monomorphemic items. For example, Bradley (1979) argues that it is the frequency of occurrence of the base morpheme (e.g., *happy*) not the frequency of the derived word (e.g., *happiness*) that determines lexical access times for words derived from "neutral" (Chomsky & Halle, 1968) or "stem-level" (cf. Selkirk, 1982) derivational affixes such as *-ness*.

The majority of experimental investigations of lexical access have investigated monomorphemic open class ("content") words.[3] If we restrict attention to these items, there are four robust and well-documented determinants of processing complexity: quality of the stimulus, the frequency or recency or occurrence of an item, whether an item is preceded by a semantically associated or a semantically unrelated item, and the lexical status of the item, i.e., whether the input is a real word of the language (see for example the review in Forster, 1976). It has also been argued (cf. Marslen-Wilson & Tyler, 1980) that the speed of recognizing an auditorily presented word depends on the position of the first phoneme distinguishing the input from all other lexical items of the language (though at present it is unclear precisely how this finding can be resolved with the finding that more frequent words are accessed more quickly than less frequent words).

These findings are explained in quite different ways in various models of lexical access (cf. Forster, 1976; Marslen-Wilson & Tyler, 1980; Morton, 1969). Reviewing the full set of findings relevant to choosing between alternative explanations or models would take us well beyond the scope of this paper. One issue, central to much recent work, is determining the stage of processing at which various factors exert their influence. For example, does the frequency of an item influence its perceptual processing, a later stage when a perceptual description of the input is used to identify the appropriate stored representation of the input, or a verification stage of, say, hypothesis confirmation? (See discussion in Foss & Hakes, 1978.) Another issue concerns what classes of items are processed in a common manner. For example, it may be that within certain limits the quality of the stimulus has little effect on the processing of closed class items, but dramatic effects on the accessing of open class items. Progress in isolating the determinants of lexical recognition times may crucially depend on discovering the principles responsible for certain lexical items behaving as a natural class with respect to perceptual operations and lexical access routines—an area which has not received much attention to date.

3.2.3. Lexical contributions to sentence processing complexity. After a stored phonological or orthographic representation of an input has been accessed,

---

[3]It is not uncommon to find some polymorphic items included in lexical access experiments; the point, however, is that the majority of studies have not explicitly manipulated the number or type of polymorphemic items.

lexical items often must be combined with other lexical items to form syntactic words, e.g., in the case of productive derivational affixes, regular inflections, compounds, and novel words. Apart from a few studies exploring whether particular morphologically complex words are stored as such in the lexicon (e.g., Bradley, 1979; Stanners, Neiser, Hernon, & Hall, 1979; Taft, 1976), this issue has simply not been addressed.

Once words are identified they must, of course, be syntactically and semantically integrated with the other words of a sentence. The general finding is that this integration is accomplished more rapidly in constrained contexts than in unconstrained contexts (see Cairns, Cowart, & Jablon, 1981, for an elegant study teasing apart word recognition times from postaccess integration times). The mechanisms underlying this effect have not really been spelled out, especially in the case of semantically integrating the morphemes, words, and phrases of an individual sentence. However, based on an analogy with investigations of the processing of connected discourse (cf. Clark & Clark, 1977), one might guess that semantically integrating words and phrases is less complex when stereotypic word meanings (or uses of words) are involved and stereotypic situations are described, since fewer bridging inferences will be required relative to the inferences needed for nonstereotypic meanings.

3.2.4. Summary. An enormous amount of attention has been devoted to lexical processing in the last 2 decades. There are myriad findings concerning lexical processing complexity, yet no clear concensus about a model of lexical processing and thus, not surprisingly, few clear-cut generalizations about the underlying principles and mechanisms involved in processing words. In part, this can be attributed to the fact that the problem is a very complicated one, since the lexicon may be viewed as an "interface" between several subsystems involving both perceptual and cognitive mechanisms and both linguistic and nonlinguistic information. But I have tried to suggest that in part the slow progress in this area may be due to the still pervasive attitude that "a word is a word" (and a "lexical item" is just a fancy name for it). Specifically, the considerations here suggest that we may need to pay more attention to modularity within the lexicon (i.e., the representations in the lexicon differ in *kind,* the vocabulary of phonological representations being quite distinct from, say, the vocabulary of syntactic representations). Further, not every lexical item is necessarily a word, and vice versa; and, distinct types of lexical items (open vs. closed class, monomorphemic vs. polymorphic, derivational affixes vs. inflectional affixes, etc.) are not necessarily represented or processed in the same way.

3.3. Semantic Processing

In the psycholinguistic literature, semantics has been construed very broadly, often subsuming everything from lexical semantics to syllogistic reasoning and the role of nonlinguistic inferences in determining the representation of meaning in longterm memory. Providing a review or full assessment of these findings would thus be impossible given the scope of this paper. There is, however, one rather surprising generalization that emerges with respect to semantic processing complexity, namely, the scarcity of evidence indicating differences in the inherent semantic complexity of particular morphemes, words or "simple" phrases (for linguistically proficient adults). If this observation accurately reflects the facts (i.e., is not an artifact of the sorts of studies that have been conducted or a reflection of the insensitivity of current experimental techniques to minimal semantic complexity differences), it may provide a basic constraint on plausible models of semantic processing. Below I expand on this observation and then explore its implications.

In general, effects of "semantic complexity" are absolutely commonplace in the literature on adult comprehension. A word occurring in a semantically unexpected or unconstrained context takes longer to process than the same word when it occurs in a semantically constrained context (Cairns et al., 1981; Ehrlich & Rayner, 1981; Inhoff, 1983; Marslen-Wilson, 1975; Marslen-Wilson & Tyler, 1980; Zola, 1982, to take just a very few examples). What one does not find are studies using semantically uninformative contexts (e.g., "The girl was very _____." or "The _____ was very nice.") where substitution of different words of equal frequency and familiarity influence comprehension times. (Note: one can find memory studies of this sort, indicating a recall advantage for "concrete" or "highly imageable" items.[4]) The question is why not? Why, for example, shouldn't we find an abundance of studies showing that words that are systematically acquired relatively late in the developmental sequence (presumably because they are semantically complex) result in longer comprehension times for adults who are completely familiar with their meaning? Or, why don't we find that more specific terms (e.g., *teacher*) take longer to comprehend than more general terms (e.g., *employee*) independent of context?

Let's briefly consider some specific examples. *Die* seems to have a simpler meaning than *kill* (cause to die) or *murder* (roughly, intentionally cause to die), but comprehension times do not reflect such differences (cf. Cutler, 1982; Fodor, Fodor, & Garrett, 1975; Fodor, Garrett, Walker, & Parkes, 1980; Gentner, 1981; Kintsch, 1974). Or, to take another example, pronouns take no longer to process than repeated definite descriptions (e.g., *the postman*) after age 5 (see Tyler, 1983) when other factors are held constant, though the complexity of processing a pronoun can vary, e.g., depending on the location or distance of its antecedent (Ehrlich & Rayner, 1982), the number of potential antecedents (Caramazza, Grober, Garvey, & Yates, 1977; Ehrlich, 1980), etc. Even for adults the use of a general term to refer to an entity introduced earlier (e.g., The

---

[4]Begg and Paivio (1969), for example, showed a memory advantage for the content of a sentence when the sentence described a concrete and easily-imaged situation.

postman . . . The man . . .) takes longer to comprehend than the use of a pronoun or repeated name (Tyler, 1983), but apparently this is due to the "semantic distance" between the two terms (Garrod & Sanford, 1977), not the inherent complexity of such terms.

Some VP-anaphors (e.g., *did*) require the presence of a linguistic antecedent and the linguistic representation of the antecedent (e.g., its "Logical Form" representation, see Carlson, 1983) must match the form of the anaphor. Hence, these anaphors have been called "surface" anaphors. By contrast, others (e.g., *did it*) do not require a linguistic antecedent, e.g., entering the recently cleaned nursery now strewn with toys, Billy might defend himself by saying "Susie did it," but "Susie did" would not be linguistically well-formed. The fact that "deep" anaphors like *did it* do not impose a matching condition on the relation between the anaphor and a linguistic antecedent (when there is one present in the discourse) is illustrated by (10b).

(10) a. The plants needed to be watered. *John did.
      b. The plants needed to be watered. John did it.

Certainly it would not be surprising to find inherent complexity differences associated with interpreting these two types of anaphors. Available experimental evidence shows that the presence of a sentence intervening between an anaphor and its antecedent interferes with the processing of surface anaphors but not deep anaphors (see Tanenhaus & Carlson, 1984); however, to date, no general or stable inherent complexity differences between these two types of anaphors have been established (see Malt, 1982, Murphy, 1984b, and Tanenhaus & Carlson, 1984).

Of all the frequent and familiar lexical items in a language, one might (pretheoretically) have expected negatives or universal quantifiers (e.g., *all, each, every*) to be inherently the most complex to understand. However, again, it is not absolutely clear that there are inherent complexities associated with processing these items. Instead, what is clear, even to intuition, is that double negatives (at least explicit ones, see Fodor, Fodor, & Garrett, 1975) are difficult to understand, e.g., *I denied that John didn't lie.* And, with respect to universal quantifiers, it might be true that they are inherently difficult to comprehend (e.g., that *All kids like candy* takes longer to comprehend than, say, *My kids like candy* or *Little kids like candy*), but I am not aware of any convincing demonstration of this. However, what is clear, again, is that universal quantifiers may lead to processing difficulties when they interact with other expressions, e.g., quantifiers or elements with inherent biases toward multiple vs. singular instantiation of entities (cf. Ioup, 1975, VanLehn, 1978). For example, Fodor (1982) argues that the "reverse" reading of (11), where there is a different girl for each boy as illustrated in (11b), is difficult to compute.

(11) Some girl loves every boy.
      a. girl   boy
      boy
      boy
      b. girl — boy
          girl — boy
          girl — boy

The processor will initially construct a single girl (i.e., a single discourse entity) in its representation of the subject noun phrase. Hence, this representation must be revised (when "every boy" is encountered) to obtain the "reverse" reading where *girl* is multiply instantiated.

In short, though, we cannot be at all sure at present that there are *no* inherent semantic complexity differences associated with individual items or constructions (for items familiar to adult perceivers) the robust findings to date are not of this sort. Regardless of whether we look at the number of components in a word's dictionary definition (e.g., *die* vs. *kill*), the specificity or generality of the term, the linguistic form of expressions that can convey the same meanings (*did* vs. *did it*), or the "logical vocabulary" of the language (negatives, universal quantifiers), it seems to be the relation of an item to the sentence and discourse context that determines its processing complexity, not the complexity of its inherent meaning or form. Let us assume for purposes of discussion that this observation is accurate or nearly so (i.e., that at most future studies will reveal minimal inherent complexity differences). What sort of model would be consistent with the observation? We will briefly examine three approaches.

Crain and Steedman (1985) suggest that the complexity of constructing a mental model for a sentence is a function of the presuppositions carried by a sentence, together with whatever information is already contained in the model set up for preceding discourse (see Johnson-Laird, 1983, for discussion of "mental models"). The general hypothesis that the semantic complexity of processing a new sentence is a function of the number and type of operations that must be performed to "update" the previous representation of discourse surely must be correct at some level (though see Ferreira & Clifton 1986, for evidence that this does not govern which particular analysis is initially postulated for certain temporarily ambiguous sentences, as was suggested in Crain and Steedman). Recent advances in formal semantics (e.g., Kamp, 1980) do seem promising with respect to the task of developing an explicit theory of discourse representations. We may hope that eventually this sort of work will lead to more explicit claims that could give real substance to the general hypothesis that semantic complexity is determined by the operations needed to "update" the current representation of discourse. Note, however, that while this approach may lead to an account of how and why context influences semantic complexity, it does not really address the problem posed above, namely, why robust inherent complexity differences have not been documented.

Fodor et al. (1975) proposed that, to understand a sentence, perceivers must only recover a representation from which the entailments or truth conditions of the sentence *could* be determined. On this view, one does not necessarily expect inherent complexity differences to exist. To understand a sentence it would be sufficient for perceivers to compute something like a surface syntactic representation of the sentence in which (roughly) each morpheme is replaced by a primitive expression in the vocabulary of the (semantic) representational system. On this view, the entailments of a word are captured by special "inference rules" or meaning postulates which may be consulted for purposes of inference tasks, but need not be consulted for simple comprehension tasks. Unfortunately, though this approach does offer an adequate explanation for the observation we've been concerned with, it has one serious drawback. Put crudely, the theory can account for the fact that we detect a difference in the meaning of (12a) and (12b), but it does not really offer any insight into the fact that when we understand these sentences we know something about the *content* of this difference, i.e., if we hear someone assert

(12)   a.   To paint a house is fun.
       b.   To burn a house is fun.

(12a) and someone asserts (12b), not only do we know that different assertions have been made, but we know something about the content of that difference, e.g., enough to give rise to the suspicion that the speaker of (a) is merely a weirdo, whereas the speaker of (b) may be an arsonist. Crucially we are aware of some aspect of the content of the difference even in the shallowest sort of comprehension task, e.g., when asked to determine whether the string is syntactically well-formed. (For a more extensive discussion of these sorts of problems with both "translation" and "semantic" theories of meaning, see Chapter 7 of Hornstein, 1984.)

Another approach to the problem is to assume that the semantic representations computed during language comprehension are extremely vague, but are "pragmatically strengthened" by contextual and real world knowledge (see Kempson & Cormack, 1981, for an example of this general approach). We might assume that with each lexical item with lexical semantic content there is stored some "heuristically useful core meaning" that is anchored, either directly or indirectly, by participating in some correspondence relation to the world.[5] Given

---

[5]There is considerable evidence for the existence of mental representations corresponding to "prototypes" (e.g., Rosch, 1975). Though there is reason to doubt that these representations constitute the linguistic representation of the meaning of a word (e.g., see Armstrong, Gleitman and

this assumption (and admittedly it's a huge one that finesses many problems), we might hypothesize the following extremely weak constraint on semantic processing: for each "content" item in a sentence, perceivers must recover either this "core meaning" or a contextually relevant component of the stored meaning that is itself anchored. This proposal is clearly programmatic at best, but it will serve to illustrate a possible solution to the puzzle we are trying to solve. As long as the entailments of a word are still represented in the lexicon (and, hence, could be determined from a syntactic representation of a sentence), we can in principle account for the following facts:

1. Perceivers are aware of more than just the existence of a distinction in the meaning of two sentences like (12a vs. 12b) (since they must recover some "anchored" component of a word's meaning).

2. The complexity of understanding different items does not necessarily increase with the number of its entailments, or the complexity or specificity of its dictionary definition (since these need not be recovered in all contexts).

3. The complexity of an item may depend on context (indeed, the recovered meaning of the item may depend on context).

Is there any virtue to this sort of approach, assuming that it could be developed into an explicit proposal specifying how relevance to context is determined, how the above aspect of semantic processing relates to compositional semantic representations, etc.? I think there may be if we take seriously the (non-truth-conditional) context dependency of semantic processing. I think the following sentences are not atypical uses of natural language.

(13) a. Martin didn't fall out of the window, he jumped.
      b. Sally didn't climb the fence, she jumped it.

In (a), what we might call the "conveyed" meaning of *jump* is the intentional nature of Martin's act; in (b) the conveyed meaning of *jump* seems to be the particular manner of movement characteristic of jumping. But surely it is our nonlinguistic knowledge which is responsible for determining that, in real world terms, intentionality is the crucial difference between falling out of a window and jumping out of it, but not the crucial difference between climbing a fence and jumping it. Due to the form of the examples in (13), there is an explicit contrast drawn between the verb in the first clause and the verb in the second. However, it

---

Gleitman, 1983), representations of this general sort might serve to "anchor" the vocabulary in which semantic representations are couched, by providing a link with experiences of the world (e.g., with perceived objects).

seems that the conveyed meaning of *jump* in (13a) is also present in a discourse like (14a) below:

(14) A. Martin is in the hospital.
      B. What happened?
      a. He jumped out of a window.
      b. He fell out of a window.

Speaker B is likely to respond to (14a) by asking "why?" indicating that the conveyed force of Speaker A's utterance is the intentional nature of Martin's act; by contrast, in (14b), Speaker B is likely to respond by asking "how?". Examples like this indicate that it is not simply the explicitly contrastive form of sentences like (13) above that is responsible for the context dependence in the interpretation of the crucial information conveyed by the verb. In other words, processing similar to that in the contrastive sentences above may be operative in general. Further, examples like (14) suggest that this type of context dependence in interpretation is not likely to fall out of, say, truth conditional semantic theories, since the truth-conditions of *jump* are the same in (13a) and (13b).[6]

It should be abundantly clear from the preceding discussion that at present we have no explicit theory predicting the relative semantic complexity of understanding various natural language expressions. Here I have suggested that there is currently no overwhelming evidence in support of there being significant inherent complexity differences between different types of simple expressions, independent of their discourse use or the context they occur in.[7] If this observa-

---

[6]It has recently come to my attention that there may be grammatical reflexes of this phenomena. For example, Szabolsci (1984) argues that in Hungarian verbs like *draw* (rajzol), *sew* (varr) and *cook* (foz), which she analyzes as meaning, roughly, "cause to become existent, in a particular fashion," cooccur with indefinite phrases but only if they occur in contexts where their "existence" predicate is most prominent, and the "particular fashion" component of their meaning is pushed to the background. (To get an impression of what's going on here, native English speakers may consider the difference between: There is a man in the garden vs. There is the man in the garden. The latter sentence is acceptable only if *there is* is interpreted as a locative expression, rather than an existential one. The similarity to the Hungarian cases is simply that when we interpret *there is* existentially, a definite noun phrase is not acceptable.) David Pesetsky (personal communication) informs me that the genitive of negation in Russian has been analyzed in similar terms, i.e., one observes the definiteness effect only when the logical content, not the nonlogical or particular fashion content, is foregrounded.

[7]This, of course, is not incompatible with the existence of correlations between the linguistic form of an expression and its discourse function. For example, phrases introducing a new discourse entity may take longer to process than those referring to an already introduced discourse entity (Murphy, 1984a). Indefinite noun phrases such as *a mayor* are often used to introduce a new entity into discourse, but they may also be used predicatively, e.g., *He is a mayor.*

tion ultimately proves to be correct, it places interesting constraints on possible theories of semantic processing. In the course of discussing various approaches that might be consistent with this observation, I have suggested that current results are more in line with the suggestion that the largest determinants of semantic processing complexity in simple language comprehension tasks are those associated with the nonlinguistic processing of real world knowledge implicated in determining the "conveyed" meaning of an expression.

4. SUMMARY

Theoretical research on linguistic complexity has been motivated by the goal of developing a precise and explanatory theory of language comprehension. Reliance on experimental measures of complexity have proven very useful in testing and refining hypotheses about language comprehension. However, as hypotheses about language processing become more subtle, it becomes increasingly important to interpret complexity results within an explicit theory of the architecture of the comprehension system specifying the relation between different subcomponents of the language processor. Considerable experimental evidence exists pertaining to the complexity of the processes involved in identifying the correct analysis of a sentence at different levels of representation (lexical, syntactic, semantic). But detailed theories of the processes involved in each of these component tasks of comprehension have emerged only recently. Thus, it is only in the last few years that attention has focused on the precise relation between processing mechanisms, permitting investigators to develop more sophisticated tests of the locus of complexity, i.e., what stage of comprehension is burdened or facilitated during the processing of linguistic inputs with various characteristics.

In the case of syntactic processing, available evidence supports the view that systematic differences exist in the complexity of alternative structures (e.g., structures violating strategies like Minimal Attachment). Further, some evidence indicates that this complexity persists despite the presence of biasing semantic information (Rayner et al., 1983), even if that information occurs in preceding sentences where it can be fully processed before the ambiguous sentence is encountered (Ferreira & Clifton, 1986). In addition to processing difficulty due to syntactic ambiguities, increases in complexity are associated with differences in the memory burden imposed by different sentence structures (e.g., Wanner & Maratsos, 1978). Finally, the complexity of syntactic processing appears to be greater when many syntactic decisions are clustered together (associated with a local region of the sentence) rather than distributed evenly over the input string.

The complexity of identifying lexical items has been a focus of investigation for well over a decade. It is clear that the frequency, length and quality of the stimulus affects the time needed to recognize monomorphemic words. However, despite the attention devoted to word recognition, little is known with certainty about the recognition of polymorphemic words. Further, the results available to date provide little evidence for the common assumption of a single mental lexicon, containing dictionary entries subsuming all different types (phonological, syntactic, and semantic) of information about a lexical item.

Studies of semantic processing indicate that the complexity of determining the conveyed meaning of a sentence is influenced heavily by context. At present there is little evidence supporting the view that individual words or phrase types are associated with robust inherent semantic complexity differences. To my knowledge, no current theory can account both for the absence of inherent complexity differences and for the apparent fact that people perceive differences in the meaning on nonsynonymous sentences even at the shallowest level of comprehension.

ACKNOWLEDGMENT

This work was supported by grants #HD18708 and #HD17246. I am grateful to Alice Davison and Chuck Clifton for comments on an earlier draft.

REFERENCES

Armstrong, S., Gleitman, L., & Gleitman, H. (1983). What some concepts might not be. *Cognition, 13*, 263–308.

Begg, I., & Paivio, A. (1969). Concreteness and imagery in sentence memory. *Journal of Verbal Learning and Verbal Behavior, 8*, 821–27.

Bradley, D. (1978). *Computational distinctions of vocabulary type*. Unpublished doctoral dissertation, MIT.

Bradley, D. (1979). Lexical representation of derivational relation. In M. Aronoff & M. L. Kean (Eds.), *Juncture*. Cambridge, MA: MIT Press.

Cairns, H. S., Cowart, W., & Jablon, A. D. (1981). Effects of prior context upon the integration of lexical information during sentence processing. *Journal of Verbal Learning and Verbal Behavior, 20*, 445–453.

Caramazza, A., Grober, E., Garvey, C., & Yates, J. (1977). Comprehension of anaphoric pronouns. *Journal of Verbal Learning and Verbal Behavior, 16*, 601–9.

Carlson, G. (1983). Logical form: Types of evidence. *Linguistic and Philosophy, 6*, 295–318.

Chomsky, N. (1965). *Aspects of the theory of syntax*. Cambridge, MA: MIT Press.

Chomsky, N., & Halle, M. (1968). *The sound pattern of English*. New York: Harper & Row.

Clark, H., & Clark, E. (1977). *Psychology and language*. New York: Harcourt, Brace, & Jovanovich.

Clifton, C., Frazier, L., & Connine, C. (1984). Lexical expectations in sentence comprehension. *Journal of Verbal Learning and Verbal Behavior, 23*, 696–708.

Crain, S., & Steedman, M. (1985). On not being led up the gardenpath: The use of context by the psychological parset. In D. Dowty, L. Karttunen, & H. Zwicky (Eds.), *Natural language parser*. Cambridge University Press.

Cutler, A. (1982). Lexical complexity and sentence processing. In G. B. Flores d'Arcais & R. J. Jarvella (Eds.), *The process of language understanding*. New York: Wiley.

Donnenwerth-Nolan, S., Tanenhaus, M. K., & Seidenberg, M. S. (1981). Multiple code activation in word recognition: Evidence from rhyme monitoring. *Journal of Experimental Psychology: Human Learning and Memory, 7,* 170–180.

Ehrlich, K. (1980). Comprehension of pronouns. *Quarterly Journal of Experimental Psychology, 32,* 247–255.

Ehrlich, K., & Rayner, K. (1981). Contextual effects on word perception and eye movements during reading. *Journal of Verbal Learning and Verbal Behavior, 20,* 641–655.

Ehrlich, K., & Rayner, K. (1982). Pronoun assignment and semantic integration during reading: Eye movements and immediacy of processing. *Journal of Verbal Learning and Verbal Behavior, 22,* 75–87.

Fay, D., & Cutler, A. (1977). Malapropisms and the structure of the mental lexicon. *Linguistic Inquiry, 8,* 505–520.

Ferreira, F., & Clifton, C. (1986). Independence of syntactic processing. *Journal of Memory and Language, 25,* 348–368.

Fodor, J. A. (1983). *Modularity of mind.* Cambridge, MA: MIT Press.

Fodor, J. A., Garrett, M. F., Walker, E. C. T., & Parkes, C. H. (1980). Against definitions. *Cognition, 8,* 263–367.

Fodor, J. D. (1982). The mental representation of quantifiers. In S. Peters & E. Saarinen (Eds.), *Processes, beliefs and questions.* Dordrecht: Reidel.

Fodor, J. D., Fodor, J. A., & Garrett, M. F. (1975). The psychological unreality of semantic representations. *Linguistic Inquiry, 4,* 515–31.

Forster, K. (1976). Accessing the mental lexicon. In R. J. Wales & E. Walker (Eds.), *New approaches to language mechanisms.* Amsterdam: North Holland Publishing.

Forster, K. (1979). Levels of processing and the structure of the language processor. In W. E. Cooper & E. C. T. Walker (Eds.), *Sentence processing.* Hillsdale, NJ: Lawrence Erlbaum Associates.

Forster, K., & Olbrei, I. (1973). Semantic heuristics and syntactic analysis. *Cognition, 2,* 319–47.

Foss, D. J., & Hakes, D. T. (1978). *Psycholinguistics: An introduction to the psychology of language.* Englewood Cliffs, NJ: Prentice Hall.

Frazier, L. (1979). Parsing and constraints on word order. In J. Lowenstamm (Ed.), *University of Massachusetts Occasional Papers in Linguistics, 5,* 177–198.

Frazier, L. (1985). Syntactic complexity. In D. Dowty, L. Karttunen, & H. Zwicky (Eds.), *Natural language parsing.* England: Cambridge University Press.

Frazier, L., Clifton, C., & Randall, J. (1983). Filling gaps: Decision principles and structure in sentence comprehension. *Cognition, 13,* 187–222.

Frazier, L., & Fodor, J. D. (1978). The sausage machine: A new two-stage parsing model. *Cognition, 6,* 291–325.

Frazier, L., & Rayner, K. (1982). Making and correcting errors during sentence comprehension: Eye movements in analysis of structurally ambiguous sentences. *Cognitive Psychology, 14,* 178–210.

Garrod, S., & Sanford, A. (1977). Interpreting anaphoric relations: The integration of semantic information while reading. *Journal of Verbal Learning and Verbal Behavior, 16,* 77–90.

Gentner, D. (1981). Verb semantic structures in memory for sentences: Evidence for componential representation. *Cognitive Psychology, 13,* 56–63.

Gordon, D., & Caramazza, A. (1982). Lexical decision for open-and closed-class items: Failure to replicate differential frequency sensitivity. *Brain and Language, 15,* 143–160.

Hornstein, N. (1984). *Logic as grammar.* Cambridge, MA: MIT Press.

Ioup, G. (1975). *The treatment of quantifier scope in a transformational grammar.* Doctoral dissertation, City University of New York.

Inhoff, A. W. (1983). *A two-stage model of on-line processing during the reading of short stories.* Doctoral dissertation, University of Massachusetts.

Jackendoff, R. (1975). Morphological and semantic regularities in the lexicon. *Language, 51*, 639–671.

Johnson-Laird, P. N. (1983). *Mental models.* Cambridge, MA: Harvard University Press.

Kamp, J. A. W. (1980). A theory of truth and semantic representation. *Report of Center for Cognitive Science,* University of Texas, Austin.

Kempson, R., & Cormack, A. (1981). Ambiguity and quantification. *Linguistics and Philosophy, 4, 2.*

Kintsch, W. (1974). *The representation of meaning in memory.* Hillsdale, NJ: Lawrence Erlbaum Associates.

Malt, B. (1982). *Anaphora and discourse structure.* Doctoral dissertation, Stanford University.

Marslen-Wilson, W. (1975). The limited compatibility of linguistic and perceptual explanation. *CLS Papers from the Parasession on Functionalism.*

Marslen-Wilson, W., & Tyler, L. (1980). The temporal structure of spoken language understanding. *Cognition, 8,* 1–71.

Morton, J. (1969). Interaction of information in word recognition. *Psych-Review, 76,* 165–178.

Murrell, G. A., & Morton, J. (1974). Word recognition and morpheme structure. *Journal of Experimental Psychology, 102,* 963–68.

Murphy, G. (1984a). *Establishing and accessing referents in discourse.* Brown University, manuscript.

Murphy, G. (1984b). *Processes in anaphoric understanding.* Brown University, manuscript.

Rayner, K., Carlson, M., & Frazier, L. (1983). The interaction of syntax and semantics during sentence processing: Eye movements in the analysis of semantically biased sentences. *Journal of Verbal Learning and Verbal Behavior, 22,* 358–374.

Rayner, K., & Duffy, S. A. (1986). Lexical complexity and fixation times in reading: Effects of word frequency, verb complexity and lexical ambiguity. *Memory & Cognition, 14,* 191–201.

Rosch, E. (1975). Cognitive representation of semantic categories. *Journal of Experimental Psychology: General, 104,* 192-233.

Selkirk, E. (1982). *The syntax of words.* Cambridge, MA: MIT Press.

Stanners, R. F., Neiser, J. J., Hernon, W. P., & Hall, R. (1979). Memory representation for morphologically related words. *Journal of Verbal Learning and Verbal Behavior, 6,* 26–32.

Szabolcsi, A. (1984, September). From the definiteness effect to lexical integrity. Presented at University of Massachusetts.

Taft, L. (1976). *Morphological and syllabic analysis in word recognition.* Doctoral dissertation, Monash University.

Tanenhaus, M., & Carlson, G. (1984). Processing deep and surface anaphors. Submitted to *Cognitive Psychology.*

Tyler, L. K. (1983). The development of discourse mapping processes: The on-line interpretation of anaphoric expressions. *Cognition, 13,* 309–342.

Van Lehn, K. A. (1978). Determining the scope of English quantifiers (Technical Report). MIT Artificial Intelligence.

Wanner, E., & Maratsos, M. (1978). An ATN approach to comprehension. In M. Halle, J. Bresnan, & G. A. Miller (Eds.), *Linguistic theory and psychological reality.* Cambridge, MA: MIT Press.

Zola, D. (1982). The effect of redundancy on the perception of words in reading. Doctoral dissertation, Cornell University.

9

Of Butchers and Bakers and Candlestick-Makers: The Problem of Morphology in Understanding Words

Janet H. Randall
Northeastern University

INTRODUCTION

What linguistic factors contribute to difficulty in reading? To answer this question, we must consider each of the processes that reading requires. From printed word to understood concept, processing written language involves roughly four sequential tasks:

(1) a. decoding the English spelling system into a phonetic representation
     b. parsing this phonetic output into linguistically relevant structural units
     c. assigning these structural units meanings
     d. mapping these meanings onto the world

To see what a reader must do to accomplish each of the tasks in (1a–d), consider the simple example of reading a string of two words: "the cat." Applying processes (1a–d) to this phrase results in the representations of (2) (see example on page 224).

First, the orthographic word forms are translated into a phonetic/phonological representation, (a). From here, a constituent structure, (b), is determined, each lexical item assigned to a category and these categories grouped into higher-level structural arrangements. Next, semantic interpretation occurs, where the meanings of individual words are determined and combined to determine a meaning for the phrase, (c). Finally, a match is made between this meaning and an entity or concept in the world, (d).

The picture looks simple but, in fact, the decoding processes can be extremely

(2)

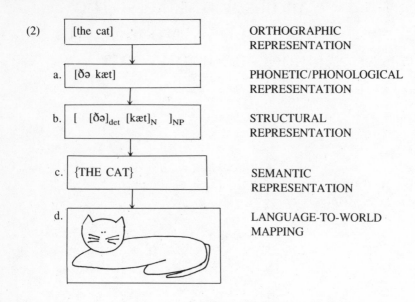

[the cat]	ORTHOGRAPHIC REPRESENTATION
a. [ðə kæt]	PHONETIC/PHONOLOGICAL REPRESENTATION
b. [[ðə]$_{det}$ [kæt]$_N$]$_{NP}$	STRUCTURAL REPRESENTATION
c. {THE CAT}	SEMANTIC REPRESENTATION
d.	LANGUAGE-TO-WORLD MAPPING

complex, because decoding at each level is potentially complicated by a variety of linguistic factors. To see what these are, we address two questions: (1) What linguistic analyses are performed on a word at each level? (2) What knowledge do these analyses require? After a coarse-grained answer to these questions for the four levels in turn, we do a fine-grained analysis of decoding from the structural level, (b), to the level of meaning, (c). Here we focus on the morphological analyses that must be performed, analyses which require us to know about the internal structures of words.

Unpacking morphologically complex words like *dancer, flatness, reglue* into their parts involves understanding what the parts are and how they may be arranged. The main portion of this chapter reports on a study of the learning of one morphological rule in English, the rule for the agent suffix, *-er*. The study shows that morphological complexity aids comprehension. In essence, acquiring morphological knowledge is acquiring a set of keys which can be used to unlock new, long, infrequent, or otherwise complex words. Moreover, knowing a morpheme like *-er* entails knowing syntactic as well as morphological facts. Because of this, syntactic and morphological decoding interact we are led to the conclusion that the relation that holds between word properties—length, frequency, complexity—and difficulty in comprehension is far from simple. We must take into account many linguistic factors if we are to have an accurate picture of how word properties cause or alleviate difficulty in reading, and under what conditions.

1. THE TASKS OF DECODING

To consider the effects of word-length and frequency, we can look at them in the context of the word-decoding tasks identified in (1), since reading is only accomplished once processes (a)–(d) are carried out on each word. We will leave aside (d), the word-to-world mappings (which involve factors beyond the linguistic), to discuss the first three levels of decoding. To see how word-length and frequency operate at each of these levels, we must first understand what each level involves.

Phonetic/Phonological Decoding

Decoding a word from its orthographic representation means identifying the word as a sequence of phonetic/phonological units.[1] Spelled words must be recast into phonetic/phonological representations, as, for example, in (3):

(3)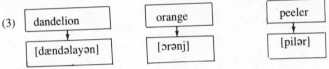

Structural Decoding

From here, each form must be assigned a categorial representation. While a form like *dandelion* can be assigned to the category [ ]$_{noun}$ in a straightforward way, often assigning a word to a category requires resolving ambiguity. *Orange,* for example, can be categorized as both a noun and an adjective.

(4)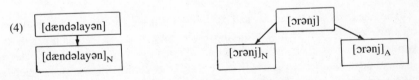

Such forms, with their dual categorial status, are clearly more complex than forms whose category is unique. But even categorially unambiguous words may pose certain puzzles. Consider words which are nouns only, but which are morphologically complex. Decoding these requires the application of what are known as morphological rules. *Peeler* provides an example.

---

[1] The phonetic/phonemic distinction is not inconsequential, and clearly not one but two levels, with rules that mediate between them, are part of the complete processing picture. We are glossing over this full account for purposes of brevity.

(5)
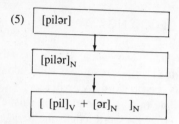

When words are combined into larger units, morphological rules must assign categories to the parts, as in (5), and also assign grammatical relationships between these parts and other words. Consider (6), the decoding of the two word sequence *orange peeler*.

(6)
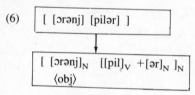

In this two word sequence, *orange* functions as the logical direct object of the second word. But when *orange* is interpreted as an adjective, the same combination of words may be related by a different rule, a rule of simple modification.

(7)
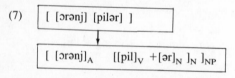

The rules assigning grammatical relations (for instance, the rule assigning the relation "object" to the first noun in (6)), do not depend on the meanings of the words involved. Rather, they depend on two other properties: the words' categories and their internal structures. To see this, consider a nonsense string such as *pote glasper*. Whatever the meaning of the contents turns out to be, the same two structural possibilities will always arise. The first word will either be the object of the second (as in "something which glasps potes") or will modify the second (as in "a glasper which is pote"). (See Levi, 1978, for additional examples.)

Semantic Decoding

A common assumption about meaning is that assigning meanings to words is a straightforward matter. This is certainly true for a subclass of the vocabulary since many simple words do have unique interpretations, e.g., *cat*:

(8)
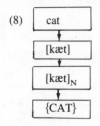

For the bulk of the lexicon, however, semantic decoding is much more complicated.

Like syntactic ambiguities, semantic ambiguities arise both at the word level and the phrase level. Again, *orange* is illustrative. Not only does this word have a dual syntactic status, in that it can belong to two different categories, it has a dual semantic status as well, meaning either "citrus fruit" or "red-yellow". However, these two types of ambiguities do not add up to two problems, since once the syntactic ambiguity is resolved, the semantic ambiguity ceases to exist. This is because in each case, each of the word's categories maps one-to-one onto a semantic representation:

(9)
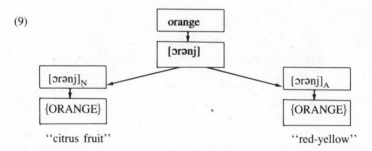

With other words, though, the problem must be solved at the semantic level; the syntax does not differentiate the two possibilities: [2]

(10)
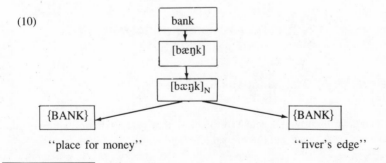

---

[2]In fact, contextual information may be needed in addition to semantic information to disambiguate "senses" of a word. See Nunberg, 1978.

We saw in (6) and (7) that when words like *orange* occur in phrases like *orange peeler*, syntactic ambiguities arise in relating a word to words in its syntactic environment. While this is true, there are also cases where ambiguities are resolved by semantic information. A phrase like *orange writer*, structurally identical to *orange peeler*, is potentially ambiguous in the same way, yet one of its syntactic possibilities is rendered unlikely by the meanings of the words involved. *Orange* is not the noun object of *writer;* it functions, rather, as an adjective, modifying it.

There are also phrases which are unambiguous at the syntactic level and branch at the semantic level.[3] A phrase like *beautiful dancer* in (11) is always interpreted as an adjective-noun sequence with *beautiful* modifying *dancer*, but two types of modification are possible. *Beautiful* can describe the dancer's ability as a dancer or the dancer's qualities as a person.

(11)

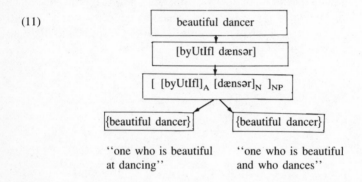

In sum, we can see that decoding a word from orthographic to semantic representations involves complexity at a number of intermediate levels. Syntactic and semantic ambiguity are two obstacles in the decoding process, facing readers of even the simplest of English sentences.

2. LINGUISTIC FACTORS IN READABILITY:
PRELIMINARIES

The Relevance of Oral Language to Written Language

It should be clear by now that much of the work that readers do in reading occurs independently of the fact that the message to be decoded is a written text. As we

---

[3]See Siegel (1980) for a detailed treatment of this example.

have just seen, understanding language requires a whole series of decoding operations beyond the orthographic; therefore, most complexities will arise regardless of the modality in which the language is presented. Spoken instances of phrases like *orange peeler* and *beautiful dancer* are as ambiguous as their written counterparts.

This may not be obvious, since one can claim that extra, more informative, verbal cues exist in spoken language than in written text. But it turns out that much verbal information is less useful than one might suppose, since auditory cues can themselves be ambiguous. Take stress, for example. In normal cases in English, the rule for stressing compound words assigns primary stress to the first member and secondary stress to the second member. The phrase *orange peeler* would have a compound stress pattern (12a) when both elements are nouns and the two form a compound noun (as in (6) above), but a nuclear stress pattern (12b) when the first word is an adjective and the two words form a noun phrase (as in (7) above).

(12) a. órange peeler
      b. orange péeler

While this might seem to be just the kind of disambiguation needed, it isn't. The distinction between (12a) and (12b) is confused by the possibilities for contrastive stress in English: (12b) may have the interpretation of (12a) if the speaker is contrasting this compound with another compound, an *orange shredder*. Conversely, (12a) may be understood with the interpretation assigned to (12b) if the speaker is contrasting a peeler which is orange with one which is blue, e.g., a *blúe peeler*.[4]

Given these facts, we can see that much of the work of decoding is not influenced by whether language is spoken or written. It is worthwhile, then, to consider how children comprehend spoken vocabulary items, since their level of comprehension of oral language and the kinds of difficulties that they encounter in this modality will certainly be relevant to their understanding of language in its written form.[5]

---

[4]For detailed discussions of English stress, see Chomsky and Halle (1968) and Liberman and Prince (1977). Roeper and Siegel (1978) characterize the rules for creating English deverbal compounds of the kind discussed here.

[5]It is relevant to point out that research on adults finds a sensitivity to morphological structure in both modalities, reading and listening. For reviews and discussion of various aspects of the question regarding reading see, among others, Henderson, Wallis & Knight (1984); Taft (1984); Fischler (1981); and Seidenberg, Tanenhaus, Leiman & Bienkowski (1982). For research addressing spoken words see Kempley & Morton (1982).

The Complex Word Problem

Morphological Knowledge. Contrary to what dictionaries would tell us, speakers of English know that the English vocabulary is not finite. Morphological rules that derive words from other words allow us to create a virtually unlimited number of new words from old ones, using a variety of word-formation devices.[6] *Reaganize, Woody Allenish, rexerox* are created using familiar prefixes and suffixes, by rules that speakers know through their experience with established words. The *-ize* rule, for instance, which makes nouns into verbs, is clear from regularities like *winter - winterize; fossil - fossilize; magnet - magnetize.* Someone learning a rule of word formation must hear a number of forms which share a particular affix, extract the common properties of these forms, and construct the general rule. The rule can then be applied to any new cases that satisfy its input conditions. Though some of these morphological rules are learned late, many morphological rules are acquired considerably before children learn to read. Berko-Gleason's (1958) classic "wug" test established that children as young as 3 years old show an awareness of how to create new words.[7]

Is Morphology Used in Comprehension? Although at first it might sound backwards, a plausible hypothesis about morphological complexity is that complex words are *easier* to understand than simple words. Think of it this way: what does it mean for a word to be complex? It means that the word contains information about such things as morphological regularities (e.g., affixes), grammatical relations (e.g., object of), and category (e.g., *-ize* = verb), information missing from the usual arbitrary relation between the form and meaning of a simple word. Consider two words of comparable length and frequency: [xxxxxx] and [yyyish]. To understand [xxxxxx], aside from the usual contextual cues, there is very little to go on. One must simply learn the meaning of the word. For the complex word [yyyish], the same contextual cues are available, but there are two additional sources of information: the base [yyy] and the *-ish* affix. However unfamiliar [yyy] might be, *-ish* reveals some insight into both [yyy] and the complex word. [yyyish] is an adjective; [yyy], either a noun (like [man] +*ish*; [fool] +*ish*) or an adjective ([yellow] +*ish*; [lively] +*ish*). Neither one is a verb.[8] These insights suggest the hypothesis that morphology is useful in the decoding of words. Complex words should be easier to decode than simple words. We will refer to this as the *Morphological Decoding Hypothesis.*

---

[6]Discussions of particular rules can be found in Siegel (1979), Aronoff (1976), Allen (1978), Roeper and Siegel (1978) and Selkirk (1982).

[7]See also Clark (1982) for further examples of children in this age range creating new words, across several languages.

[8]There is a body of experimental evidence on this point. Seidenberg et al. (1982) found that syntactic cues were used to disambiguate words during reading within 200 msec after a word is identified.

A different hypothesis is suggested by the usual variables measured by read-ability formulas.[9] Readability formulas consider word-length and vocabulary "difficulty" (determined by frequency) to be correlated with complexity, and complexity, in turn, to be correlated with text difficulty. Under this hypothesis, knowledge of a word's internal structure is irrelevant to decoding and so mor-phological complexity should play no role in aiding comprehension. Under this assumption, morphologically simple words and morphologically complex words will be treated alike.

We can contrast the predictions made by these two hypotheses easily. In the next section, I outline some research on children's acquisition of words display-ing simple and complex morphology.[10] The results provide strong evidence in favor of the Morphological Decoding Hypothesis, showing that children actively use structural information to understand new words, analyzing them (and some-times mis-analyzing them) into linguistically significant subparts. These analyses (and misanalyses) that learners impose on the language must be taken into account in any adequate theory of readability.

3. OF *PILOTS* AND *FLIERS*: ACQUIRING THE VOCABULARY OF AGENTS

Two Types of Agents

The vocabulary of English contains two types of words for referring to someone who typically engages in a particular occupation or activity:

(13)	a.	pilot	b.	flier
		chef		baker
		ballerina		singer
		dentist		diver
		nurse		climber
		cabbie		drummer
		soprano		dancer

The words in (13a) are all simple nouns from the standpoint of morphology; they are not grammatically related to the words for the activities that the agents pursue. In contrast, the words in (13b) are morphologically complex, derived from activity verbs by the addition of the *-er* suffix. Each noun in (13b) is transparently related to the verb inside it: a *singer* is "someone who *sings*."

---

[9]See Klare (1963) for a review and Davison (1984) for discussion and critique of this research.
[10]The research discussed here is originally reported in Randall (1985).

What *Pilots* and *Fliers* Have in Common

The two sets of agents (13a) and (13b) behave alike in several respects. Semantically, both types show the ambiguity of modification discussed earlier in the section on Semantic Decoding: *a beautiful ballerina* and *a beautiful dancer* both have readings in which *beautiful* refers to (a) how well the agent performs the activity and (b) what kind of person the agent is.

When ambiguity is resolved, though, to the extent that they are synonymous, the two types are interchangeable. Though not all dancers are ballerinas, and not all chefs are bakers, the ones who are can be described by both words. The *-er* affix on one does not make one more or less correct. Either can be used when the word fits the world.

How *Pilots* and *Fliers* Differ

There are many respects, however, in which simple and complex agents are not interchangeable. Their dissimilarities lie at the syntactic level. Because of their derivational relationships to verbs, complex agents can appear in a wider range of syntactic contexts than simple agents (Randall, 1984a, 1984b, 1985). In particular, agents derived from verbs that take direct objects take direct objects as well. They "inherit" the direct object of the verb they contain. Simple agents, with no relation to verbs do not allow an object. (In the examples below, an asterisk indicates that a form is ungrammatical.)

(14) a. sing sad songs
              fly supersonic aircraft
              bake fancy pastries
              dance tangos
     b. a singer of sad songs
              a flier of supersonic aircraft
              a baker of fancy pastries
              a dancer of tangos
     c. *a soprano of sad songs
              *a pilot of supersonic aircraft
              *a chef of fancy pastries
              *a ballerina of tangos

Yet, while a complex agent may inherit its underlying verb's direct object, it may not inherit any other of the verb's complements. In this respect, complex agents pattern with simple agents. (15) shows their behavior with prepositional phrases (PPs):

(15) a. sing into a microphone
              fly through the clouds

    bake with a convection oven
    dance around the room
  b. *a singer into a microphone
    *a flier through the clouds
    *a baker with a convection oven (on the intended interpretation)
    *a dancer around the room
  c. *a soprano into a microphone
    *a pilot through the clouds
    *a chef with a convection oven (on the intended interpretation)
    *a ballerina around the room

This is not to say that complements may not appear at all. Although PP complements of the verb may not be inherited as complements of the derived noun,
nouns themselves can take complements. A phrase like *a horse with a hat* is
well-formed, where the PP [with a hat] is a complement of the NP [a horse].
Agent nouns just by virtue of being nouns permit these kinds of complements.
  Consider an example like (16):

(16)   a diver without a mask

There is an interpretation for this phrase, but it is not the inherited object reading.
It may mean only "a diver who, in all respects, is without a mask," not
"someone who dives without a mask." The complement *without a mask* tells us
about the diver, not the diving. Pictorially, (16) may refer to Fig. 9.1c but,
crucially, not to 9.1b:

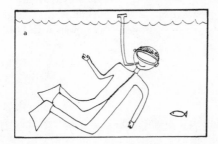

FIGURE 9.1.

As expected, the same is true for the synonymous phrase containing the simple agent, (17).

(17)   a frogman without a mask

Here, again, only Fig. 9.1c is correct.

To summarize, morphological complexity is relevant to whether or not an agent permits a direct object complement. Only agents derived from verbs allow them. Morphological complexity is not relevant, however, to the interpretation of any other complements, for example, the complements in (15) or (16). With respect to these phrases, complex and simple agents behave identically. Such phrases, when they appear, must be interpreted as a complement of the entire agent noun, i.e., as a "noun complement." It is this fact which makes (16) and (17), in all relevant respects, identical in meaning.

4.   TESTING CHILDREN'S COMPREHENSION OF AGENTS

The Morphological Decoding Hypothesis

We can test whether morphological cues are used by children in vocabulary comprehension. A simple test would be to look at groups of simple agents and complex agents matched for frequency and length. If complex agents were comprehended more easily than simple agents, we could conclude that children use morphological information to help them decode the meanings of agent words. But a stronger case could be made if we examine the comprehension of agents with PP noun complements such as (18).

(18)   a.   a diver without a mask
          b.   a frogman without a mask

As discussed above, the correct interpretation of (18a) and (18b) is to treat them identically. Both phrases correspond only to Fig. 9.2c because in both phrases the PPs function as noun complements. Thus if children were to treat the forms alike, we would have evidence that they understand both *diver* and *frogman* as nouns and *without a mask* as a noun complement. Although this is evidence that they interpret these phrases as an adult would, it is not evidence either for or against the Morphological Decoding Hypothesis.

However, we would have strong and specific evidence in favor of the Morphological Decoding Hypothesis if children were to interpret *without a mask* as a noun-complement phrase in (18b) but as a verb-complement phrase in (18a). It would be the presence of the verb inside the noun *diver* which could lead them to this error. They would understand (18a) to mean, essentially, a "dive without a mask *-er*," i.e., someone who typically dives without a mask. Since this morphological difference is the *only* relevant difference between the two forms, Morphological Decoding would necessarily be responsible for their differential treatment.[11]

Method

Subjects.   Eighteen children between the ages of 3 and 7 (mean age 5.1) were tested. All were enrolled in a day-care center in Amherst, Massachusetts, and all were native English speakers. In addition, 12 adult subjects, students at the University of Massachusetts, were tested.

Pretests.   Two pretests were designed to test the comprehension of (1) the noun-complement interpretation of PPs and (2) the verb-complement interpretation of PPs, to ensure that both interpretations were available to the subjects.

Pretest 1 tested subjects' comprehension of PPs as noun complements as in (19), where the phrase *without a hat* functions as a complement of the noun *horse*.

(19)   a horse without a hat

The subject was asked to select all the pictures that matched the phrase from an array such as Fig. 9.2.

FIGURE 9.2.

---

[11]It happens that the noun *frogman* is a compound, made up of two nouns. This morphological fact is not relevant to the issue at hand since there is no verb or other complement-taking category inside the compound.

Figure 9.2b is the crucial test of the noun-complement reading of this phrase. It is a correct choice (along with 9.2a) *despite* the fact that a hat appears in the picture. If a subject didn't understand the noun-complement reading of the PP and were merely looking for any pictures *without a hat,* she would choose 9.2a and not 9.2b. Four arrays were presented and only subjects with perfect scores on all four were considered as having passed.

Pretest 2 examined subjects' comprehension of PPs as verb complements. The subject heard four phrases of the form in (20),

(20)   a man diving without a mask

in which the PP *without a mask* functions as a complement of the verb *diving.* For each phrase the subject saw an array modeled on Fig. 9.1 and was asked to choose all of the pictures from the array which matched the phrase. A correct response requires two pictures: picture c, in which no mask appears at all, and crucially, picture b, in which a mask appears but the diver is not using it for diving. If a subject were not aware of the verb-complement interpretation of the PP and merely chose any picture "without a mask," she would not choose picture b. Thus, by choosing picture b, the subject indicates an understanding of the PP as a verb complement. Once again, only those subjects with a perfect score of four correct responses were considered as having passed. All of the children and all of the adults passed both of the pretests.[12]

The Experiment.   Once it was established that subjects understood that a prepositional phrase could act as a noun complement (Pretest 1) or a verb complement (Pretest 2), it was possible to test how such a PP was interpreted when it modified a noun derived from a verb. If complex agent nouns like *diver* are treated differently from simple agent nouns like *frogman,* then the Morphological Decoding Hypothesis is supported.

The Morphological Decoding Hypothesis was tested using the two types of agent phrases in (18) above. They are repeated here as (21).

(21)   a.   a diver without a mask
       b.   a frogman without a mask

Given the array in Fig. 9.1, only picture c is correct for both (21a) and (21b). Notice that this contrasts with the correct response pattern for Pretest 2 (also based on Fig. 9.1) for which both pictures b and c must be chosen. Sentences were constructed on the model of (21), with the morphologically complex agent examples (the a cases) parallel to the verb-complement examples in Pretest 2. To perform correctly on the noun-complement readings here the subject must choose

---

[12]Distractor sentences were included in the pretests for which the correct answer did not require two pictures, to keep subjects from using a strategy based on the number of pictures chosen.

TABLE 9.1

		Children	Adults
MORPHOLOGICALLY COMPLEX AGENTS	*1	0%	0%
a diver without a mask	*2	82%	0%
	3	100%	100%
MORPHOLOGICALLY SIMPLE AGENTS	*1	0%	0%
a frogman without a mask	*2	0%	0%
	3	100%	100%

one picture to match each phrase, in contrast to the two pictures required for the correct verb-complement readings of Pretest 2.[13] Distractor sentences kept subjects from developing a response strategy based on the number of pictures chosen.

Results

The results are quite striking. Table 9.1 shows the percentage of responses in which each picture was included in subjects' choices, across subjects. (An asterisk indicates that the picture does *not* match its phrase.) The responses to the two types of agent phrases are identical in all conditions but one: the children's responses to picture 9.1b. To the simple agent phrases (e.g., *a frogman without a mask*) the children responded correctly 100% of the time, never choosing the incorrect picture b. To the complex agent phrases (e.g., *a diver without a mask*) the children's responses were incorrect 82% of the time, in choosing picture b to satisfy the phrase.

It is informative to compare these results to the results of Pretest 2, which tested children's knowledge of verb-complement PPs in phrases like *a man diving without a mask*, in which the PP is a complement of the verb *diving*. These appear in Table 9.2.

Comparing Tables 9.1 and 9.2, we see that the children treated the complex agent phrases more like verb-complement phrases than like simple agent noun complement phrases. That is, the phrase *a diver without a mask* was interpreted more like the phrase *a man diving without a mask* than like *a frogman without a mask*, in terms of what the PP *without a mask* was understood to modify.

TABLE 9.2

		Children	Adults
VERB-COMPLEMENT PP	*1	0%	0%
a man without a mask	2	100%	100%
	3	100%	100%

---

[13]A full explanation of counterbalancing procedures along with a complete set of materials for the Pretests, this experiment and the experiments which follow are reported in Randall (1985).

It is important to keep in mind that the phrase *without a mask* is impossible to interpret in isolation. It is much like the simple noun *bank*, discussed earlier, whose meaning is unclear between its two possible readings, "edge of a river" and "place for money." Out of context, the phrase is ambiguous and allows either interpretation. Given this, the fact that the children responded correctly to the PP in Table 9.2 reveals that they *understood* that the phrase in this context is used to modify a verb. If they did not understand this, and interpreted it as a noun complement here, they would have rejected picture b. Considering the responses on Table 9.1 in this light, it is reasonable to claim that the misinterpretation of complex agent complements is not due to a problem in understanding either of the two possible readings for the PPs. Complex agents are difficult in precisely the way predicted by the Morphological Decoding Hypothesis: derived nouns and their complements are treated like the verbs from which they are morphologically derived.

Discussion

The data so far provide strong evidence that morphological decoding is what is responsible for children's difficulty with morphologically complex -*er* agent phrases. In passing the Pretests, learners showed that they understood that the same PP may function alternately as a complement to a verb (*diving*) or to a noun (*frogman*), and that its interpretation in a particular context depends upon which of these categories of words it is modifying. When confronted with nouns like *diver*, however, which are in a sense "in between" a verb and a noun, the children faltered, interpreting the PP complements to these words incorrectly, as verb complements instead of noun complements. But now we confront the following question: why should learners misanalyze these forms?

One hypothesis is that learners have difficulty with the morphological relationship that holds between a complex noun and the verb on which it is built. The relationship can be stated as a rule, given in (22). As shown by the double-pointed arrow, (22) may be understood to function in either direction, either to add the -*er* affix to a verb to form a noun, or to analyze an -*er* noun into its subcomponents, a verb and the -*er* nominalizing affix.

(22) $[\quad]_V + [\text{-er}] \leftrightarrow [\quad \text{er}]_N$

There are two problems that a learner could be having with this rule. It may be that she does not know that the element on the right is a noun; that is, she may understand that the word is a single unit but not know to what category it belongs. Let us call this the *category* problem. Or, she might think that the base words inside derived words are available to the syntax, so that the rules for interpreting complements can "see inside" complex words into their make-up. This would allow a PP complement to modify not only the word [diver], which is a noun, but also the verb [dive] inside it. While for adults, derived words are "opaque" to this kind of analysis by complements, for children they may not be.[14] Let us call this the *opacity* problem. Before trying to uncover which of these two problems is responsible for the learners' mistakes, it is useful to ask what, exactly, learners of this age know about the *-er* rule in (22), since if it were shown that they already control it, then a different explanation would be in order.

A study by Clark and Hecht (1982) looked at how children use a variety of word-formation devices (the *-er* rule among them) to coin novel agent and instrument nouns. For tasks requiring both production and segmentation, the results showed that *-er* agents are acquired throughout the age range of the children in the present study (3.9 to 6.0), the oldest of their groups giving 83% correct responses. This suggests that rule (22) is *not* yet mastered, and that one of the two problems outlined above is indeed responsible for learners' difficulty. But which is it? If it turned out that children who have mastered the *-er* rule still misinterpret the complements to *-er* nouns, then the problem is arguably opacity. Their ability to create *-er* words appropriately would show that they recognize *-er* words as nouns, yet it would not show an understanding that such nouns are opaque to complements. If, on the other hand, children understand the opacity condition immediately upon mastering the *-er* rule, then learners are facing a category problem. Until they master the category change invoked by the *-er* rule, they would continue to treat the derived word as a verb and its complements as verb complements.

The test, then, is whether there is a correlation between mastery of the *-er* rule and mastery of PP complements. If so, the problem is with category; if not, it is with opacity. To answer this question, Experiment II was performed.

5. EXPERIMENT II: AN ERROR OF CATEGORY OR OPACITY?

Experiment II was designed to see if a correlation holds between children's control of the *-er* rule and their correct interpretation of the complements of complex agent *-er* forms. Such a correlation would point to an error in category labeling, a problem with the "right-hand side" of rule (22). Until children understand *-er* forms as members of the category *noun*, they cannot treat *-er* complements as noun complements. However, there may be no correlation: children who have mastered the *-er* rule may still fail to control complementation. Then the problem would lie with learning a separate fact: that derived forms are opaque, i.e., that the words inside them are inaccessible to further linguistic operations, like taking complements.

---

[14]Versions of an "opacity" condition have been discussed in the linguistics literature. See Pesetsky (1979); Kiparsky (1982); Randall (1985).

The question is an interesting one, since if opacity "comes for free," then learning is simpler overall. Linguists have claimed that much linguistic knowledge does come for free, as a result of links among a small number of interacting grammatical principles. Such a system would make the task of language acquisition less complex, the learner's choices fewer. If general principles such as opacity were the "unmarked case," bound to all rules of word-formation, and if children assumed this from the outset, then individual opacity conditions would not need to be learned case by case for each rule in the grammar. The claim that constraints like opacity govern how children piece together the grammar has been investigated in a number of experiments in recent years,[15] and several putative "universal principles" have emerged. The present study, then, could suggest an additional candidate and if so, would have implications for the theory of language acquisition overall.

Method

Subjects. A new group of 12 subjects, all between the ages of 5 and 7 were tested, their mean age, 6.2. All were native English speakers.

Materials and Design. Experiment II replicated Experiment I (including the two Pretests) with one addition, a production test for -*er* agent forms. The details of the replication are as described above. The production test was given between the Pretests and the Experiment. It consisted of four short stories, in which a nonsense verb was used to describe an activity for which English lacks a one-word equivalent, for example, the activity of unrolling a roll of paper on a table. While listening to the story, subjects was a picture of someone engaged in the activity, as in Fig. 9.3.

FIGURE 9.3.

Each story required the listener to repeat the nonsense verb and to supply a properly inflected form of the verb in the middle of the story. At the end of the story, an -*er* form was elicited. The story corresponding to Fig. 9.3 appears in (23):

---

[15]See, for discussion, Goodluck (1986) and references she cites.

(23) This little girl knows how to *zib*.
      Can you say that? (*Zib.*)
      What is she doing in this picture? (*Zibbing.*)
      What would you call someone whose job is to *zib?* (A *zibber.*)

To be considered as having mastered the rule for creating words in *-er*, a subject had to produce all 4 *-er* nonsense forms.

Results and Discussion

The results, shown in Table 9.3, indicate a correlation between the mastery of *-er* affixation and the correct treatment of the PP complements to complex agent nouns.

In 11 out of 12 cases, the subjects who mastered the *-er* rule for novel forms were exactly those subjects who correctly understood the PP as a noun-complement phrase when it occurred with complex agents, while the subjects who had not mastered the *-er* rule did not correctly interpret the PP complements. In only one case did a subject understand how the *-er* rule worked but fail to interpret the PPs correctly.

The correlation explains children's lack of understanding of PP complements. It is a category problem. They do not yet control the category membership of *-er* nouns, and therefore treat these nouns like the verbs from which they are derived. As a result, the complements of complex agent nouns are treated as verb complements, and receive the incorrect interpretation found in Experiment I.

Beyond this, the correlation points to a link between complementation and a principle of grammar. It suggests that morphological opacity, or the inability for the internal parts of complex words to be analyzed by syntactic rules, is a general principle of grammar, and is information which emerges in learners alongside word-formation rules. It is not something which needs to be learned separately, and it is certainly not something which must be taught.

TABLE 9.3

	PRODUCTION TEST	
	-er not mastered	-er mastered
PP incorrect	5	1
PP correct	0	6

6. AN ALTERNATE HYPOTHESIS: WORD LENGTH AND FREQUENCY

Could these results be explained by the factors involved in Readability Formulas? The two factors to examine are word length and frequency.

TABLE 9.4

AVERAGE NUMBER OF LETTERS	
Simple agents	6.25
Complex agents	6.13

TABLE 9.5

FREQUENCY	
Simple agents	9.75
Complex agents	17.50

Word Length

If subjects' difficulty with morphologically complex agents were due to word length, then it would be because the morphologically complex agents were longer than the morphologically simple agent nouns. In fact, the average length of the two types of agents used in the study was almost identical, as shown in Table 9.4. The length of the complex agents was slightly less than that of simple agents.

Frequency

An argument from frequency would demand that complex agents be significantly less frequent than simple agents. The Kučera and Francis (1967) norms, averaged for the two classes of agents, are given in Table 9.5.

In fact, the complex agents occurred approximately twice as often as the simple agents, exactly opposite to what an explanation based on word frequency would require. It is interesting to note that these averages are based on word tokens alone and do not include any related words; plural and possessive forms of the agents are not included. Of course, a complex agent has many more words related to it than a simple agent does: the verb it contains, and all of this verb's inflected forms. Including these words would increase the difference between the two types, making the argument from frequency even weaker. We can conclude from these data that the difficulty learners experience with complex agents is not related to the frequency of these forms in the language.[16]

---

[16]Cutler (1981) cites two lines of research bearing on this issue. First, a number of studies suggest that uninflected forms and forms inflected for tense and number appear to be represented together in the mental lexicon. Second, studies which use these combined frequencies produce stronger frequency effects than studies which do not. Together, these suggest that word frequencies should be tabulated by taking items along with their full inflectional paradigms. In fact, with the Kučera and Francis frequency count, which does not separate the frequencies of homophonous words, this would be impossible, since complex agents are typically formed from verbs which have noun homonyms (e.g., drum, dive) which are not strictly part of the verb's inflectional paradigm.

7. CONCLUSIONS

In this chapter we have been considering a perspective on word difficulty which takes into account factors beyond those traditionally associated with Readability Formulas. A brief overview of the kinds of work the reader must do in order to fully decode a sentence uncovered a host of linguistic factors: phonological/phonetic, morphological, syntactic, and semantic. We looked closely at the morphological factors, at two types of agent words: morphologically simple forms (like *frogman*) and their morphologically complex counterparts (like *diver,* built from the simple units *dive* and *-er*). We found that morphological complexity influences children even before they learn to read. Decoding morphologically complex agents affects how children interpret words that follow them; decoding morphologically simple agents causes no such difficulty.

In these two studies we have shown that morphologically complex agent nouns are comprehended differently from morphologically simple agent nouns. We showed, further, that these differences are not predictable from the length or frequency of the two types of agents. The differences are predictable from the morphological structure of the nouns, the fact that complex nouns are derived from verbs while simple nouns are not. The subjects of Experiment I, who were in the process of acquiring the *-er* suffix as a general means of forming a noun from a verb, could correctly interpret a prepositional phrase complement when it occurred with a simple noun, but not with a complex noun. For complex nouns, they treated the PP as if it were modifying a verb. Interference came from the fact that the subjects were doing a morphological analysis of these nouns and basing their interpretation of the PPs on the verbs inside.

As revealed in Experiment II, once the *-er* suffix is learned, children can interpret complex nouns as nouns without interference from their internal parts and, as a result, can correctly interpret PP modifiers. Learning that a suffix changes a word's category has ramifications for how we interpret other parts of the sentence, because of the linguistic relationships among suffixes, categories, and complements. The information about complements clicks into place when a suffix like *-er* is mastered, so that learning this single fact influences comprehension on a much larger scale.

To put it another way, knowledge of the *-er* suffix entails more than just knowledge of one rule of word formation; it entails knowledge of the syntactic structure of the surrounding phrase and its semantic interpretation. Thus the presence of a component of a word affects not only the interpretation of the word but also the interpretation of the sentence. The presence of the affix also interacts with the linguistic knowledge of the hearer or reader. It hinders comprehension for children who haven't learned it, while aiding those children who have learned it in their comprehension of more than just the affixed word itself. It allows them to assign the appropriate syntactic structure to other constituents in the sentence and ultimately arrive at their proper semantic interpretations. Furthermore, the presence of a known element such as -er or -ish makes an unknown complex word more easily interpretable than an unfamiliar morphologically simple word. Hence, morphological complexity cannot be said to have a constant effect on text comprehension. As we have seen, in some instances it contributes to difficulty, while under other conditions it facilitates processing. Studies like the one reported here suggest that the relation between difficulty of comprehension and properties of words is far from simple, and must be investigated in further detail as part of an attempt to understand how language is processed and comprehended.

ACKNOWLEDGMENT

I would like to thank the Killam Foundation for their support during the time when these ideas were developing and the Northeastern University Research and Scholarship Development Fund for a grant which allowed me to write this chapter. I am also grateful to a number of colleagues and friends who provided provocative discussion: Chuck Clifton, Carole Counihan, Irene Fairley, Judy Shepard-Kegl, Mark Seidenberg and Larry Solan. Finally, I thank Kinley Roby, who let me use the department's Lanier.

REFERENCES

Allen, M. (1987). *Morphological investigations*. New York: Garland.
Aronoff, M. (1976). *Word formation in generative grammar*, Linguistic Inquiry Monograph #1. Cambridge, MA: MIT Press.
Berko-Gleason, J. (1958). The child's learning of morphology. In A. Bar-Adon & W. Leopold (Eds.), *Child Language*. Englewood Cliffs, NJ: Prentice-Hall.
Chomsky, N., & Halle, M. (1968). *The sound pattern of English*. New York: Harper and Row.
Clark, E. (1982). The young word-maker: a case study of innovation in the child's lexicon. In E. Wanner & L. R. Gleitman (Eds.), *Language acquisition: the state of the art*. New York: Cambridge University Press.
Clark, E., & Hecht, B. (1982). Learning to coin agent and instrument nouns. *Cognition, 12*, 1–24.
Cutler, A. (1981). Making up materials is a confounded nuisance, or; will we be able to run any psycholinguistic experiments at all in 1990? *Cognition, 10*, 65–70.
Davison, A. (1984). Readability formulas and comprehension. In G. G. Duffy, L. R. Roehler, & J. Mason (Eds.), *Comprehension instruction*. New York: Longman.
Fischler, I. (1981). Research on context effects in word recognition: Ten years back and forth. *Cognition, 10*, 89–95.
Goodluck, H. (1986). Developing grammars: Language acquisition and linguistic theory. In P. Fletcher & M. Garman (Eds.), *Language acquisition: Studies in first language development* (2nd ed.). New York: Cambridge University Press.
Henderson, L., Wallis, J., & Knight, D. (1984). Morphemic structure and lexical access. In H. Bouma & D. G. Bouwhis (Eds.), *Attention and performance X: Control of language processes*. Hillsdale, NJ: Lawrence Erlbaum Associates.

Kempley, S. T., & Morton, J. (1982). The effects of priming with regularly and irregularly related words in auditory word recognition. *British Journal of Psychology, 73,* 441–454.

Kiparsky, P. (1982). Lexical morphology and phonology. In I.-S. Yang (Ed.), *Linguistics in the morning calm.* Seoul, Korea: Hanshin.

Klare, G. R. (1963). *The measurement of readability.* Ames: Iowa State University Press.

Kučera, H., & Francis, W. N. (1967). *Computational analysis of present day American English.* Providence, RI: Brown University Press.

Levi, J. N. (1978). *Syntax and semantics of complex nominals.* New York: Academic Press.

Liberman, M., & Prince, A. (1977). On stress and linguistic rhythm. *Linguistic Inquiry, 8,* 249–336.

Nunberg, G. (1978). *Pragmatics of reference.* Unpublished doctoral dissertation, City University of New York.

Pesetsky, D. (1979). *Russian morphology and linguistic theory.* Unpublished manuscript, MIT.

Randall, J. H. (1985). *Morphological structure and language acquisition.* New York: Garland.

Randall, J. H. (1984a). Thematic structure and inheritance. *Quaderni di Semantica, 5,* 92–110.

Randall, J. H. (1984b). Morphological complementation. *MIT Working Papers in Linguistics, 7,* 70–85.

Roeper, T., & Siegel, M. E. A. (1978). A lexical transformation for verbal compounds. *Linguistic Inquiry, 9,* 199–260.

Seidenberg, M. S., Tanenhaus, M. K., Leiman, J. M., & Bienkowski, M. (1982). Automatic access in the meanings of ambiguous words in context: Some limitations of knowledge-based processing. *Cognitive Psychology, 14,* 489–537.

Selkirk, E. (1982). *The syntax of words.* Linguistic Inquiry Monograph #7. Cambridge, MA: MIT Press.

Siegel, D. (1979). *Topics in English morphology.* New York: Garland.

Siegel, M. E. A. (1980). *Capturing the adjective.* New York: Garland.

Taft, M. (1984). Evidence for an abstract lexical representation of word structure. *Memory and Cognition, 12,* 264–269.

10 Factors of Linguistic Complexity and Performance

Carlota S. Smith
University of Texas, and Center for Advanced Study in the Behavioral Sciences

The linguistic features of a sentence make it relatively simple or complex, and one might expect linguistic performance to reflect some features of complexity. This chapter addresses questions about the relation between linguistic complexity and performance. Some empirical research with young children is reported, within a theoretical framework for dealing with complexity. The experimental question was whether and how aspects of linguistic complexity affect comprehension and production. This chapter is organized as follows: Section 1 (p. 249) outlines the theory of linguistic complexity and discusses the linguistic structures that were tested experimentally; Sections 2 and 3 (pp. 256 and 262) present the experiments and their results; Section 4 (p. 266) considers the experimental tasks; Section 5 gives a detailed discussion of linguistic complexity (pp. 270).

Psycholinguistics is concerned with the psychological processes underlying linguistic performance. Much psycholinguistic research focuses on the structure and strategies of the human parser, and its interaction with other systems. In studying comprehension, for example, investigators may seek to determine the processes involved in the construction of a parse tree (cf. the pioneering work of Kimball 1973, and the paper by Frazier in this volume). Such research addresses questions about how parse trees are constructed. The properties of the parse tree itself are taken for granted, as are the other aspects of the linguistic structure of a sentence. This approach leaves a rather surprising gap: We know little about whether and how linguistic structure affects performance.

It is hard to imagine that linguistic structure has no effect at all on performance, and in fact such a view is not generally held. Miller and Chomsky (1963), for instance, discuss the processing difficulties of sentences with multiple embeddings, and Chomsky's early papers point out that transformations tend to reduce abstract structure, and thereby simplify the task of the speaker or hearer. More recently, various efforts to elucidate the relation between the linguistic grammar and performance have been made, so far without notable success.[1] But informally the notion prevails that linguistic complexity increases processing time and perhaps processing difficulty. This notion is quite plausible; but not easy to investigate in the absence of an independent characterization of linguistic complexity.

In the field of child language acquisition, linguistic complexity is generally thought to influence language development. The topic is occasionally discussed; but the contributions of cognitive development and processing capacity to acquisition have received more attention. It seems fair to say that researchers assume that linguistically complex structures are learned later than simple structures, other things being equal. Again, this assumption seems entirely plausible; but it has not been tested seriously.[2]

It is reasonable to suppose that linguistic complexity is a component in linguistic processing and language development; perhaps it is an important component. To give content to this plausible idea, and to make it testable, an independent theory of linguistic complexity is required. What is needed is a way of gauging the linguistic complexity of a sentence which is independent of performance factors. This chapter presents a theory of linguistic complexity and some experimental studies in child language acquisition which test that theory.

The theory of complexity is set in the framework of the linguistic theory known as the Government and Binding theory (cf. Chomsky, 1981).[3] This theory focuses on features of linguistic structure that are important for the discussion of linguistic complexity. The Government and Binding theory (GB) has a modular organization: it is composed of separate, interacting modules that account for the lexical, syntactic, interpretive, and phonological properties of

---

[1]In the 1960's attempts were made to relate the processing of a sentence to its derivation in generative grammar of the type presented in Chomsky's "Aspects of the Theory of Syntax," that is, the Standard Theory. The Derivational Theory of Complexity, an interesting attempt along these lines, was abandoned after research showed it to be untenable; for discussion, see Section 5.1 below. More recently, two different approaches have been proposed: in one, the relation between a linguistic grammar and performance is said to be "indirect," cf. Berwick & Weinberg, 1982; Berwick, 1983. Another approach suggests a different organization of the grammar, cf. Bresnan, 1978, and Ford, Bresnan, & Kaplan, 1982. For comments, see Steedman, 1985.

[2]Researchers in reading and in writing have developed indices of written sentences and surface linguistic complexity, some of them both sophisticated and successful, cf. Bormuth (1966), Botel, Dawkins, & Granowsky (1973), Kintsch and Vipond (1979) and references in this volume.

[3]There are currently several competing general theories in linguistics, notably in addition to the Government and Binding Theory, Lexical Functional Grammar (cf. Bresnan, 1982) and Generalized Phrase Structure Grammar (cf. Gazdar, Pullum, Klein, & Sag, 1985). Their similarities are more striking than their differences, except in the relation between surface structure and semantic representation.

linguistic structure. This organization is well adapted to the assessment of different types of complexity presented here. The GB approach to sentence interpretation is of particular interest; the approach is discussed below.

The Government and Binding theory within generative grammar provides a rich set of linguistic structures at the syntactic, semantic, and phonological levels (Chomsky, 1981; Van Riemsdijk & Williams, 1986). The structures associated with a given sentence represent what the speaker or hearer knows about that sentence. The various levels are all relevant to the generation and interpretation of a sentence, including material that is not phonetically realized. This suggests that factors besides those of surface structure are relevant to the processing of a sentence.

According to the theory of linguistic complexity outlined in section 1, the complexity of a sentence is assessed at the different levels of the grammar. For a given sentence a complexity profile is constructed, that assesses its complexity in terms of its associated grammatical structures. If a sentence is complex at a given level, its complexity might be reflected in experimental situations which pertain to that level. Experimental testing of the theory requires presenting sentences of different complexity profiles to subjects in a task that involves the comprehension or production of the sentences. In these tests sentences were presented to young children, partly because they are often more likely than adults to produce interesting verbal data in an experimental situation.

The experimental studies were designed to investigate the relation between linguistic complexity and performance. They were jointly planned and conducted by Anne van Kleeck and myself (Smith & van Kleeck, 1986). The most general experimental question was whether linguistic complexity would affect the performance of young children in two familiar experimental tasks, toy moving and imitation. The stimuli for these tasks were sentences that varied in linguistic complexity. The possible outcomes were three: linguistic complexity might not affect the children's performance; it might affect their performance consistently; it might affect performance inconsistently.

The effect of linguistic complexity on performance was expected to depend to some extent on the task, especially considering that young children are not expert talkers. In fact, substantial differences in the effect of linguistic complexity on the two tasks did emerge. Because the differences were so substantial, the results have important methodological implications for the use and interpretation of these tasks as measures of comprehension or processing load.

1.   LINGUISTIC COMPLEXITY

1.1.   The Components of Linguistic Complexity

I suggest that linguistic complexity is a property of individual sentences, and is a result of several factors in combination. I take it that grammatical factors contribute to complexity at each component. Thus I distinguish the following types: systematic complexity, surface syntactic complexity, interpretive complexity, and phonological complexity.

These factors are assessed for sentences. For a given sentence a complexity profile is constructed, that indicates its complexity at each level. A sentence may have high complexity of one type and low complexity of another, and there are some interactions between components, discussed below: for example, sentences that are high in interpretive complexity (with missing elements) tend to be low in amount, or length in number of words. Perhaps the most complex sentences are high in complexity of all kinds.

Not all types of linguistic complexity can be expected to have an effect on performance. It may be that certain factors make little or no difference, whereas others with little *cost* in grammatical terms—such as length, number of words— make a big difference. In section 5 I discuss three of the components of complexity in the framework of linguistic theory; I do not discuss the fourth component, phonological complexity, in this chapter.

1. Surface Complexity

Surface syntactic complexity assesses a sentence at surface structure, which is the linguistic level at which all syntactic rules have applied; interpretive and phonological rules have not yet applied. (I follow essentially the organization of the grammar in GB theory.) For the purposes of this discussion the syntactic surface structure of a sentence is a tree with labeled bracketing of its preterminal nodes (see example 1 below). Terminal nodes are words, morphemes, or empty categories; nonterminal nodes are phrasal categories. Empty categories (e) indicate morphemes that have no overt form, as in 3b below.[4]

The determinants of surface complexity are Amount, Density, and Ambiguity. Amount refers to the number of linguistic units in a sentence: it involves words and morphemes. The amount of a sentence contributes to its surface complexity. The longer and more morphologically complex a sentence is, the higher its complexity. Ambiguity involves the surface structure interpretation of a sentence. Sentences with more than one bracketing, or category interpretations, are ambiguous.[5] Number of interpretations contributes to complexity: the more bracketings and interpretations of a surface structure, the higher its complexity.

---

[4]Theta roles (agent, patient, etc.) and referential indices are also indicated in surface structure, according to some versions of the Government and Binding theory. Their interpretation will not be considered here.

[5]These two types of ambiguity are illustrated by two well-known examples. Surface structure ambiguity: "They are flying planes" has two bracketings, according to whether "flying" is part of the verb or part of the object nounphrase; different category interpretations, the subject nounphrase of "Visiting relatives can be boring" has two interpretations (Adj Noun) the relatives who visit, and (Ving Noun) to visit (one's) relatives.

Density of structure refers to the way linguistic material is distributed in a sentence. Material may be distributed quite evenly among the units of a sentence (that is, NP, PP, etc.); or many words may appear in one unit. When relatively many words are compressed into one unit or constituent, the constituent is dense. Compare 1 and 2:

1 [Mary wrote NP[a letter] PP[to her family]]
2 [Mary wrote NP[a letter PP[about the meeting]]]

1 has a simple object NP followed by a PP; 2 has a complex object NP, consisting of an NP and a PP. The object of 2 is denser than that of 1 on two counts: it has more words and more nonterminal node structures within a phrase. See section 5.2 for further discussion of the component of density.

2. Interpretive complexity

The linguistic structures associated with a sentence include those of semantic interpretation. Semantic interpretation is many-faceted; I discuss here expressions that appear in surface structure without lexical specification (empty categories) or whose position in surface structure does not represent their semantic scope (quantifiers, tense, aspect, negation).

In GB the interpretation of such expressions is made at a linguistic level known as Logical Form. The structures of Logical Form are homologous to those of surface structure, in that the same categories and phrases appear in each. Logical Form represents structurally the semantic scope of quantifiers and other expressions, and specifies the interpretation of empty categories. The position or specification of an expression may be different in surface structure and Logical Form. Rules convert the surface structure of a sentence to its Logical Form. (This does not, of course, exhaust the semantic meaning of a sentence.)

In the simplest sentences there is little difference between surface structure and scopal semantic structure. Complexity arises when the structures are not one-to-one. There are three main ways that interpretive complexity can arise: (a) the reconstruction or interpretation of empty categories; (b) the positioning of words or morphemes to conform to their semantic scope; and (c) the bringing together of discontinuous constituents.

(a) Empty categories in surface structure require interpretation, and thereby contribute to the interpretive complexity of a sentence. Consider for example the interpretation of 3a and the rough surface structure for that sentence given in 3b.

3 a Mary wanted to visit the zoo.
   b [Mary want+past [e [to visit the zoo]]]

To understand the sentence the empty category e must be identified with the subject of the main clause, Mary. Note that we can say this much without committing ourselves as to how the interpretation takes place.

(b) Semantic scope. Certain quantifiers, tense and aspectual morphemes, negatives, etc., have semantic scope over a sentence. Others may have scope over verb phrases, adverbials, or other constituents. For example, consider 4, which has a negative. The sentence has two interpretations, as shown:

4   The leaves of the sequoia do not wither for years
(i)   (not) the leaves of the sequoia wither for years
       It is not the case that the leaves of the sequoia wither for years
(ii)   the leaves of the sequoia wither (not) for years
       The leaves of the sequoia wither, but not for years

The position of the negative in (3) is fixed in surface structure, but the interpretations may differ in terms of scope at LF. In (i) the negative has scope over the entire sentence, in (ii) it has scope over the adverbial only. In Logical Form, semantic scope is based on the syntactic relationship of c-command:[6] a form c-commands material over which it has scope, and nothing can be in the scope of an element like a negative if the negative does not c-command it. Rules of Logical Form convert surface structures to structures of Logical Form, moving forms when needed to conform to their semantic scope (Chomsky, 1981).

(c) Discontinuous constituents are forms that appear separate from each other in a sentence, yet are interpreted as a unit; examples include auxiliary forms such as "be+ing," and extraposed relatives. They are discussed briefly in 5.3.

Sentences are relatively hard to process to the degree that their surface syntactic structure differs from scopal semantic structure, or Logical Form. Examples will be shown in the discussion below of the experimental sentences.

3.   Systematic Complexity

Systematic complexity deals with constraints on the rules that produce syntactic structures. Generally speaking, the rules operate without constraints, producing the full range of possible structures. But some words or phrases cannot appear generally: they have limited distributions. Such words or phrases add to the complexity of a sentence because they constrain the rules. The simplest situation is one in which the rules operate freely, without constraints. For example, there is a well-known set of words and phrases known as "negative polarity" items; they do not appear freely but require a negative of some kind in sentences in which they appear. The examples in 5 have one such phrase, "lift a finger."

---

[6]C-command is a technical term concerning tree structure. The form A c-commands a form B if the node directly dominating A also dominates B. For instance, in the sentence:

John said [that he was tired].

the subject NP "John" c-commands the embedded subject "he." C-command relations are crucial to co-reference. See Chomsky, 1981, van Riemsdijk & Williams, 1986 for discussion.

5 a I didn't lift a finger to help her
   b* I lifted a finger to help her

The second sentence is odd at best as a literally meant sentence, and ungrammatical on the idiomatic interpretation. Systematic complexity is discussed briefly at the end of the chapter, though it was not varied in the experimental sentences.

The linguistic complexity of a sentence may arise in one or more of the main components. In the following section I present the structures used in the experiments with children, and their characteristics in terms of the theory sketched here.

1.2. The Experimental Sentences

Three adverbial structures that differ in complexity were chosen as the linguistic focus of our study. In these structures adverbs introduce full, partially reduced, and maximally reduced clauses: the following sentences illustrate.

6 John called Mary before he visited Sam
7 John called Mary before visiting Sam
8 John finished supper before Mary

I refer to sentences with these adverbial clauses according to the structure of the clause: 6, an "S" sentence, has a full clause; 7, a "Ving" sentence, has a partially reduced clause; and 8, an "NP" sentence, has a maximally reduced clause. The sentences differ in surface structure complexity and interpretive complexity in a complementary manner that makes them particularly suitable for experimental work. Those higher in surface complexity are lower in interpretive complexity, and vice versa.

Surface complexity: the sentences differ in amount, that is, in number of words and morphological structure. They have the same density, assuming that the phonetically unrealized elements are present in surface structure. The surface structures of 6–8 are given in the rough tree diagrams of 9–11 (details and irrelevant factors are ignored):

9 tree for [John called Mary [before [he visited Sam]]]

10   tree for [John called Mary [before [e visit+ing Sam]]

(10)
```
              S ————————————
         NP        VP              PP
        John    V     NP      P        S'
             called  Mary  before      S
                                   NP        VP
                                    e     V      NP
                                       visit + ing  Sam
```

11   tree for [John finished supper [before [Sam e e]]

(11)
```
              S ————————————
         NP        VP              PP
        John    V     NP      P      S'
             finished supper before   S
                                  NP        VP
                                  Sam    V      NP
                                          e      e
```

The full clause is longest, the Ving clause shorter, the NP clause shortest. The NP clause is simplest, with least surface complexity, the Ving clause is next, with one more word and some morphological complexity, and the S clause has the highest amount because it is longest.

Interpretive complexity: the sentences differ as to whether they have empty categories to be interpreted, so they differ in interpretive complexity. Note that the correct interpretation of an empty category involves more than one decision: minimally, one must decide that there is an empty category and find its antecedent. (I make no suggestion as to how these decisions are actually made in performance.)

The full sentence has no empty categories. It requires only the standard interpretation for sentences of English, e.g., that tense and aspect have wide scope in scopal semantic structure.

The Ving sentence requires that an empty category be interpreted, which is the subject of the adverbial clause. There is only one interpretation of this structure, namely that the subjects of the main and adverbial clause are the same. Thus in 10 the empty category must be identified with the subject of the main clause, roughly as in 12b.

12   a   Surface structure
     b   John called Mary [before [e visiting Sam]]
     b   Interpretation
         John called Mary [before (John's) visiting Sam]]

The NP sentence requires the interpretation of the two empty categories that appear in surface structure. In 13 they are the subject and verb of the adverbial clause, and the interpretation of the sentence is indicated in 13b.

13   a   Surface Structure
         John finished supper [before [Sam e e]]
     b   Interpretation
         John finished supper [before [Sam (finished) (supper)]]

note that NP sentences are ambiguous if the main verb is reversible, as in 14.

14   John called Mary before Sam

On one reading the lone adverbial NP is the subject of the reduced clause, on the pattern of 13; though on another reading the lone NP is the object of the reduced clause. The two readings are indicated in 15 a and b.

15a   Surface: John called Mary [before [Sam e   e]]
Interpretation: John called Mary before Sam called Mary
  b   Surface: John called Mary [before e   e Sam]]
Interpretation: John called Mary before John called Sam

The factor of ambiguity contributes to the interpretive complexity of the NP sentences, all of which have reversible verbs (see discussion on p. 261).

In interpretive complexity the experimental sentences are in the following order (beginning with the simplest): S, Ving, NP. This order reverses the order of surface complexity.

Sentences with adverbials of the three types were constructed for these experimental studies. Adverbial structure was the main variable. Thus the structures varied in surface structure complexity and interpretive complexity, as elucidated earlier. Note that in the test sentences the factors of structure and amount are inextricably entangled. But this could not have been avoided by holding length constant. If we had lengthened the reduced (NP) sentences, the lengthening material would have made some sentences different from others. In a second experiment, discussed below, length was held constant.

A second variable was transitivity in main and dependent clauses. Transitive clauses have a subject, verb, and direct object (''The dog chased the cat''); intransitive clauses have a subject and verb only (''The dog slept''). The variable of transitivity was included to explore and control the factor of length, because transitive clauses are longer by one noun phrase than intransitive clauses. Only S and Ving sentences were varied in this way. Had NP sentences varied in transitivity, they would also have varied in ambiguity: transitive clauses are ambiguous in NP structures whereas intransitives are not (cf. ''John called Sue before Sam'' and ''John slept before Sam'').

Reversible verbs appeared in the experimental sentences to make sure that the subjects attended to syntactic structure. If the verbs are not reversible subjects can correctly act out a sentence simply by choosing the most plausible action. We chose to exclude the possibilities of implausible actions such as ''The milk drank the dog.''

The temporal connectives "before" and "after" were used with each structure; Clark (1973) provides a useful study of the acquisition of these connectives. This variation does not affect syntactic complexity. They have the same syntactic constraints, though there are some differences in interpretation (Heinämäki, 1974; Smith, 1978). The sentences talked about animals (cow, horse, walrus, tiger) and actions (intransitive: jump up, sleep; transitive: tickle, chase, kiss). Examples follow, giving the structures used in the experimental sentences. The full list is presented in the appendix.

16   S dependent clause
    a.   Both clauses (S1, S2) transitive
          The cow kisses the tiger before the horse chases the walrus
    b.   S1 transitive, S2 intransitive
          The cow chases the horse before the tiger sleeps
    c.   S1 intransitive, S2 transitive
          The horse sleeps after the walrus tickles the cow
17   Ving dependent clause
    a.   Both clauses transitive
          The tiger chases the horse after tickling the cow
    b.   S1 transitive, S2 intransitive
          The cow tickles the walrus before sleeping
    c.   S1 intransitive, S2 transitive
          The tiger jumps up after kissing the horse
18   NP   dependent clause
        Both clauses transitive [8]
        The cow kisses the walrus after the tiger

2.   THE EXPERIMENTS

2.1.   The Tasks

The experimental structures were presented to young children in two tasks, toy-moving and imitation. These tasks make rather different demands of subjects. Therefore, if linguistic complexity affected performance, we expected it to make a difference in one or both of these tasks. And, if performance were affected differently according to task, the pattern of results would differ for the two tasks. We discuss each task briefly before presenting the experiments and results.

It was expected that toy-moving and imitation might lead to slightly different results, owing to their different requirements, but that the results would be of essentially the same nature. This could only be the case if the tasks involve the same competence, which might be described as that of accessing and using grammatical knowledge in performance. Such a formulation suggests that, though types of performance differ, there is some sort of unitary access to grammatical knowledge.   But the results and analysis presented here indicate that the use or access to such knowledge is not unitary but task-dependent. The tasks of toy-moving and imitation involve different performance abilities and perhaps different access to and use of linguistic knowledge.

Toy-moving as a task focuses almost entirely on understanding: The subject hears a sentence and acts it out with toys. This means that the subject must be able to decode the incoming stream of speech into its linguistic parts and to hold it in memory at least long enough for understanding, perhaps also long enough for acting out. In acting out sentences subjects indicate precisely how they understand the basic roles talked about in the sentence, such as agent and patient. Toy–moving is also informative about other aspects of interpretation, such as empty elements or pronouns (cf. Solan, 1983). Since the experimental sentences vary as to how much interpretation they require, the task is an appropriate one for these sentences.

Since toy-moving requires understanding and interpretation, one might expect interpretive complexity to be an important factor in toy-moving tasks.

Imitation tasks are based on the interaction between structure and memory. The subject hears a sentence and repeats it immediately. The strategy for constructing experimental sentences is based on length: One uses sentences long enough to overload the subject's short-term memory, so knowledge of structure makes a difference in the subject's performance. Very short sentences can be imitated by rote; very long sentences cannot be imitated even if the subject controls the structure. For children 3;6 to 6;0, sentences of 5 words or less are very short, sentences over 14 words are very long. (See the discussions of imitation in Daneman & Case, 1981; Keller-Cohen, 1975.)

In repeating a sentence the subject is required to reproduce its surface structure, not necessarily to understand or interpret it. For this reason imitation is a task that focuses on structure rather than on interpretation. There is some evidence that subjects do not entirely suspend understanding in imitation tasks; see the discussion in Section 4. Considering the requirements of the task we would expect surface structure complexity to be an important factor in sentences presented for imitation. It was indeed the case that this kind of complexity was important.

2.2. The Toy-Moving Study

a. The Experiment.[7] The experimental sentences were presented to 44 children, ranging in age from 3.6 to 6.0, in a toy-moving task. The subjects were divided into three groups according to age:

18 Subject Groups
Group I: 3;6 to 4;6 years
Group II: 4;6 to 5;0 years
Group III: 5;0 to 6;0 years

---

[7]For detailed technical presentation of the experiments and of the analysis of the results, see Smith and van Kleeck, 1986.

The S and Ving structures were tested six times each: three times with "before" and thrice with "after." The NP structures were tested twice with each connective. Two filler sentences with the connective "when" were also presented. Throughout, the same toy animals were visible and within reach. Sentences with S structure adverbials talked about three or four animals; the other types talked about two or three animals. The sentences were presented in two blocs. The experimenter presented the sentences, and an assistant noted the child's actions. If the child asked for a sentence to be repeated, the experimenter complied without comment.

b. Results. The results are presented summarily here. Except in the analysis of errors I omit detailed tables and statistical support for my claims; see Smith and van Kleeck (1986) for full presentation of these matters. I focus here only on the material that is necessary to follow the argument.

Response categories. There were three main response categories: Correct, Error, and Single Clause.[8] Error responses are those that do not conform to the standard adult interpretations of the whole sentence. Single Clause responses act out a single action, usually that of the first clause (recall that all stimulus sentences talked about two actions).

Findings: the main finding was that children knew something about all three structures, but that the degree of control differed according to interpretive complexity, not surface structure or length. S structures, the longest, were best controlled, Ving structures next, NP structures least. The variable of interpretive complexity thus strongly affected the results.

To justify this conclusion it is necessary to consider both Correct and Error responses. It will be seen that NP structures were the most difficult, from the viewpoint of Correct and Single Clause responses. Details of the Error responses further differentiate the Ving and S structures. Ving structures were more difficult than S structures, in that the errors indicated considerable confusion about the Ving structure and little confusion about the S structure.

The Correct and Single Clause responses showed that S and Ving sentences were considerably easier than NP sentences. The NP sentences were highest in interpretive complexity. The percentage of Correct and Error responses was strikingly similar for S and Ving sentences, as example 20 indicates.

---

[8]The analysis began with 5 categories, which were reduced to 3 after analysis. Two original categories, Reverse and Failure, were eliminated. Reverse responses (that reversed the correct clause order with no other error) were combined with Correct responses into a single Correct category. This step was taken because Reverse responses indicated only the effect of the "after" connective and were not affected by the experimental variables. It is well-documented that order of mention and temporal connective affect performance, and that "after" is often interpreted as "before:" see Clark, 1973; Keller-Cohen, 1975. There were very few Failure responses so this category was combined with the Error category.

20   Toy Moving: % of Responses by Structure

	Correct	Single clause	Error
S:	56	21	20
Ving:	55	21	23
NP:	42	36	18

The structures that elicited relatively many Correct responses elicited few Single Clause responses, and vice versa. Single Clause is a minimal response in this experiment, since an essential fact about all of the experimental sentences is that they talk about two actions.

The effect of the other variables, length and age of subject, was also analyzed. Length did not affect the responses in a consistent manner. That is, the shorter S and Ving structures, which contained intransitives, did not pattern with any particular type of response. There was a significant relation between age and success. The oldest children gave a significantly greater number of Correct responses than the two younger groups, and significantly few Single Clause responses. The youngest children gave significantly more Single Clause responses than the others. (For details see the references noted above.)

The Error responses to S and Ving sentences show that the children's knowledge of Ving structures was less solid than their knowledge of the S structure.[9] Consider first S structure error responses. In most errors one or more of the NP's was incorrect, although both actions of the stimulus sentence were acted out correctly. Two types of errors predominated. Most frequent was Doubling, in which one animal did double duty by participating in two actions where the sentence mentioned two different animals. Also frequent was Interchange, in which agent-patient roles are changed within or across clauses. Many responses had more than one error; almost all errors involved the animals rather than the actions. To appreciate the error pattern, it is useful to keep in mind that S structure sentences have two full clauses; they talk about 3 or 4 animals and 2 different actions. Since these sentences contain no empty categories, the subject's main task in understanding is to remember the nouns and verbs and act them out in the correct relation to each other.

Doubling errors all have the effect of reducing the number of animals involved in the action: one animal plays two roles. Among the various Doubling strategies that the children used, the most frequent was Same Subject, in which one animal acted as subject of main and adverbial clause. This response may be due partly to the toy-moving task itself. Investigators have noticed that children prefer to use a single toy as agent in acting out multiple actions (Hamburger, 1980; Huttenlocher, Eisenberg, & Straus, 1968; Legum, 1975).

---

[9]There were few Error responses to NP structures; they will not be discussed here; but see Smith & van Kleeck, 1985.

The other frequent response type was Interchange. There were also a few verb errors, and some errors using an animal not mentioned in the sentence, called Outside. This error was possible for sentences with an intransitive clause; such sentences mention 3 animals and 4 animals were present. The frequencies are presented in example 21:

21   Error responses to S structure
       % of all Error responses
          Doubling   64.0
       Interchange   22.0
          Outside   9.5
             Verb   4.5

The small percentage of Verb and Outside errors suggests that the children did not have difficulty in understanding the S sentences globally. Outside errors might be expected in cases of general confusion. Recall that such errors were possible only for sentences with intransitive clauses, but the transitivity variable, as noted above, did not significantly affect children's responses. Intransitives did not tend to elicit Outside responses.

We interpret these errors to mean that the children had reasonably good control of the S structure, but that it tended to overload their memory.

Ving sentence errors. The characteristic errors to Ving structures gave the wrong interpretation for the empty category. (Since the characteristic errors were different for the different structures, directly comparable tables cannot be given.) The most frequent response chose an NP adjacent to the empty category as subject of the adverbial clause, as shown in 22:

22   The   cow chases the horse before e   tickling the sheep
(correct) Cow chase   horse   cow tickle   sheep
Adjacency Cow chase   horse   horse tickle   sheep

In the Outside response an animal not mentioned in the sentence participates as subject or object of the second action. These two error types, in which the subjects of the two clauses are different, accounted for over 50% of the error responses to Ving structures. The other Error responses preserved the equal subject interpretation but showed confusion elsewhere: the children used an Outside animal as subject, interchanged the animals mentioned, or confused or interchanged the verbs.

The frequent Adjacency and Outside responses indicate that the children were confused about how to interpret the empty category. One might question this interpretation by arguing that for Ving, as for S sentences, the children's main difficulty was not structural, but rather involved keeping straight the animals and roles in the stimulus sentence. Since an important feature of work with toy moving is the interpretation of error responses, I consider this possibility briefly here. If the children's error responses to both S and Ving sentences were due to the same difficulty, we would expect them to respond similarly to both structures. But the response patterns were actually quite different for the two types. The children responded to S structures with a same-subject interpretation (the most frequent Doubling strategy) 38% of the time. For Ving structures this response, which was the correct one, occurred 55% of the time. The difference in use of the adjacency strategy is even more striking: it occurred 37% of the time with Ving structures and 9.7% of the time with S structures.

The error responses to S and Ving structures, then, are due to their difference in interpretive complexity. The Ving structure requires interpretation; the S structure does not. The Adjacency strategy was a response to the empty subject of the Ving structure. Its frequency, together with the frequency of Outside responses, shows that the children did not fully control the Ving structure.

Ambiguity in NP structures: The NP sentences have two interpretations, one with the adverbial NP as subject and one with the NP as object of the adverbial clause. There is some evidence in the literature that young children are unaware of syntactic ambiguity (Kessel, 1970). If this is correct, the NP sentences would be high in interpretive complexity for our subjects because they have two empty categories rather than because of their ambiguity. However, the children's responses in this experiment indicate awareness of the two possible interpretations. The point is demonstrated below.

The ambiguity of the NP sentences is located in the lone NP: it can be taken as subject or object of the adverbial clause. Since the data in this experiment is behavioral, the children's responses indicate how they interpreted the lone NP's. Consider the interpretations given to NP sentences. As 23 shows, the NP's were interpreted both as subjects and objects by the group as a whole. The example includes only correct responses.

22)   NP Subject and Object Interpretations
        (group as a whole)
          Subject   Object
            40   60

These figures in themselves do not indicate whether the NP structure was ambiguous for individual children. They might result from a situation in which the NP structure was unambiguous for all the children, so that some children always interpret the lone NP as subject, but others always interpret it as object. It is now necessary to ask whether individual subjects were consistent in their interpretations of the lone NP. Of the 44 subjects, 36 were not consistent: they interpreted the lone NP as either subject or object. This inconsistency indicates that most of the children were aware of both interpretations of the NP structure or were responding randomly, knowing that the interpretation involved an action with a lone NP of S_2 as a participant. Of the 8 who were consistent, 5 treated the NP as subject and 3 treated it as object; the 8 did not belong to one particular age group.

c. Conclusions. In the toy-moving experiment, interpretive complexity significantly affected the children's responses. The most complex structure is the NP adverbial clause: it has two empty categories; it also has surface structure complexity because of its ambiguity. There were relatively few Correct responses to NP structures and relatively many Single Clause responses. The next most complex is the Ving adverbial clause: it has one empty category. There were relatively many Correct and Error responses. The Error responses indicated lack of knowledge of the Ving structure. The lowest in interpretive complexity is the S adverbial clause, which elicited relatively many Correct and Error responses. The Error responses indicated confusion, and inability to use knowledge rather than lack of structural knowledge.

Surface structure complexity did not affect the children's responses in this experiment. The experimental sentences differed in amount, number of words and morphological complexity; they did not differ in density. Transitivity did not affect the responses.

It is not surprising that toy moving, which is essentially an interpretive task, is sensitive to interpretive complexity. However the pattern of effect of length is somewhat surprising: not only did transitivity fail to affect the results, but the shortest sentences were the most difficult.

3. THE IMITATION STUDIES

Two imitation studies were conducted, continuing the investigation of the adverbial structures. One used the sentences of the toy-moving experiment, in spite of their variation in length. The other controlled carefully for length. These studies will be discussed in somewhat less detail than was presented for the toy-moving study. The reason for this rather summary treatment is that the error responses were informative, and considered closely, in the toy-moving study; in the imitation study the correct responses play the major role.

In both, the sentences were presented in blocs by the experimenter, and the children were instructed to "say what I say." If a child asked for a sentence to be repeated, the experimenter complied without comment.

Study 1. The experimental sentences varied from 7 to 11 words; there were 18 in all, exactly as in the toy-moving experiment. The usual caveats about holding length constant were ignored because we wished to compare the effect of these sentences in the two tasks.

There were 18 subjects, ages 3;7 to 6;2 years. Some had participated a few months earlier in the toy-moving experiment, but enough time had elapsed to make it most unlikely that they would remember the sentences. There was no indication that these children did remember them. The subjects were divided into 3 groups on the basis of age.

Responses were scored as Correct or Error; the Correct category included responses with peripheral errors such as change of article or number. Other changes, including change of tense and pronoun, were not treated as peripheral. (For detailed discussion see Smith & van Kleeck, 1986.)

The results of this experiment were unequivocal: length predicted the distribution of correct responses. Correct responses were infrequent to sentences of 8 words or less; they were quite infrequent to sentences of more than 9 words. Since the NP structures are consistently short, this meant that the factor of length overrode the other factors. The percentages of correct responses are presented in 24. The children over 5 years, those of Group III, did well with all three structures; variation occurred for the two younger groups.

24   Imitation Study 1
     Percent Correct Responses

	Group III	Group II	Group I
S clause	80%	36%	25%
Ving clause	90%	33%	36%
NP clause	92%	71%	54%

There were too few error responses for statistical analysis (but see the discussion in Smith & van Kleeck, 1986).

These results only confirm the familiar wisdom about imitation as an experimental task: length is the crucial property in stimulus sentences. Since length is a property of surface structure this finding accords with the expectation that the task be sensitive to surface structure, but it gives little other information. A second imitation study was then run, that focused on structure.

Study 2. In this study subjects were presented with sentences of equal length; the main variable was structure of the adverbial clause. There was no variation of transitivity or connective. The intention was to explore as fully as possible imitation responses to the three types of adverbial clause.

The experimental sentences all had 9 words, transitive clauses, and the connective "before." In order to keep length constant, we varied the noun phrases and verb phrases. Noun phrases consisted of proper names (one word) or two (determiner + noun); verbs consisted of one word (verb) or two (verb + preposition). For example:

25   Michael caught the cat before Pete tickled the dog (S)
     The clown kissed the giraffe before petting the dog (Ving)
     The monkey waved to the cow before the elephant (NP)

There were four exemplars of each structure; the test sentences appear in the appendix. The sentences were presented in one session, interspersed with fillers of different structures. There was at least one filler before each stimulus sentence and three fillers before the first test sentence.

The subjects were 10 children, aged 4;0 to 5;0. The first study showed that this age group is most responsive to the imitation task. Children older than 5 generally imitated almost all of the sentences correctly, and children younger than 4 tended to imitate almost none of them correctly.

The results of this experiment, surprisingly, supported those of the previous study: the NP sentences were easiest, Ving sentences less easy, S sentences most difficult, as 26 indicates.

26   % Correct Imitation Responses for all Subjects

	S	Ving	NP
	25%	45%	75%

There was little significant variation in the group as a whole.

The error responses, though limited in number, were revealing. The errors discussed are all in response to S and Ving sentences. The categories Omission, Change, and Semantic Change, covered almost all of the error responses. I discuss each briefly. An omission response omitted one or more words, as in the second line of 27:

27   Omission error
Stim: The walrus kissed the cow before chasing the horse
Resp: The walrus kissed the cow before the horse

It is interesting that omission responses were almost all syntactically well-formed. There were no responses which changed structure; the children never responded to e.g., 27 with something like "The walrus kissed the cow before chasing." Some omission responses were not quite grammatical, however. 28 illustrates:

28   S: The walrus kissed the cow before the horse chased the dog
     R: The walrus kissed the cow before chased the dog

For the response to be well-formed the verb form would have to be changed.

Responses which made a syntactic change were scored as Change. An omission often occurred in such responses, as in the response of 29:

29   Change error
     S   The walrus kissed the cow before the horse chased the dog
     R   The walrus kissed the cow before chasing the dog

The category Semantic Change covered responses that changed the name of an animal or the action, or both. There were some Semantic Change responses with more than one such change; the majority had one or two changes. As is well-known, responses tend to preserve rather closely the semantic domain of the original. Examples are given in 30:

30 Semantic Change errors
    S   The horse chased the walrus before hitting the cow
    R   The horse kissed the walrus before hitting the cow
    R   The dog chased the walrus before hitting the horse
    etc.

There were a number of responses with more than one error, usually one or more semantic errors and another type. They were coded according to grammatical error.

Comparison of the error patterns for S and Ving structures shows that the children had more difficulty with the former. S structures elicited some ungrammatical responses, whereas Ving structures did not, and S structures elicited more semantic change errors. Example 31 gives the actual numbers of error responses.

31 Error responses to S and Ving structures
    N = 40

	Omission	Change	Semantic Change
S	10	2	19
Ving	11	1	7

Evidently a factor other than length must be invoked to explain these results. One possibility would be to look for another type of property that differentiates the structures; another, to claim that the structures are not interpreted in imitation and that the NP structure is simpler. However, this would beg the question of what makes one structure simpler than another. Instead I shall continue to explore the hypothesis that imitation crucially involves surface structure.

Considering carefully the different surface structures associated with each adverbial clause, we notice that they differ in the number of surface nouns and verbs. The differences pattern clearly with the imitation results: The fewer the nouns and verbs, the easier a sentence was to imitate. The examples of 32 illustrate; the number in parentheses gives the number of nouns and verbs in each sentence.

32 Michael caught the cat before Pete tickled the dog (S:6)
    The horse kicked the dog before chasing the cow (Ving:5)
    The snake looked at the turkey before the rabbit (NP:4)

What mattered for the experiment was the number of high-content words in a sentence, that is, the nouns and verbs. Although unexpected, such a number is not inconsistent with the view that imitation crucially involves surface structure. There is a phonological explanation for the results, as Richard Meier has pointed out to me. Meier suggests that the NP sentences may be relatively easy to imitate because they have few major stresses. The subjects and objects of these sentences consist of two or more words that make up one phonological word; only the noun receives major stress. In contrast the other sentences contained more phonological words. The NP sentences may also have been shorter in total duration.

At the lexical level nouns and verbs can be considered complex because they are relatively constrained, and constraining. Such constraints are assessed at the level of systematic complexity. Both cooccurrence requirements (e.g., combinations such as "The dog elapsed" must be blocked) and syntactic factors constrain the appearance of a particular noun or verb in a sentence. Therefore the strong effect of nouns and verbs suggests that semantic and lexical properties are important in imitation. This topic is pursued in a discussion of the two experimental tasks.

4. THE EXPERIMENTAL TASKS

4.1. Imitation

The pattern of correct responses to the imitation task suggests that semantic and phonological factors may play a role in imitation. This is somewhat surprising since imitation is generally considered to focus primarily on surface structure.[10] We now consider the task more closely. There are two kinds of issues to consider: What are the processes involved in imitation and what degree of grammatical analysis is involved in imitation. This discussion is based on the theory of imitation in Daneman and Case (1981); see also Case, Kurland, and Goldberg, 1982.

In the task of imitation a subject hears a sentence and is required to produce the same sentence. This involves a minimum of three stages: the input must be decoded, to some extent; held in memory, and (re)produced, assuming that the imitation involves more than reproduction by rote. If the reproduction were by rote, decoding would be merely the phonological form. Minimally, to reproduce a spoken stream of speech, the listener must segment it in some way; the next minimal step is to identify the segments with lexical items. It is in order to force subjects to a more structural decoding that the length of imitation sentences is carefully controlled. The idea is that if the length of a sentence taxes subjects' memories, they will use their structural knowledge to enable them to hold the sentence in memory, cf. Miller and Selfridge (1951). Imitation tasks typically present a subject with a list of sentences and ask only that they be repeated. There are no connections with the context and no consequences: The sentences follow one another whether or not the subject repeats on or all of them correctly. I return to this point below.

---

[10]Though Keller-Cohen (1975), presents data in which lexical factors also make a difference. Keller-Cohen showed that children were more likely to be successful in imitating sentences with familiar temporal connectives than with temporal connectives they did not understand.

The basic notion behind the task of imitation is to arrange things so that subjects are forced to structure the input in order to keep it in short-term memory. Unfortunately, the notion of structure here is vague, since structures at various levels of detail qualify. Suppose for example an input sentence structured so that a subject is able to hold it in short-term memory. It might be partially structured, perhaps into major constituents; or structured into constituents but without labeled bracketing; or more fully structured. And the sentence might be partially or fully interpreted, though I assume that syntactic and semantic processing occur in parallel, as Marslen-Wilson and his colleagues have convincingly argued (Marslen-Wilson & Tyler, 1980; Waltz & Pollack, 1985). What makes analysis problematic is that there is nothing in the logic of the imitation task that requires or rules out a given level of structuring and comprehension.

This unfortunate situation is partly due to our limited understanding of imitation, but it is also due to the flexible nature of comprehension. There is almost an unlimited number of possibilities for partial comprehension: it is not an all-or-nothing affair. Further, no clear line separates one degree of comprehension from another. It should also be noted that degrees of comprehension vary depending on the circumstances under which a person listens to a sentence. Cocktail party conversation makes certain demands, following instructions makes others. As noted above, the context of the imitation task does not require detailed comprehension.

Some evidence is available from errors. I now consider the typical errors, looking for clues about the degree of grammatical analysis involved in imitation. I make the basic assumption that for a sentence to be fully comprehended it must be fully structured and interpreted.

One type of error reported in the literature involves grammaticality. When asked to repeat sentences with grammatical errors people tend to correct the errors automatically: instead of reproducing ungrammatical sentences, subjects produce grammatically correct versions of the sentences. For example, 33a presents an ungrammatical sentence; 33b a typical response.

33 a John wants go to the store
    b John wants to go to the store

In responses such as 33b there is no evidence that subjects are aware of their failure to correctly repeat the sentence presented to them. The relevant work involves young children whose knowledge of grammatical structure is uneven and often incomplete (Menyuk, 1971; Smith, 1970). Automatic corrections of this type are taken as evidence of subjects' knowledge of grammatical structure. The corrections indicate, as expected, that people tend to structure grammatically the sentences of imitation tasks. They suggest a degree of analysis beyond segmentation into constituents. Other errors such as those classified as structure-violating in Smith (1970) show that misanalyses of imitation sentences tend to be well-behaved with respect to surface grammatical structure.

Another type of error is semantic substitution, which must involve recoding of input which has been processed. Subjects tend to change articles, names, common nouns, verbs, tenses of imitation sentences. The changes are almost invariably within the same semantic domain as the word that they replace, hence the label of substitution. For example, "the" might be substituted for "a," "laugh" for "laughed," "Joe" for "John," "go" for "run" (see Keller-Cohen, 1975; Smith, 1970, for discussion). The examples of Semantic Change given in the preceding section are illustrative.

Errors like this give some information about the organization of the mental lexicon. From the viewpoint of understanding, they are also informative. They suggest that in the imitation task sentences tend to be only partially comprehended. These errors would be serious in the real world, or in tasks involving interaction with a toy world. But in the imitation task they are trivial, since it really doesn't matter whether a particular sentence mentions John or Jim. The semantic substitution errors indicate that some semantic processing occurs in imitation, but that it is often incomplete and tends to stop short of full understanding.

We now ask whether the errors that occur in imitation responses reflect difficulties at the stage of comprehension, memory, or production. It seems likely that the errors of ungrammaticality occur at the second stage. The idea is that with a structured ungrammatical sentence one must hold in memory the structure and a footnote of sorts about the error. When memory is overloaded the footnote drops (see the discussion in Smith, 1970).

However, this account does not generalize convincingly to other errors, that is, grammatical errors of the structure-violating type, and semantic substitution errors. If a sentence is correctly structured in comprehension, why should the structure be changed in remembering? In order to answer this question one would have to appeal to additional factors. Again, if a sentence is fully comprehended, it is hard to explain why some of it should fail to be stored in memory or produced. The simpler and more convincing explanation is that these types of errors indicate difficulty at the stage of production.

But now we seem to have no account for the effect of nouns and verbs in the second imitation experiment. I shall adopt the processing account given by Daneman and Case. In their 1981 article Daneman and Case give a convincing account of the task of imitation. They suggest that short-term memory is a crucial factor in imitation; and that "placing forms in memory" requires attention to all the features of a sentence as recognition does not. "Semantic and syntactic features must be dealt with as independent units for production . . . these features needn't be treated as independent units for recognition." According to Daneman and Case, production requires that each part of an utterance be processed sequentially and placed briefly in short-term memory.

This account can be adapted to our experimental results: Subjects may have found the S and Ving sentences difficult because the nouns and verbs required particular attention when placed in short-term memory. Apparently nouns and verbs have extra weight. The extra weight may be due to the strong semantic and syntactic constraints on nouns and verbs, that is, their systematic complexity. If this is so then imitation partly engages the meaning system in a sense not heretofore appreciated.[11]

Pulling these threads together, it seems that the results of the imitation study that controlled for length are due to difficulties at the second and third stages of the imitation process. Nouns and verbs are apparently weighty at these stages; in the terms of the theory of complexity, they are relatively high in systematic linguistic complexity. We arrive, then, at an account of imitation that involves both surface structure complexity and systematic complexity. (This would probably have to be modified with a theory of linguistic complexity that included phonological factors.) We conclude that in decoding the imitation task tends to involve surface structure and partial, rather automatic semantic interpretation. In short-term memory and production the task engages systematic factors as well.

4.2. Toy-Moving

The toy-moving task involves interpretation, as noted above. The subject must arrive at an understanding of a sentence presented in order to act it out. Considering the task a little more closely, one sees that this understanding need not be complete. To act out a sentence it is necessary to understand the words, and the thematic roles ascribed to the relevant referents, but it may not be necessary to understand fully the grammatical structure of the sentence, especially if the sentence is multiclausal. This observation has as corollary the fact that the task does not indicate unequivocally the grammatical structure ascribed to it by subjects. Thus, a subject may successfully act out a sentence without giving a clear indication of how it is structured for that subject.

The controversy about relative clauses may be due in large part to this fact. There is an extensive literature on the topic, in which different researchers give different interpretations to toy-moving data on sentences with relative clauses. It has been claimed that children understand sentences with relatives as conjunctions (Tavakolian, 1981); extraposed relatives (Sheldon, 1974); or as relatives attached sometimes to the main VP and sometimes to the root S (Solan & Roeper, 1978). A useful summary and comparison, with some new data, is presented in deVilliers, Flusberg, Hakuta, and Cohen (1979). This controversy could not have stayed alive if toy-moving responses indicated the grammatical structure that a subject ascribes to an experimental sentence.

---

[11]For discussion of the relation between imitation and the grammatical and meaning system, see Brown and Fraser (1963) and later critical papers.

4.3. The Two Tasks

The experimental tasks engage different aspects of children's ability to use language. The point is uncontroversial; what is added in the work reported here is a new level of specificity. Using a variable that is independent of linguistic performance, linguistic complexity, we were able to be quite specific (though certainly not exhaustive) about differences between the tasks. These differences suggest a cautious answer to the nontrivial methodological question of how the tasks relate to each other. The two are often taken to be complementary. Indeed, it was as complementary tasks that they were selected for the experimental work discussed above.

The pattern of results reported here suggests task difference rather than complementarity. This means that it may not be possible to make predictions about children's general competence from their performance on a particular task. This is not to say that tasks of comprehension and imitation never have similar patterns of results (see Lust,Solon, Flynn, Cross, & Schuetz, 1981, for a report of just such a case). When similar patterns occur it is reasonable to assume both knowledge of the linguistic material, and comparable development of the performance factors involved in accessing linguistic knowledge. But performance on one task does not necessarily indicate what kind of performance the other task might elicit. Therefore the results of either cannot be taken as more than partial evidence of children's linguistic and performance abilities.

5.   REMARKS ON LINGUISTIC COMPLEXITY

In this final section I give a somewhat more careful theoretical discussion. I begin with brief comments on theories of linguistic complexity, and then consider how this theory might be specified formally. Surface structure complexity and interpretive complexity receive particular attention, with detailed consideration of some important examples. The discussion is intended as a step toward the fuller development of this theory of linguistic complexity.

5.1.

There are, evidently, several ways of approaching linguistic complexity. The challenge is to develop a coherent theory that has an interesting relation to linguistic performance. Although not all aspects of linguistic complexity are likely to affect performance, it is not unreasonable to seek a theory that identifies factors that are relevant to performance. The effects of linguistic complexity in the experiments discussed above suggest that the modular theory presented here identifies some factors that interact with performance.

This theory avoids some of the difficulties that beset the Derivational Theory of Complexity (DTC). The DTC, which seemed promising in the early '60s, proved inadequate. (See Fodor & Garrett, 1967, for a discussion of the rise and fall of the DTC.) In that theory the complexity of a sentence is due to the length of its derivational history. The more rules involved in the derivation of a sentence, the more complex. The idea is quite plausible especially if one believes in the psychological reality of grammars. But the DTC was a failure in relating linguistic complexity to psycholinguistics, that is, to performance: length of derivational history did not correlate as predicted with ease or difficulty in performance. Many types of sentences that are complex according to the DTC were easier in performance than related sentences that are less complex. Deletion is a dramatic example of the inadequacy of the approach. The DTC predicts sentences that have undergone the rule of deletion to be more complex than sentences that have not. For example, short passives, that have deleted agent-phrases, are predicted to be more complex than full passives; comparatives with deletion such as 34 are predicted to be more complex than longer comparatives.

34 a   Susan plays croquet better than Jim does
    b   Susan plays croquet better than Jim

Experimental work showed that the predictions of the DTC were not borne out.[12]

The complete theory of complexity must specify formally how to assess structures at the levels of systematic, surface structure, interpretive, and phonological complexity. It would be premature to attempt such a specification now, but some comments can be made about surface structure and interpretive complexity. I do not deal with systematic complexity in this section, in spite of its relevance to the imitation results. The reason for this omission is that constraints on words and phrases are given in lexical entries. To present a proposal for systematic complexity it would be necessary to consider closely the form and range of lexical entries. Such a task is beyond the scope of this paper. I discuss in the following part-sections the structures assessed at the levels of surface complexity and interpretive complexity.

5.2.   Surface Structure Complexity

A formal assessment of surface complexity must assign a degree of complexity to each component and put them into a composite. The components are length, density, and ambiguity. One way of doing this might be to assign a number to each component, perhaps with some type of weighting, and somehow combine

---

[12]It should be noted that the DTC was framed and tested in the Standard Theory, set out in Chomsky (1965). How it would fare if adapted to current theories is not obvious; Berwick (1983) presents an optimistic account of an adapted DTC and the Government and Binding theory. See also the references in for LFG in note 1.

the numbers into one. But since each of the components is quite unlike the other, combining them seems undesirable, at least at this stage. Therefore I shall set out the main determinants of complexity without making a proposal about how they might be combined. Two of the components, length and density, lend themselves naturally to numerical assessment; for ambiguity, the third component, a number seems less natural but not difficult to arrange. One could simply give a 1, in this component, for each structural interpretation of surface structure. Thus a sentence would be assigned 1 if it had one reading; 2 if it were ambiguous; etc.

Length involves both words and morphemes, and should be gauged by two counts: number of words, and number of certain types of morphemes. I assume a morphological analysis that differentiates between types of morphemes, such as inflectional and class-changing morphemes, at the level of surface structure.[13] I have also assumed that only the latter should be counted as contributing to complexity. Thus in the informal assessment of the experimental sentences in Section 1.2, I considered the form Verb+ing to have more complexity than verbs with inflectional suffixes. The form is nominal because of the class-changing -ing suffix. This assumption might be changed or modified in future work, especially when languages other than English are considered. The length factor of a sentence would be indicated by a number indicating how many words, and how many morphemes (of certain types) appear in that sentence.

The factor of density concerns the distribution of words in a sentence. Both amount and abstract structure contribute to density, an attribute of constituents and of sentences in which the constituents occur. Consider amount first. Words may be distributed more or less evenly throughout a sentence, or a few may appear in one or more constituents. When many words are compressed into one constituent, that constituent is dense. For example, 35 and 36 have the same number of words but their organization is different:

35   [NP[The green boat] easily overtook NP[the white boat]]
36   [NP[None of the green boats] finished the race]

Again, consider the objects of 2 and 3, repeated here as 37 and 38. The object NP in 37 has a determiner and noun; the object NP in 38 has more words and more abstract structure (nonterminal tree nodes).

37   [Mary wrote NP[a letter] PP[to her family]]
38   [Mary wrote NP[a letter PP[about the meeting]]]

The differences between the dense and sparse constituents of these sentences might be partially indicated according to number of words per constituent. So for

---

[13]Inflectional morphemes indicate tense, number, etc.; class-changing morphemes form nouns from verbs, adjectives from nouns, etc.

example, the words in 37 and 38 might be counted according to their appearance in main constituents, as in 39:

39   (sentence 2) 1, 2, 2, 3
(sentence 3) 1, 2, 5

This count of density is not quite satisfactory, however, because it fails to consider the factor of nonterminal nodes, that is, abstract syntactic structure. Abstract syntactic structure is a linguistic feature; little is known at this time about its effects on processing.

Dense constituents tend to have relatively many abstract nodes in surface structure. This is because in dense constituents intermediate nodes usually relate the parts of the constituent to each other. In terms of x-bar theory, intermediate nodes are neither maximal projections nor per-terminal nodes that dominate lexical items; they are generally double-bar nodes (Jackendoff, 1977). In contrast, sparse structure have few abstract, intermediate nodes. To see the difference, examine the tree diagrams in 40 and 41, which give roughly the structures of 37 and 38. I will assume a pruning convention in which non-branching intermediate nodes are pruned.[14]

(40)

```
              S
   NP                VP
  Mary        V    NP         PP
            wrote a letter  P    NP
                            to  her  family
```

(41)

```
              S
   NP         VP
  Mary     V      NP
         wrote  a letter  PP
                         P     NP
                       about  the meeting
```

In 40 an object NP and a following PP are attached directly to VP; whereas 41 has the intermediate node N'' to which the PP is attached. Thus sentence 38 is denser than sentence 37 in terms of structure as well as amount.

The surface structure complexity measure should include an indication of abstract structure, because long constituents may vary in structure. Not all long constituents have the same proportion of words and intermediate nodes. For example, some conjunctions do not have intermediate nodes: 41 is a NP conjunction, and 42 seems a plausible structure for it.

---

[14]The need for rules of tree-pruning was originally noted in Ross (1967); tree-pruning rules delete in surface structure (and perhaps other places as well) nonbranching preterminal nodes.

41   NP[the dog and the cat and the rabbit]

42   NP

NP   and   NP   and   NP

Again, consider NP's with more than one prenominal modifier. Such modifiers may have hierarchical structure with more than one intermediate node, or they may be on the same bar level (essentially a conjunction structure, whether explicit or not). The NP's in 43 indicate several possibilities; for simplicity their constituent structure is given with brackets.

43   a.   NP[bright [autumn [leaves]]]
      b.   NP[blue and white [stripes]]
      c.   NP[tall narrow [buildings]]
      d.   NP[three hundred fifty [boats]]
      e.   NP[[none [of the]] [green [boats]]]

These examples show that constituents should be evaluated for abstract structure as well as for number of words. If a constituent contains intermediate nodes the number of such nodes should be indicated in the complexity index for surface structure for the sentence in question.

A fuller treatment of the topic of density would require careful consideration of other points involving X-bar theory and is beyond the scope of this paper.[15]

In sum, the formal assessment of surface structure complexity for a sentence considers amount, density, and ambiguity. Amount and density deal with the number and distribution of words and morphemes in the major constituents of a sentence and the number of intermediate nodes in major constituents. Amount and distribution can be represented by a set of numbers corresponding to the major constituents of a sentence. If a major constituent has nodes of abstract structure, the relevant number will be augmented by a subscript indicating the number of abstract nodes in that constituent. The notion of density, involving the distribution and structure of words in constituents, is thus represented by a subscripted number for each of the major constituents of a sentence. A second number can indicate the number of syntactic analyses for the sentence, that is, whether the sentence is syntactically ambiguous.

5.3. Interpretive Complexity

Interpretive complexity arises when the semantic structure that shows scope relations of a sentence is not congruent with its surface structure. It differs from

---

[15]It would be difficult to work out a detailed proposal at this time since some of these matters are far from settled in the Government and Binding theory. Cf. Chomsky's (1986) recent proposal that there are two nonlexical XP's.

the other types of complexity considered here because it involves a comparison between two levels of structure, rather than properties of one level.[16] The notion depends on an interpretive level such as Logical Form in GB. At least three types of interpretive complexity can be identified: empty categories, discontinuous constituents, semantic scope.

Empty categories appear in surface structure and are reconstructed or interpreted in scopal semantic structure. They can arise by movement or deletion, or they may be generated directly. Empty categories are interpreted according to the principles of Binding Theory, themselves under debate. There are interesting questions in this area about how the application of such principles contributes to linguistic complexity, but it would be premature to attempt a detailed characterization at this point. Therefore the contribution of empty categories to complexity will be assessed in the simplest possible manner, by counting. Each empty category in surface structure will contribute one unit to complexity. The more empty categories, the higher the interpretive complexity of a sentence.

Discontinuous constituents are elements that go together syntactically or semantically but that are not adjacent in surface structure. Some examples are given in 44:

44   a   Mary is swimming (be+ing)
     b   A man came in wearing a red hat (a man wearing . . .)
     c   They collect objects for their gallery
         from the Civil War (objects from the Civil War)

In early generative theory such elements were syntactically related in underlying structure: they were generated together and then separated by a movement process. Current theories generate some or all such constituents separately and relate them in interpretation.

Since they must be related to each other for interpretation, discontinuous constituents contribute to the interpretive complexity of a sentence. Perhaps the contribution should be assessed by the number of linguistic units to be brought into adjacency, or according to the number of linguistic units to be moved.

At the level of Logical Form the structure of a sentence indicates the scope of quantifiers and sentence operators. Elements that have semantic scope over all or part of a sentence appear at Logical Form in positions that c-command the material in their scope. The scope may be an entire sentence, an embedded sentence, or a constituent of a sentence.   A standard example concerns a quantifier with wide scope, as indicated very roughly in 45 (for the wide scope reading of the object NP).

---

[16]Perhaps the phonological component, when investigated from this point of view (cf. Chomsky, 1981, would require more than one factor of linguistic complexity.

45   a.   Everyone owns a logic text
    b.   Rough logical form for 35a
        [(a logic text, x) (everyone, y) y owns x]

The point is that the NP in object position at surface structure has scope over the whole sentence at Logical Form. Again, consider the interpretation of elements indicating temporal location, tense and adverbs; semantically they have scope over a sentence, which is indicated structurally at Logical Form (Dowty, 1979; Smith, 1978).

46   a.   Mary fed the cat at dawn
    b.   Rough Logical Form for 36a
        [(past, at dawn) Mary fed the cat]

The structures of Logical Form are scopal semantic structures and they differ roughly as indicated from surface structure.

Such elements contribute to interpretive complexity. I shall again take a tentative, even programmatic, approach to the formal assessment of their contribution. At this stage I shall merely propose that each linguistic unit that moves in Logical Form contributes to the interpretive complexity of a sentence. As for empty categories and discontinuous constituents, we will simply have a number that corresponds to the number of units affected. At a later stage it may be desirable to refine this crude approach.

The component of interpretive complexity analyzes certain differences between linguistic details. In accounting for this component, one deals with some of the same difficulties that faced the DTC. Differences between levels are analyzed by linguistic rules, and linguistic rules may be irrelevant for performance. (Recall that, of the many theories of linguistic complexity that are in principle available, we are attempting to construct a theory that is relevant for performance.) There is an important constraint imposed by the theory proposed here that limits the possibilities for irrelevance. This theory considers only differences that appear in the structures of the two levels: Intermediate forms and stages are not taken here to contribute to complexity.

This chapter has developed a linguistic approach to linguistic complexity, and has presented experimental studies investigating its effect on the performance of young children. Linguistic complexity affected the children's performance in the two tasks used. The effects varied with the tasks, showing that the relation between performance and linguistic complexity depends on the type of performance involved.

ACKNOWLEDGMENTS

This chapter was written while the author was a Fellow at the Center for Advanced Study in the Behavior Sciences. I gratefully acknowledge the support of the Center and of the Spencer Foundation. I would like to thank Alice Davison, Georgia Green, S. A. Kendall, Richard Meier, Howard Schuman, and Anne van Kleeck for helpful discussion of the chapter. The research on which it is based was supported by the National Science Foundation and the Center for Cognitive Science at the University of Texas.

REFERENCES

Berwick, R. C. (1983). Transformational grammar and artificial intelligence: A contemporary view. *Cognition and Brain Theory, 6,* 383–416.
Berwick, R. C., & Weinberg, A. (1982). Parsing efficiency, computational complexity, and the evaluation of grammatical theories. *Linguistic Inquiry, 13,* 165–192.
Bormuth, J. (1966). Readability: A new approach. *Reading Research Quarterly, 1,* 79–132.
Botel, M., Dawkins, J., & Granowsky, A. (1973). A syntactic complexity formula. In W. H. MacGinitie (Ed.), *Assessment of problems in reading.* Newark, DE: International Reading Association.
Bresnan, J. (1978). A realistic transformational grammar. In M. Halle, J. Bresnan, & G. Miller (Eds.), *Linguistic structure and psychological reality.* Cambridge, MA: MIT Press.
Bresnan, J. (Ed.). (1982). The mental representation of grammatical relations. Cambridge, MA: MIT Press.
Brown, R., & Fraser, C. (1963). The acquisition of syntax. In C. Cofer & B. Musgrave (Eds.), *Verbal behavior and learning: Problems and processes.* New York: McGraw-Hill.
Case, R., Kurland, D., & Goldberg, J. (1982). Operational efficiency and the growth of short-term memory span. *Journal of Experimental Child Psychology, 33,* 386–404.
Chomsky, N. (1965). *Aspects of the theory of syntax.* Cambridge, MA: MIT Press.
Chomsky, N. (1981). *Lectures on government and binding.* Dordrecht: Foris.
Chomsky, N. (1986). *Barriers.* Cambridge, MA: MIT Press.
Clark, E. (1973). How children describe time and order. In C. A. Ferguson & D. I. Slobin (Eds.), *Studies of child language development.* New York: Holt, Rinehart and Winston.
Daneman, M., & Case, R. (1981). Syntactic form, semantic complexity, and short-term memory: Influences on children's acquisition of new linguistic structures. *Developmental Psychology, 17,* 367–79.
deVilliers, J. G., Flusberg, H. T., Hakuta, K., & Cohen, M. (1979). Children's comprehension of relative clauses. *Journal of Psycholinguistic Research, 8,* 499–518.
Dowty, D. (1979). *Word meaning and Montague grammar.* Dordrecht, Holland: Reidel.
Fodor, J., & Garrett, M. (1967). Some reflections on competence and performance. In J. Lyons, & R. Wales, (Eds.), *Psycholinguistics papers.* Edinburgh: Edinburgh University Press.
Ford, M., Bresnan, J., & Kaplan, R. (1982). A competence-based theory of syntactic closure. In J. Bresnan (Ed.), *The mental representation of grammatical relations.* Cambridge, MA: MIT Press.
Gazdar, G., Pullum, G., Klein, E., & Sag, I. (1985). *GPSG.* Cambridge, MA: Harvard University Press.
Hamburger, H. (1980). A deletion ahead of its time. *Cognition, 8,* 389–416.
Heinämäki, O. (1974). The semantics of English temporal connectives. Unpublished dissertation, University of Texas.
Huttenlocher, J., Eisenberg, K., & Straus, S. (1968). Comprehension: The relation between perceived actor and logical subject. *Journal of Verbal Learning and Verbal Behavior, 7,* 527–530.
Jackendoff, R. (1977). *X-Bar syntax: A study of phrase structure.* Cambridge, MA: MIT Press.
Keller-Cohen, D. (1975). *The acquisition of temporal reference.* Indiana University Linguistics Club.
Kessel, F. (1970). The role of syntax in children's comprehension from ages six to twelve. *Monographs of the Society for Research in Child Development, 35*(6).

Kimball, J. (1973). Seven principles of surface structure parsing in natural language. *Cognition, 2,* 15–47.

Kintsch, W., & D. Vipond (1979). Reading comprehension and readability in educational practice and psychological theory. In L. G. Nilsson (Ed.), *Perspectives on memory research.* Hillsdale, NJ: Lawrence Erlbaum Associates.

Legum, S. (1975). *Strategies in the acquisition of relative clauses* (Southwest Regional Laboratory Technical Note, TN2-75-19). Southwest Regional Laboratory.

Lust, B., Solan, L., Flynn, S., Cross, C., & Shuetz, T. (1981). A comparison of null and pronominal analysis in first language acquisition. In V. Burke & J. Pustejovsky (Eds.), *Proceedings of the 11th Annual Meeting of the New England Linguistics Society.* Amherst, MA: University of Massachusetts.

Marslen-Wilson, W. & Tyler, L. (1980). The temporal structure of spoken language understanding. *Cognition, 8,* 1–72.

May, R. (1985). *Logical form: Its structure and derivation.* LI Monograph 12.

Menyuk, P. (1971). *The acquisition and development of language.* Englewood Cliffs, NJ: Prentice-Hall.

Miller, G. A., & Chomsky, N. (1963). Finitary models of language users. In R. Luce, R. Bush, & E. Galanter (Eds.), *Handbook of mathematical psychology* (Vol. 2). New York: Wiley.

Miller, G. A., & Selfridge, J. (1951). Verbal context and the recall of meaningful material. *American Journal of Psychology, 63,* 176–185.

Ross, J. (1967). Constraints on variables in syntax. MIT dissertation.

Sheldon, A. (1974). The role of parallel function in the acquisition of relative clauses in English. *Journal of Verbal Learning and Verbal Behavior, 13,* 272–281.

Smith, C. S. (1970). An experimental approach to children's linguistic competence. In J. Hayes (Ed.), *The acquisition of language.* New York: Holt, Rinehart & Winston.

Smith, C. S. (1978). The syntax and interpretation of temporal reference in English. *Linguistics & Philosophy.*

Smith, C. S., & van Kleeck, A. (1986). Linguistic complexity and performance. *Journal of Child Language.*

Solan, L. (1983). *Pronominal reference: Child language and the theory of grammar.* Dordrecht, Holland: D. Reidel.

Solan, L., & Roeper, T. (1978). Children's use of syntactic structures in interpreting relative clauses. In H. Goodluck & L. Solan (Eds.), *Papers in the structure and development of child language.* University of Massachusetts Occasional Papers.

Steedman, M. (1985). LFG and psychological explanation. *Linguistics and Philosophy, 8,* 359–385.

Tavakolian, S. (1981). The conjoined clause analysis of relative clauses. In S. Tavakolian (Ed.), *Language acquisition and linguistic theory.* Cambridge, MA: MIT Press.

Waltz, D., & Pollack, J. (1985). Massively parallel processing: A strongly interactive model of natural language interpretation. *Cognitive Science, 9,* 51–74.

van Riemsdijk, H., & Williams, E. (1986). *Introduction to the theory of grammar.* Cambridge, MA: MIT Press.

APPENDIX

List of Stimulus Sentences

1. Toy Moving and Imitation 1

The sentences are in blocs according to structure and do not indicate the order of presentation.

1. The cow chases the horse before the tiger sleeps.
2. The horse sleeps before the walrus kisses the cow.
3. The cow kisses the tiger before the horse chases the walrus.
4. The horse tickles the walrus after the tiger kisses the cow.
5. The tiger jumps up after the horse tickles the cow.
6. The horse kisses the tiger after the walrus jumps up.
7. The horse sleeps when the cow tickles the walrus.
8. The walrus sleeps when the tiger chases the cow.
9. The tiger jumps up before chasing the cow.
10. The cow tickles the walrus before sleeping.

Author Index

Italics denote pages with bibliographic information.

Subject Index